Democracy's Value

Democracy is a flawed hegemon. The collapse of communism has left it without a serious institutional competitor in much of the world. In many respects this is, no doubt, a good thing. Democracy's flexibility, its in-built commitment to equality of representation, and its recognition of the legitimacy of opposition politics are all features of political institutions that should not lightly be discounted. But democracy has many deficiencies. It is all too easily held hostage by powerful interests; it often fails to protect the vulnerable or otherwise to advance social justice; and it does not cope well with a number of features of the political landscape. Intensely felt political identities, the drawing and redrawing of boundaries, and global environmental problems are among the most urgent. In short, although democracy is valuable it fits uneasily with many other political values and is in many respects less than equal to the demands it confronts.

In this volume (and its companion, *Democracy's Edges*) some of the world's most prominent political theorists and social scientists present original discussions of these urgently vexing subjects. *Democracy's Value* deals principally with the nature and value of democracy, with particular attention to the tensions between it and such goods as justice, equality, efficiency, and freedom. *Democracy's Edges* contains meditations on one of the most enduring problems of democratic politics: how to establish the boundaries of democratic polities democratically. These books provide an accessible extension of the state-of-the-art in democratic theory.

IAN SHAPIRO is Professor of Political Science at Yale University. He has written widely on contemporary political and social theory, with particular recent emphasis on democratic theory. His books include *The Evolution of Rights in Liberal Theory* (1986), *Political Criticism* (1990), *Pathologies of Rational Choice Theory* (with Donald Green, 1994), *Democracy's Place* (1996), and *Democratic Justice* (1999). He has also edited numerous books, including, since 1992, the NOMOS series.

CASIANO HACKER-CORDÓN is a doctoral student at Yale University. His work centers on contemporary political philosophy and social theory.

D1364103

Contemporary Political Theory

Series editor

Ian Shapiro

Editorial Board

Russell Hardin   Stephen Holmes   Jeffrey Isaac
John Keane   Elizabeth Kiss   Susan Moller Okin
Philippe Van Parijs   Philip Pettit

As the twenty-first century approaches, major new political challenges have arisen at the same time as some of the most enduring dilemmas of political association remain unresolved. The collapse of communism and the end of the Cold War in the east reflect a victory for democratic and liberal values, yet in many of the western countries that nurtured those values there are severe problems of urban decay, class and racial conflict, and failing political legitimacy. Enduring global injustice and inequality seem compounded by environmental problems, disease, the oppression of women, racial, ethnic and religious minorities, and the relentless growth of the world's population. In such circumstances, the need for creative thinking about the fundamentals of human political association is manifest. This new series in contemporary political theory is intended to foster such systematic normative reflection.

The series proceeds in the belief that the time is ripe for a reassertion of the importance of problem-driven political theory. It is concerned, that is, with works that are motivated by the impulse to understand, think critically about and address problems in the world, rather than issues that are thrown up primarily in academic debate. Books in the series will be interdisciplinary in character, ranging over issues conventionally dealt with in philosophy, law, history, and the human sciences. The range of materials and the methods of proceeding should be dictated by the problem at hand, not the conventional debates or disciplinary divisions of academia.

Democracy's Value

Edited by

Ian Shapiro and Casiano Hacker-Cordón

CAMBRIDGE
UNIVERSITY PRESS

PUBLISHED BY THE PRESS SYNDICATE OF THE UNIVERSITY OF CAMBRIDGE
The Pitt Building, Trumpington Street, Cambridge, United Kingdom

CAMBRIDGE UNIVERSITY PRESS
The Edinburgh Building, Cambridge CB2 2RU, UK
40 West 20th Street, New York, NY 10011–4211, USA
10 Stamford Road, Oakleigh, Melbourne 3166, Australia
Ruiz de Alarcón 13, 28014 Madrid, Spain
Dock House, The Waterfront, Cape Town 8001, South Africa

http://www.cambridge.org

First published 1999
Reprinted 2001

Printed in the United Kingdom at the University Press, Cambridge

Typeset in 10/12pt Plantin   [CE]

A catalogue record for this book is available from the British Library

ISBN 0 521 64357 0 hardback
ISBN 0 521 64388 0 paperback

To the memory of Richard Ashcraft

Contents

List of contributors   *page* xi
Preface   xiii

1. Promises and disappointments: reconsidering
   democracy's value   1
   IAN SHAPIRO and CASIANO HACKER-CORDÓN

Part I: Minimal democracy   21

2. Minimalist conception of democracy: a defense   23
   ADAM PRZEWORSKI

3. Does democracy engender justice?   56
   JOHN E. ROEMER

4. Democracy and other goods   69
   PARTHA DASGUPTA and ERIC MASKIN

Part II: Beyond minimalism   91

5. Democracy and development: a complex relationship   93
   PRANAB BARDHAN

6. Death and taxes: extractive equality and the development
   of democratic institutions   112
   MARGARET LEVI

7. Democracy and development?   132
   JOHN DUNN

8. State, civil society, and social justice   141
   IRIS MARION YOUNG

9. Republican freedom and contestatory democratization   163
   PHILIP PETTIT

10. Contestatory democracy versus real freedom for all   191
     PHILIPPE VAN PARIJS

Index   199

Contributors

Pranab Bardhan *Department of Economics, University of California, Berkeley*

Partha Dasgupta *Department of Politics and Economics, Cambridge University*

John Dunn *King's College, Cambridge University*

Casiano Hacker-Cordón *Department of Political Science, Yale University*

Margaret Levi *Department of Political Science, University of Washington*

Eric Maskin *Department of Economics, Harvard University*

Philip Pettit *Department of Philosophy, Australian National University*

Adam Przeworski *Department of Politics, New York University*

John E. Roemer *Department of Economics, University of California, Davis*

Ian Shapiro *Department of Political Science and the Program in Ethics, Politics, and Economics, Yale University*

Philippe Van Parijs *Faculty of Economic, Social, and Political Sciences, Université Catholique de Louvain*

Iris Marion Young *Department of International and Public Affairs, University of Pittsburgh*

Preface

This volume and its companion, *Democracy's Edges*, grew out of a conference on "Rethinking Democracy for a New Century" held at Yale in February 1997. The conference was sponsored by Yale's Program in Ethics, Politics, and Economics, with financial support coming from Yale's Olmsted Fund, Castle Fund, and Kempf Fund. Thanks are due to Kellianne Farnham for going well beyond the call of duty in organizing the conference and helping us assemble the manuscript. We are also pleased to record our gratitude to John Haslam of Cambridge University Press for his interest in the project from the beginning, and for facilitating the timely appearance of the volumes.

IAN SHAPIRO

CASIANO HACKER-CORDÓN

1   Promises and disappointments: reconsidering democracy's value

Ian Shapiro and Casiano Hacker-Cordón

Democrats expect much of democracy. They expect to participate in making the collective decisions that govern them. They expect these decisions to be informed by extensive public deliberation. They expect those who lead public discussion and implement the collective will to be held accountable for their actions by the electorate. Democrats also expect democracy to help make the world a better place. They believe it will diminish injustice and oppression, and bring reason to bear on the organization of collective life. Nor does this exhaust the list. Democracy is often touted as diminishing the likelihood of war, protecting human freedom, and facilitating economic growth. It might be going too far to say democracy is all things to all people, but it is fair to say that there is a strong propensity to associate democracy with a wide array of activities and outcomes that people value.

In reality, democracy often disappoints. Both in its operation and its consequences it fails to live up to the promise people associate with it. Usually, democratic participation is fleeting, accountability is little more than nominal, and the true mechanics of "democratic" decisions are obscure. Far from reducing injustice and oppression, grinding poverty in the midst of opulent wealth persists in democracies across the world. Democracies find sustenance in prejudice as often as in reason, and they seem compatible with policies that single out vulnerable minorities for maltreatment. Democracies manage to avoid war only with one another. Economic growth can occur as well without democracy as with it, and when the two go together it is unclear that the latter has much causal responsibility for the former. At best we can perhaps say that the democratic ideal lives in adaptive tension with the political realities in most so-called democracies. At worst it provides a misleading gloss for practices that scarcely deserve the name.

This has been true from the beginning. The ancient understanding of democracy centered on the egalitarian idea of ruling and being ruled in turn. Yet citizenship was so restricted in the slave-owning and patriarchal "democratic" Greek city-states where the ideal was developed that in reality this turned out to be a decidedly superficial egalitarianism. Among those recognized as citizens a measure of truncated democracy prevailed, perhaps, yet this proved compatible with the maintenance of a social order that few today could defend as even minimally democratic. On inspection, ancient democracy turns out to have lived more in the minds of philosophers than in the realities of politics on the ground. Nor has any subsequent form of political organization lived up to the egalitarian dimension of the ancient ideal. To be governed by it, a society would have to be small and homogeneous. It would have to be marked by high levels of like-mindedness and trust among citizens, underpinned by common interests on most major issues of collective concern. The world would have to be comparatively simple, requiring few technical or professional skills for governing. It also would have to be a world in which no permanent political bureaucracy was required.

Some of these features were exhibited in the small principalities Jean-Jacques Rousseau (1968 [1762]) had in mind when writing *The Social Contract*, but even he was forced to abandon the ancient ideal of ruling and being ruled in turn. He replaced it with two ideas that were to become building blocks in the theory of representative government. One was the idea of the "general will," which he famously – if imprecisely – described as the "sum of the difference" which results from finding "the sum of individual desires" and subtracting "the pluses and minuses which cancel each other out." The other was the notion of a lawgiver, among whose tasks was to discern and act on the general will. In these ideas we see in embryonic form a view of a type of democracy in which such institutional devices as electoral systems express the population's will, which in turn operates to direct and constrain the actions of public officials. It is often described, following Schumpeter (1942), as the classical theory of democracy, even if it is really a neoclassical view: an adaptation of the ancient theory to what were thought to be the realities of eighteenth-century European politics.

Rousseau was still thinking of homogeneous principalities in which the entire populace could meet in the town square, a far cry from politics in modern democracies. Their landscapes are large, sometimes continental, with populations of multiple millions. They are marked by conflicting interests revolving around market dynamics, gender, racial, and cultural divisions. They are governed by professional politicians who must work with autonomous bureaucracies over which they exert limited control, not to mention transnational forces and institutions before which they often stand powerless. Citizen oversight over politicians who "represent" them is arguably *de minimus* when compared to the influence exerted by well-heeled financial contributors in an age of multimillion-dollar television campaigns. Voters do little, even, to set political agendas. As political participants they are but infinitesimal voices in periodic retrospective judgments as to how a government has done. The administration can be returned to office, or rejected in favor of the alternative (usually there is only one) that will be similarly judged in the not too distant future. This reality bears scant resemblance to the classical ideal of representative government in accordance with a general will, not to mention the ancient one of ruling and being ruled in turn.

Perhaps Rousseau's ideal can be rethought by reference to the distinction between ideal and non-ideal theory, yet still retain a purchase on contemporary politics. What we have come to know as representative government might not be fully representative, but, on this line of thinking, we would identify it as a reasonable second-best approximation, given contemporary conditions. Modern electoral procedures might not rationally encapsulate the collective will, but perhaps they do as well as can be done among large heterogeneous populations. And modern democracies might not be inclusively egalitarian, but what is the force of this criticism if no more inclusive system has been shown to be durable in the contemporary world? Likewise with the other goods people associate with democracy. Its failure to deliver on expectations that it will reduce injustice and inequality, attenuate violent conflict, or promote sustained economic growth is cast in a different light if in the non-ideal world of the second-best. To describe a system as democratic, on this view, is partly to make a comparative judgment capturing how well it approximates the ideal as compared with the going alternatives. The oft-repeated epithet to the effect that democracy is the worst system of government, except for the others, rests on considerations of this kind.

I   Minimalist democracy

Alluring as the comparative tack might be, it understates the difficulties that modern political theorists have identified at democracy's core. As Adam Przeworski argues in chapter 2, democracy's main operating principle – majority rule – turns out to be a poor device for achieving even second-best approximations of the classical ideal. There are good reasons to doubt that majoritarian politics converge on common interests in modern polities, that politicians in any meaningful sense are constrained by elections to represent voters' interests, or that they even pursue policies – such as egalitarian redistribution – that would benefit an unambiguous majority of the citizenry. Przeworski makes a powerful case that the principal arguments that have been advanced to the effect that democracy can be expected to achieve these results are unsuccessful. Accordingly, if democracy is to be defended it must be on minimalist grounds, detached from the classical expectation that it can rationally represent a general will, not to mention the widespread impulse to argue that it produces ancillary benefits such as egalitarian redistribution. While on a pure operation of democratic procedures in the light of the median-voter model, people have good deductive reasons to expect egalitarian redistribution, in actual practice such is not the case. One explanation for this, among the several Przeworski discusses without endorsing, is the mechanism of the state's structural dependence on capital. Voters, who know that capitalists make decentralized decisions in reaction to state policies, must factor in the deadweight losses that should be expected if redistributive policies are pursued beyond a certain point – as when high marginal tax rates result in declining investment. Accordingly, they temper their redistributive demands, reinforcing a circumstance in which democratic governments are structurally dependent on private capital. At any rate, whether the state's structural dependence on capital explains it or not, it is patently clear that really existing democracy is "compatible with a fair degree of inequality."

In the modern world driven by endemic conflicting interests, democracy's value derives not from the promise of redistribution, but rather from the possibility it holds out of managing conflict peacefully. This is the core idea Przeworski adapts from Schumpeter's *Capitalism, Socialism and Democracy* (1942), the work that is perhaps singly most responsible for the twentieth-century abandonment of the classical theory of democracy. Schumpeter modified classical democratic theory not only by junking the idea of the general will, but also by delinking democracy's legitimacy from any pretense that politicians represent voters. Instead, Schumpeter modeled his democratic theory on the neoclassical theory of price competition: just as firms compete for business in market systems, would-be political leaders compete for votes. Although political elites must in some minimal sense be responsive to voters on this view (or at least less unresponsive than their competitors), democracy is not fundamentally about representation; it is about selling a product – governmental output – in exchange for votes. The *sine qua non* of democracy, on this view, is institutionalized competition for power. Losers accept defeat in return for peace and the possibility of victory in the future. Winners are kept sober by what Przeworski describes as the "flexing muscles" inherent in majority rule. At best, majority rule is "a reading of the chances of violent conflict," and is, at the very least, a source of information about values, passions, and interests that should be taken into account if elections are to continue as a peaceful substitute for rebellion. It does not always work, but when it does "the miracle of democracy is that conflicting political forces obey the results of voting. People who have guns obey those without them. Incumbents risk their control of governmental offices by holding elections. Losers wait for their chance to win office. Conflicts are regulated, processed according to rules, and thus limited. This is not consensus, yet not mayhem either." Przeworski thus endorses Engels's description of ballots as "paper stones," but not his deprecation of them. To those who reject this view as too minimal to be worth valuing, his answer is straightforward: tell that to the billions in the world who currently live without it.

John Roemer, in chapter 3, pursues further the view that it is a mistake to expect democracy to deliver many ancillary benefits. Just as those on the Left were misguided, in the 1960s, when they identified socialism as the confluence of all good things, Roemer thinks we should resist similar temptations with democracy today. In particular, he is skeptical of attempts to insist on an internal relationship between democracy and justice. Arguing that the question "does democracy engender justice?" can be interesting only if we avoid settling it by definition, he endorses Przeworski's minimalist conception of democracy, and asks whether, as a causal matter, it should be expected to promote justice – or at least to diminish injustice. The answer, he argues, turns partly on how we comprehend justice and partly on what the distribution of interests and values is in the society in question. Roemer is willing to concede that democracy can generally be expected to promote justice of a purely procedural kind, but this is not the kind of justice that is widely embraced in the literature, and not the kind that Roemer believes ought to command allegiance. The justice that interests Roemer would involve significant diminution in income inequality in virtually all of today's market economies. How should we think about the likelihood that democracy will promote that?

Exploring this question leads Roemer to tackle the question "why do democracies based on universal suffrage not redistribute downwards more than they do, as many nineteenth-century liberals feared and some on the Left hoped that they would?" In contradistinction to the notion that the state is structurally dependent on private capital, Roemer's solution to this puzzle relies less on speculations about prudent calculations on the part of voters, and more on the complexities of their preferences. He agrees that some factors which lead voters not to press for greater redistribution are rooted in their beliefs about its likely effects on the economy and, perhaps, themselves. Roemer speculates that these beliefs might change as voter sophistication increases and expert opinion diverges less than it does now, favoring more redistribution. Yet there are more profound obstacles to redistribution in many democracies. Roemer observes that in circumstances where there is a high degree of agreement on values other than those relating to distributive issues, as in the Nordic countries, democracy does in fact lead to pressure for downward redistribution. But when politics are multidimensional, for instance if a left/right dimension with respect to distributive concerns is intersected by an authoritarian/libertarian dimension concerning "values," as in the United States, then vote-maximizing parties might well find it to be in their interest not to advocate strongly redistributive policies. If justice requires significant redistribution, Roemer does not think we should expect democracy to deliver much of it in this type of circumstance.

Przeworski and Roemer both offer incisive critiques of those who think democracy should be valued because it converges on the right decisions, is genuinely representative, or that it promotes other values democrats often care about, such as egalitarian justice. Trenchant as these critiques are, there is a still more fundamental one that they do not take up, deriving from Kenneth Arrow's (1951) famous impossibility theorem. Arrow showed that unless significant restrictions are placed on individual preferences, any collective decision procedure that satisfies some quite minimal conditions is subject to the possibility of "cycles" in which every apparent majority can be beaten by some other majority. Arrow's result questions the coherence of all procedures of collective decision-making. In response, democratic theorists have developed a vast literature geared to undermining, avoiding, reinterpreting, restricting, or otherwise escaping from the apparently devastating implications. If this cannot be done, it is commonly assumed that libertarians – who often try to draw sustenance from Arrow's findings – appear to have a home run. If all procedures of collective decision-making are as internally flawed as the theorem suggests, how can collective action ever be deemed legitimate?

In fact the libertarian conclusion does not follow, since it assumes, implausibly, that a scheme of collective action is an alternative to a scheme of private action (Shapiro 1996). The latter is in fact parasitic on the former. The institutions of private property, contract, and public monopoly of coercive force that libertarians characteristically favor were created and are sustained by the state, partly financed by implicit taxes on those who would prefer an alternative system. The real question, for democrats, is not "whether or not collective action?" but whether or not democratic modes of managing it are superior to the going alternatives. Enter Partha Dasgupta and Eric Maskin. In chapter 4 they demonstrate that once the question is thus conceived, majority rule can indeed be shown to avoid the possibility of Arrovian cycling over a broader range of preference orderings than any other procedures of collective decision-making. Maskin's demonstration, in an earlier work, of majority rule's robustness in this sense was limited to cases where the population is odd, because it could not deal with populations that are evenly divided. Here Dasgupta and Maskin demonstrate that the result holds when populations are large, and the knife-edge case is thus exceedingly unlikely. Accordingly they can conclude that to the extent that Arrow identified a genuine problem for the practice of collective decision-making, majority rule avoids it more than the going alternatives.

Dasgupta and Maskin's defense of the reasonableness of democratic procedures of collective decision-making extends beyond the realm of pure theory. They are less skeptical than Przeworski and Roemer of general claims about democracy's ancillary benefits, but concede that benign authoritarian regimes can sometimes deliver greater benefits than do democracies. Yet they caution that the common belief that "benevolent authoritarianism is a sure-fire route to sustained economic betterment is a belief in an incongruent object: sustained benevolent authoritarianism." Dictatorships are prone to turn nasty in tough times or when opposition develops, and they are subject to chronic information problems. In any case, anecdotally based observations about benign authoritarianism are not supported by systematic data. Dasgupta and Maskin note that the available evidence weighs against those who contend that democracy is a luxury good that poor countries can ill afford. While causal arguments about the relations between democracy and human well-being are notoriously difficult to establish, they leave little doubt that, statistically speaking, poor countries that enjoy greater political and civil liberties also experience greater improvements in life expectancy at birth, real per capita income, and infant survival rates (but such is not the case with literacy).

Important as competitive elections are, on Dasgupta and Maskin's view, they are not sufficient for effective democratic government. They must be accompanied by mechanisms of accountability at every level of administration, lest government be captured by powerful interest groups. They buttress this contention via an examination of collective management of local common-property resources among rural communities in poor countries. Since Garrett Hardin's (1968) seminal discussion of the "tragedy of the commons," it has been conventional to assume that common resources will inevitably be eroded by self-interested actors. In the absence of sanctions, each individual has an incentive to overgraze the common pasture, free-riding on the collective

bounty until it is destroyed. While Dasgupta and Maskin are skeptical of
this as an argument for privatizing all common resources, they are
equally skeptical of proposals to police the commons by a centralized
state. The former excludes some from any access to the resources in
question, while the latter assumes, unwisely, that central governments –
even democratic ones – have the requisite knowledge to police commons
effectively. They take note of a burgeoning empirical literature which
tends to show that although large-scale commons, such as ocean fisheries, rain forests, or clean air, are often eroded by the logic of individual
incentives, this is not generally true of small commons which function as
risk-pooling devices in poor communities. Partly because the players
know one another, partly because their behavior is observable, and
partly for other reasons, these communities do manage to use common
resources efficiently.

Yet Dasgupta and Maskin do not idealize local communities. The
systems of local norms through which commons are policed can be
exclusionary, they can operate to the disproportionate benefit of some,
and they can become inefficient if those who work most on commons
(often women, in rural areas) and thus have the most pertinent local
knowledge about them, are excluded from systems of local decision-
making. As with national democracy, at the local level democracy works
in tandem with efficiency by helping bring relevant knowledge to bear
on decisions about governance. That is partly why Dasgupta and
Maskin find it desirable. This leads them to argue that enlightened
governments will seek to foster democracy in the procedures by which
local communities regulate themselves rather than obliterate local
control through either privatization or direct assertions of central power.
Introducing mechanisms of democratic accountability wherever power
is exercised is, in their view, the best course to pursue as far as
promoting well-being is concerned. Yet they are careful to emphasize
that it will not guarantee prosperity. Rather, it will encourage "the
creation of a social and economic environment where citizens have a
chance to thrive."

II   Beyond minimalism

But perhaps more can be said. Perhaps democracy has predictable
effects on the organization and operation of a country's economy.
Pranab Bardhan takes up this much-debated question in chapter 5, also
with particular emphasis on developing economies. Noting that systematic empirical evidence concerning democracy's effects on the
economy is inconclusive, he tries to make the case that democracy is

more conducive to development in some contexts than in others, that
different kinds of democracy may be more important at some phases of
development than in others, and that, taking all the imponderables into
account, it makes better sense to bet on democracy rather than against it
as far as development is concerned. In the course of his discussion
Bardhan shows that there is neither decisive reason nor compelling
evidence to suppose democracy to be better or worse equipped than
authoritarianism at solving precommitment problems that are important
for economic development, that while it may be reasonable to expect
less bribery in the bureaucracies of democracies, this may be more
damaging to development than bribery that arises under authoritarianism, but that it is sometimes easier for authoritarian rulers to sacrifice
development to other goals than it is for elected governments. He notes
that democratic accountability mechanisms may be better for heading
off developmental catastrophes, such as famines, than authoritarian
systems, but they may be worse at dealing with endemic hunger and
nutrition. "Sometimes in a democracy it seems easier to focus political
attention to dramatic disturbances in a low-level equilibrium, than to
the lowness of the level itself."

Turning to the issue of what kind of democratic accountability is most
conducive to development, Bardhan notes that in developing countries,
where much economic activity occurs in far-flung villages at the edges of
the informal sector, local political power may be most significant. Yet he
notes that there are no one-to-one relationships between national
democracy and local accountability. Whereas Chinese local Communist
Party officials have sometimes been quite responsive to local needs, in
large parts of northern India rampant absenteeism of salaried teachers
in village schools and doctors in rural public health clinics results from
the absence of effective systems of local accountability. Solutions to such
difficulties can be hard to come by. Increasing local accountability can
be regressive in its effects in inegalitarian circumstances, as in the
reassertion of "states' rights" in the American context or the decentralization of financing of local schools which leads to the secession of the
rich. Efforts to democratize at the local level can also destroy traditional
systems of common resource management, and the new self-governing
forms of local association that democrats envisage might fail to even-
tuate or be corrupted by agents with ulterior motives. Democratization
can also lead to populist pressures for protectionism and preferential
policies that benefit strategically well-placed groups. In the short term
these can advance development, but in the longer term they can
produce dependent interest groups that should be expected to manufacture continual pressure to abolish sunset clauses, and preserve infant

industry and other remedial protections. Bardhan notes that authoritarian governments have found these pressures easier to resist than democracies when they are committed to development. But partly because there is less likely to be pressure on them to be committed to development in the first place, on balance Bardhan concludes that pressing for democracy – without romanticizing it – is to be preferred.

It would seem, then, that in addition to democracy's inability to guarantee advances in government's representativeness or rationality and its detachment from values of equality and justice, its capacity to foster economic development is speculatively contingent at best. If so, one is bound to wonder why democracy emerged at all. Przeworski's answer to this question, it will be recalled, is that, when it can be self-sustaining, democracy offers a solution to the Hobbesian problem: it gives losers in the political process a reason not to reach for their guns; but as Margaret Levi notes in chapter 6, a rigorous argument has yet to be made establishing that democracy, thus conceived, should be expected to sustain itself rather than fall apart. Moreover, there are other solutions to the Hobbesian problem, most obviously Hobbes's own. If democracy's only contribution is that sometimes it can avoid the anarchic violence of a war of all against all, authoritarianism can achieve that result as well. The question remains, therefore, why democracy should have survived, against the odds, when it delivers so few of the goods people commonly associate with it and even its minimalist value is debatable.

This is the question Levi takes up, and reverses. Instead of asking what norms and values democracy might be thought instrumental in promoting, her concern is with the norms and values that promote democracy. Perhaps democracy is an institutional expression of other values, or it is a by-product of other purposes. If so, understanding democracy's nature and its place in the social order will require attention to those values and purposes. Surprisingly, she notes, despite the rivers of ink that have flowed in attempting to account for democracy's origins, the standard explanations fail to square with the available evidence. We have serviceable explanatory accounts of the emergence of constitutionalism, and of so-called "proto-democracy" – the limited expansion of the franchise to include elites whose involvement is sought in joint projects with the state. But this is a far cry from the mass extension of the franchise characteristic of modern democracy. Why would people seek to achieve this, and why would non-democratic rulers accede to it?

Among other things, governments seek to raise revenue and fight wars, for which they must extract both money and soldiers from the population. In principle this can be done by force, but it is costly, and in some cases the required institutional wherewithal is unavailable. Levi suggests that a "contingent consent" on the part of the population can facilitate government's extraction of the relevant resources. Contingent consent involves "a norm that sometimes means a citizen will act in a way counter to self-interest but only if she is convinced that she is not a sucker within her reference group and that government actors are acting in ways that promote democracy and its long-term benefits." In Levi's view, it is the demand for egalitarian fairness that gives rise to democratic expectations. In the area of conscription, for example, governments found that insisting on universality (and thus refusing to allow discriminatory exemptions for wealthy and powerful constituents) produced more active compliance from the masses. Similarly, she argues, democratization provided "a means for popular discussion and approval of the war and conscription policy," making wars more difficult to fight without popular support but more effective when it was forthcoming. Levi proposes that we conceive of the demand for "no taxation without representation" in a similar fashion. Confronted with obligations to deliver up taxes, people pushed for democracy to ensure that the burden would be equitably enforced against all. Rulers discovered that the bargain was worth making because it reduced the costs of ensuring tax compliance. Democracy arises, on this account, when large numbers of unenfranchised persons control resources that the state needs, and they have a view of fairness "that implies relative equality and voice." If empirical research turns out to support Levi's contention, it may also shed light on a conundrum noted by Roemer: that in democracies no matter whose interests political parties actually represent, they claim to be fairly representing the interests of all.

In chapter 7 John Dunn registers skepticism at any attempts to find general relationships between democracy and development, or between democracy and the needs of governments to secure widespread compliance with their extractive ambitions. He notes that democracies have emerged as a consequence of a great many factors, among them the departure of colonial governments, the arrival of victorious occupying forces, threats of international sanctions, the loss of nerve by military rulers, and angry insurrections on the part of local populations. Moreover, he points out, claims about the relations between democracy and the extractive ambitions of governments are often so ill-specified and contradictory as to defy all possibility of systematic evaluation – as when democracies are simultaneously said both to be congenitally incapable of taxing adequately and hence fiscally profligate, and unable to resist taxing too much for redistributive or rent-seeking purposes. If there is a generalization to be had about the forces that give rise to democracy,

Dunn thinks about it in negative terms: no such generalization is likely to be persuasive unless it includes the motivations of those who fight for democracy and create democratic institutions. On the basis of his "skeptical, historical approach which sees normative categories as inexpugnable from the understanding of political causality," we should not expect democracy to be a mere by-product of political bargaining. Important as bargaining often is in politics, those who fight for democracy typically seek something more "in which a miscellany of free agents deliberate freely with one another and choose interactively what is to be done through the apparatus of public choice." As a description of the way politics actually works, this is typically "impertinent," but that is because it captures a political aspiration; it is not a category of social-scientific prediction.

Important as the aspiration of those who design and manufacture democratic institutions might be, Dunn and Levi agree that on their own they cannot account for the growth of modern democracies. Much conventional wisdom in political science implicitly denies this by focusing exclusively on elite pacts as the only – or at any rate the principal – means by which democracies are brought into being. But as Levi helpfully points out, unless more widespread demands for democratic inclusion emanate from civil society, anti-authoritarian elites will have scant reason to endorse a universal franchise, let alone insist upon it. Of course, Levi could be right that democracy develops partly due to widespread expectations that the state should be made to promote egalitarian justice and fairness, while at the same time Przeworski and Roemer could be right that in fact democracies fail to do this. Indeed, part of the Schumpeterian move in democratic theory is motivated by the perception that this disjunction is real. Because democracy will not deliver on expectations about egalitarian justice and fairness, the argument goes, it is important to detach democracy from these expectations. Hence Samuel Huntington's (1991: 165–9) contention that elites who sell out on constituents' demands for social justice are more likely to consolidate democracy than those who do not, and Guiseppe Di Palma's (1990: 23) insistence that the democratic ideal should be disengaged "from the idea of social progress" if it is to endure.

Nor is it only the Schumpeterians who perceive the disjunction. As Iris Young points out in chapter 8, in recent years libertarians, communitarians, and post-Marxists of various stripes have sought to delegitimate the democratic state by appeal to similar arguments. Whereas Schumpeterians seek to diminish demands on democratic states by casting off ancillary agendas that are likely to fail in a democracy (with damaging results), these commentators think it is misguided to rely on democratic states as instruments for advancing such agendas for the same reason. However, they draw a different implication: that egalitarian justice and fairness is better pursued, if at all, through the institutions of civil society. Young questions this turn, arguing that we should decline the available invitations to abandon the role of a democratic state in advancing social justice. These claims generally turn on a combination of appeals to the alleged virtues of "strong" civil societies and the vices of democratic states that become hostage to sectional interests or the bureaucrats who manage them, and generally lack the capacity for efficacious action. Dismissing neither claim, Young argues instead that both are overstated and underanalyzed. On her telling, the claim that strong civil institutions promote social justice is true of some aspects of social justice and some civil institutions only.

On Young's account, social justice is about the absence of domination that promotes self-determination as well as the absence of oppression that facilitates self-development. Civil institutions are a lot better at fostering the former than the latter. Whereas self-determination often flourishes best in the voluntary contexts of human association that are characteristic of civil institutions, self-development requires the development of skills and capacities – what Amartya Sen (1992) calls "capabilities" – for which the needed resources are typically maldistributed. Particularly given the ubiquitous character of market systems and the systematic inequalities they bring with them, Young thinks it is sheer fancy to suppose that capabilities will be anywhere near as widely developed as they might be without a regulatory state geared to regulating the market, acting where it fails, redistributing through the tax system, providing and maintaining infrastructure and other public goods, and generally serving as guarantor of people's basic interests. Mindful of the arguments about the limitations of state capacity, Young cautions against misleading comparisons of state failures with civil society successes. She points out that despite the state's failures when it has embarked on totalizing ventures, it has been comparatively successful when its activities have been limited to fostering the capacities for self-development. It is in this area that a democratic state can and should promote social justice. Young would not dissent from the proposition that democratic states have often failed to do this, but for her the appropriate resulting imperative is to try to get them to do it better in future.

A conventional objection to claims, such as Young's, that democratic states are needed to prevent domination is that they can actually foster it. This is the stock libertarian critique of democratic government, although as Philip Pettit notes in chapter 9 it has been around for some time. An influential strand of political ideology in the West has persistently condemned democracy as particularly threatening to liberty at least since Sir Robert Filmer (1991 [c. 1633]: 275) insisted that "there are more laws in popular estates than anywhere else, and so consequently less liberty." In the nineteenth century this critique took the form of worries about majority tyranny, most commonly associated with the names of Alexis de Tocqueville and John Stuart Mill. During the second half of the twentieth century, in the wake of the post-Arrovian public choice literature, the libertarian critique has become yet more trenchant: what appears as majority tyranny might not even be that. Majoritarian processes all too easily lend themselves to capture and manipulation by well-organized minorities to advance their particular interests. On these accounts, one might be persuaded by Young's discussion of the sources of domination and oppression, yet remain skeptical that centralized authority wielded by a democratic state is the appropriate response. Instead one might conclude that the cure is worse than the disease. In addition to democracy's problematic interactions with the values of justice, equality, rationality, representation, and development, there appear to be enduring tensions between it and the demands of human freedom or liberty. No discussion of democracy's relations with other values would be complete without attending to these tensions. They are Pettit's central preoccupation.

Before one can determine whether and to what degree democracy undermines liberty, the relevant terms must be defined. With respect to liberty, Pettit counsels avoiding Isaiah Berlin's famous dichotomy between "negative" conceptions (in which freedom is regarded as noninterference) and "positive" conceptions (in which self-mastery is the motivating idea). Instead he argues for a republican conception, "akin to the negative one in maintaining that what liberty requires is the absence of something" yet akin to the positive conception "in holding that that which must be absent has to do with mastery rather than interference." Liberty consists, for Pettit, "not in the presence of self-mastery, and not in the absence of interference by others, but rather in the absence of mastery by others." In short, for Pettit as for Young, liberty consists in the absence of domination.

Is democracy better placed than the going alternatives to maximize liberty by limiting or preventing domination thus construed? This is the question we must answer to be able to decide whether democratic institutions can shoulder the burden Young believes that they should. To answer it, one must first settle on a particular view of democracy. Here Pettit's proffered candidate is what he describes as "contestatory democracy." Conventional majoritarian democracy cannot pass muster from his point of view because it can indeed foster domination. Majority rule may express the will of the people, but "the people" exist severally as well as collectively and it is in their several existence that majoritarian politics threatens them with domination. Pettit is aware that the libertarian option of "not having" collective action is chimerical for reasons we have already discussed. For him the institutional design challenge for democratic theory is thus to build and sustain democratic institutions that can limit domination more than the going alternatives. His notion of contestatory democracy draws on the oppositionalist impulse in democratic theory, traceable at least to Locke's (1965 [c. 1681]) discussion of the right to resist and emphasized in the contemporary literature by Robert Dahl (1956), Barrington Moore (1989), and Shapiro (1996: chaps. 5 and 8) among others. On this view democracy is as much about the freedom to oppose collective decisions as it is to participate in making them.

Because we all have good reasons to fear domination through the actions of governments, we also have good reasons to embrace forms of democracy that can institutionalize the right to oppose those actions. Opposition here cannot mean a veto power, however. Giving individuals vetoes, is in effect, to embrace unanimity rule, privileging whatever forms of domination might be built into the prevailing status quo. Rather, Pettit has in mind a variety of institutional devices, ranging from constitutional constraints, to the insistence on publicity of deliberation and debate, to multicameral institutions that facilitate the second-guessing of legislative decisions, to fora for local consultation in which people can force a reconsideration of decisions and help "edit" them as they apply in particular cases. In extreme cases consociational solutions and even separation may be justified, if it will create populations who are better placed to participate in contestatory democracy. Pettit thinks we should be hostile to opaque institutions that undermine contestatory democracy, even if such institutions are internally democratic, as well as to apparently democratic devices such as the citizen-initiated referendum, where reason-giving is not required and the majorities that prevail are under no compulsion to reconsider their policies in light of the claims of those who are harmed by them. On Pettit's account, those who value liberty ought to comprehend it in republican terms and embrace contestatory democracy as its most feasible institutional ally. This conclusion dovetails neatly with Young's ideal of a democratic state as geared to the prevention of domination and oppression. To the charge that the cure may be worse than the disease, Pettit's answer must be that the medical metaphor misleads. The question is not: "whether collective action?" Rather it is: "what sort of collective action?" Contestatory democracy, he argues, is better geared than the alternatives to institutionalizing mechanisms that limit the state's potential for tyranny.

One might be persuaded that contestatory democracy is the best available device to preserve republican liberty, yet still remain skeptical that the republican conception captures every worry that champions of freedom have in mind when they question democratic politics. This skeptical stance motivates Philippe Van Parijs's response, in chapter 10, to Pettit's argument. For Van Parijs, freedom is not to be valued as an end in itself but rather as a component of justice. To get at this issue, he contrasts Pettit's account with his own view of "real" freedom, asking how the latter should be expected to fare under contestatory democracy. Van Parijs defines real freedom as a supplement to purely formal freedom in that it encompasses "the means and not just the right" to do what one may wish to do. Anatole France's famous quip to the effect that the poor are free to sleep under the bridges of Paris captures what is at stake here. Purely formal or legal freedoms, while not without value, are seldom sufficient to make people meaningfully free. When Van Parijs advocates "real freedom for all" he is calling for universal availability of the resources needed to make their legal freedoms meaningful, and he wants to know how a contestatory democracy would affect their distribution.

Van Parijs concedes that in many circumstances contestatory democracy will vindicate real freedom as well as republican freedom. After all, Pettit defines republican freedom rather robustly when he says that exercises of power will be non-arbitrary – and hence compatible with republican freedom – only if they are "forced to track the interests and judgments of those on whom they are imposed." Moreover, Pettit construes adequate contestation to require a significant measure of deliberation. As Van Parijs notes, theorists of deliberative democracy have generally held that, in pluralist societies, meaningful deliberation requires both strong protection of fundamental liberties and strongly egalitarian distribution of the means needed to pursue the good life. With republican freedom and its connotations construed in this expansive fashion there is evidently considerable overlap with Parijs's real freedom, so that if contestatory democracy is the best bet for protecting the former it follows a fortiori that it will often be sufficient to vindicate the latter.

But not always. Even if it falls well short of a veto power, as Pettit insists that it must, for contestatory democracy to work at all, minorities who lose in the electoral process must be able to slow down collective action significantly, effectively paralyzing government while their claims are reheard. The danger is government by filibuster, and Van Parijs points out that this would be particularly likely in multilingual polities such as Belgium or the European Union. In such settings it is more difficult for minority voices to be heard, for Pettit's consultative editing to take place, and for legislative and administrative procedures to be seen by all to be impartial. These considerations suggest that if a smoothly functioning contestatory democracy is the most important value, then preserving or developing multilingual polities such as Belgium or the European Union is a bad idea. Better to divide the world into monolingual republics which can be efficient contestatory democracies internally, and avoid the costs of achieving meaningful contestation across linguistic boundaries. South Africa now has eleven official languages. If citizens regularly invoked their rights to transact any public business in their native tongue, South Africa would be a better contestatory republic than it is now. The country would also grind to a halt, however, devoting vast public resources to achieving the required translations in the process. Yet if this potential consequence were invoked as a reason to divide up the country, the chances that the injustices of apartheid could be rectified by governmental action would be greatly reduced. The same is true in Belgium, on Van Parijs's account. Dividing the country into its linguistically more homogeneous components would mean splitting up a social security system that currently redistributes from richer to poorer areas. Furthermore, he speculates, the newly autonomous fiscal components would engage in cut-throat fiscal competition with one another, "leading to lower redistribution within each of the components." In short, to the extent that real freedom requires significant redistribution across linguistic lines, contestatory democracy becomes its enemy not its ally.

The debate between Pettit and Van Parijs brings us full circle. The force of Van Parijs's critique is, in effect, to suggest that contestatory democracy will work best among internally homogeneous groups that are not perceived by substantial subgroups to be beset by inherited injustices that it is part of government's job to remedy. This sounds remarkably like the sort of conditions that Przeworski argued would be needed for the classical model of democracy to operate. Yet as we noted at the outset, even the ancient polis can be held to have fitted the description only from a myopic standpoint that excludes attention to women and slaves. One wonders if there are any countries in the modern world that do not contain significant perceptions of inherited injustice, reinforced by linguistic identities and cultural affiliations.

More generally, Pettit is surely right to conceive of contestation as important to ensure that disempowered and marginalized voices are heard in any democratic process worthy of the name, but this is not the only case we need to be concerned about. The difficulty is that the institutional devices he recommends for achieving this end – bills of rights enforced through judicial review, multi-cameralism, and other forms of stickiness in collective decision-making process – can all too easily be hijacked to serve the interests of disproportionately powerful minorities rather than disproportionately powerless ones. The Lochner era in the United States, when a conservative Supreme Court acting in the name of the Bill of Rights struck down masses of redistributive and other social legislation passed by Congress, is one sobering reminder of this possibility. The Court's refusal, since its 1976 decision in *Buckley v. Valeo*, to allow meaningful regulation of money in American politics on the grounds that this violates the First Amendment is another. The Clinton administration's decision to dismantle large parts of the welfare system on the grounds that these can be better managed by the several states – where more effective contestatory politics can and will take place – is a third.

This is not to say that contestatory democracy is a defective ideal any more than the ancient notion of democracy was. It is, rather, to acknowledge that democratic aspirations will always be at odds with reality in a world that is riven by widespread inequalities and injustices. People find democracy appealing partly because its universalist ethic holds out the possibility of undoing, or at least mitigating, many of the evils they see around them. Nowhere has this been more obvious in recent years than in the fights against communism and apartheid, where people demanded meaningful rights of democratic participation as engines for transforming their societies away from appalling cumulative effects of arbitrary power. That democracy gains popular legitimacy from the promise it holds out in this regard cannot be surprising. Why else would people want it, if not to make the world, if not better, at least less bad? That democracy typically fails to deliver fully in this regard – that it remains, perhaps forever, something of an impertinent ideal – should be no less surprising. Democracy invariably disappoints. But if we respond to this reality by abandoning the aspirations people associate with democracy, the danger is that we will end up with an ideal that will not merit enduring allegiance. Przeworski is right that the benefits of minimal democracy are manifest in circumstances where it is absent; but once minimal democracy has been established, people will inevitably expect, and demand, more from it than peace. The challenge remains, therefore, to come up with forms of political organization in which the chasms between democracy's promise and its disappointments can be bridged better, and more often.

REFERENCES

Arrow, Kenneth. 1951. *Social Choice and Individual Values*. New Haven: Yale University Press.

Dahl, Robert A. 1956. *A Preface to Democratic Theory*. Chicago: University of Chicago Press.

Di Palma, Guiseppe. 1990. *To Craft Democracies: An Essay on Democratic Transitions*. Berkeley: University of California Press.

Filmer, Sir Robert. 1991 (c. 1633). *Patriarcha and Other Writings*. Edited by Johann P. Sommerville. Cambridge and New York: Cambridge University Press.

Hardin, Garrett. 1968. "The tragedy of the commons." *Science* 162: 1243–8.

Huntington, Samuel P. 1991. *The Third Wave: Democratization in the Late Twentieth Century*. Norman: University of Oklahoma Press.

Locke, John. 1965 (c. 1681). *Two Treatises of Government*. Edited by Peter Laslett. New York: Mentor.

Moore, Barrington, Jr. 1989. *Liberal Perspectives on Soviet Socialism: A Comparative Historical Perspective*. New York: Columbia University, The Averill Harriman Institute.

Rousseau, Jean-Jacques. 1968 (1762). *The Social Contract*. Harmondsworth: Penguin.

Schumpeter, Joseph A. 1942. *Capitalism, Socialism, and Democracy*. New York: Harper.

Sen, Amartya. 1992. *Inequality Reexamined*. New York: Russell Sage Foundation; and Cambridge, MA: Harvard University Press.

Shapiro, Ian. 1996. *Democracy's Place*. Ithaca: Cornell University Press.

Part I

Minimal democracy

2   Minimalist conception of democracy: a defense[1]

Adam Przeworski

What is democracy other than a set of rules ... for the solution of conflicts without bloodshed?
(Bobbio 1984: 156)

Introduction

I want to defend a "minimalist," Schumpeterian, conception of democracy, by minimalist, Popperian, standards. In Schumpeter's (1942) conception, democracy is just a system in which rulers are selected by competitive elections. Popper (1962: 124) defends it as the only system in which citizens can get rid of governments without bloodshed.

By "conception," I mean a description that has value connotations, where the move from the empirical to the evaluative is definitional. Although Schumpeter (1942: 269) says that, in contradistinction to the classical doctrine, he offers "another theory which is much truer to life and at the same time salvages much of what sponsors of the democratic method really mean by this term," following Skinner (1973: 299), I think he does more: by designating the system he describes as "democracy," he appeals to evaluative, not just empirical, intuitions associated with this term. For one could easily say, "a system in which all people do is to choose among elites has nothing to do with 'democracy,' which is a system in which people rule." Indeed, Dahl (1971: 8), who agrees with most of Schumpeter's description, avoids making his move by reserving the concept of "democracy" to the ideal realm and inventing a neologism to designate the real world phenomenon: "since (in my view) no large system in the real world is fully democratized," Dahl says, "I prefer to call the real world systems ... polyarchies." So to defend Schumpeter's conception, I need to do both: to argue that his empirical description is accurate and that what he describes merits being positively valued.

[1] I appreciate comments by Joshua Cohen, Fernando Limongi, Bernard Manin, Alberto Paredes, Ignacio Sanchez-Cuenca, and James Vreeland.

Since neither the position I wish to defend nor the claim in its favor are new, what do I defend them from? Perusing innumerable definitions, one discovers that democracy has become an altar on which everyone hangs his or her favorite *ex voto*. Almost all normatively desirable aspects of political, and sometimes even of social and economic, life are credited as intrinsic to democracy: representation, accountability, equality, participation, justice, dignity, rationality, security, freedom, . . ., the list goes on. We are repeatedly told that "unless democracy is x or generates x, . . ." The ellipsis is rarely spelled out, but it insinuates either that a system in which governments are elected is not worthy of being called "democracy" unless x is fulfilled or that democracy in the minimal sense will not endure unless x is satisfied.[2] The first claim is normative, even if it often hides as a definition. The second is empirical.

Now, from the normative viewpoint, we could care foremost about x and treat any method of achieving it as morally neutral. Then the absence of x would speak against the method. For example, one could assert, as Skinner (1973: 303) does, that a system in which only some people rule cannot be properly termed a genuine "democracy" even if it is a competitive oligarchy. But if elections are valuable in themselves,[3] then the question arises whether there are good reasons to expect that the method of selecting governments has causal consequences for anything else. If there are no such reasons, then the critique of minimalism is purely hortatory. If elections are valuable and if they do not cause x, the absence of x is not sufficient to reject elections as a definitional feature of democracy. To bemoan perhaps yes, but to reject not.

Yet, from the empirical perspective, it may turn out that systems based on contested elections do not endure unless some x's hold. If democracy must generate some conditions – say John Stuart Mill's "high wages and universal reading" – just to last, then the minimalist defense of the minimal conception breaks down. More than elections are needed for elections to be held.

This is pretty much the outline of the chapter.

---

[2] Widely cited statements in this vein are Weffort 1992 and Schmitter and Karl 1991, but the phrase is ubiquitous. Here is Shapiro (1996: 108): "If democracy does not function to improve the circumstances of those who appeal to it, its legitimacy as a political system will atrophy." Even Kelsen (1988 [1929]: 38) poses the threat that "Modern democracy will not live unless the Parliament will show itself an instrument appropriate for the solution of the social questions of the hour."

[3] I am not certain how this claim relates to Shapiro's (1996) notion of democracy as a "subordinate foundational good." If democracy is "foundational" because other good things can be expected to follow from it, then I do not think it is foundational. In turn, while I agree that democracy is neither the only nor the highest nor the most universal good, I am not certain to what values is democracy "subordinate."

Theorems of democracy

Are there good reasons to think that if rulers are selected through contested elections then political decisions will be rational, governments will be representative, and the distribution of income will be egalitarian?

This is what I mean by "theorems": propositions of the form "if rulers are selected by freely contested elections, then . . . ." The consequences I discuss are not the only outcomes of conceivable interest. We could ask whether governments that are elected will obey laws, whether their actions will be limited in the sense that they would never do some things to citizens, whether laws passed by elected legislatures will be never collectively injurious, . . .; I leave the list open as an invitation to the reader.

It may be that answers to such questions are conditional on some institutional features that are not universal to democracies: for example, governments may be representative only in systems characterized by "clarity of responsibility" (Paldam 1991; Powell and Whitten 1993), itself a result of majoritarian electoral rules. Yet, even if my holy grail is institutional design, I do not consider such institutional variations systematically. I ask throughout whether elections are *sufficient* to generate the particular outcomes. Thus, while I assume throughout that all of Dahl's (1971) conditions defining elections as contested hold, my purpose is to examine the consequences of the bare fact that governments are freely elected, whatever the methods of election, other institutional features, cultural traditions, or social conditions.

My method is eclectic and opportunistic, which means that "theorems" should not be taken too seriously. Whenever the structure of the problem is sufficiently clear, I rely on deductive arguments. Whenever systematic empirical evidence exists, I bring to bear the "facts." But I also do not shy from trusting authorities, looking for intuitions in particular historical events, or simply asserting prior beliefs.

Democracy and rationality

Is democracy rational, in the eighteenth-century sense of this term?

This is a threefold question: (1) *Existence*. Is there something that can be considered as a welfare maximum defined over the political community, some state of the world which is best for all: general will, "voeu national," common good, public interest? (2) *Convergence*. If there is, does the democratic process identify it? (3) *Uniqueness*. Is the democratic process the unique mechanism that converges to this maximum?

The question whether democracy is rational in the sense that it satisfies these three conditions evokes five distinct responses, depending on whether (1) (a) such a welfare maximum is thought to exist prior to and independent of individual preferences, (b) it is thought to exist only as a function of individual preferences, whatever these might happen to be, or (c) it is thought not to exist at all, because of class or some other irreconcilable divisions of society; and whether (2) the democratic process is thought to converge to the maximum.

Condorcet, as well as Rousseau,[4] believed that the general interest is given a priori and that the democratic process converges to it. Conservatives in France and England at the time of the French Revolution, as well as contemporary ideologists of various authoritarianisms, maintain that such a prior welfare maximum does exist but that the democratic process does not lead to it. Economic theorists of democracy, notably Buchanan and Tullock (1962), held that the public interest is tantamount to the verdict of the democratic process, which thus identifies it. Arrow (1951) demonstrated that even if such a maximum does exist, no process of aggregation of ordinal preferences will reveal it.[5] Finally, Marx and his socialist followers argued that no such general interest can be found in societies divided into classes.

The foundational argument that democracy is rational in the above sense was put forth by Condorcet in 1785 (1986): there exists some state of the world which is best for all; hence, one "correct" decision. If each individual is endowed with reason, that is, each person is more likely to vote for rather than against the correct decision, then an assembly is more likely to make the right decision than each individual separately. Indeed, as the size of the assembly increases relative to the majority required to adopt a decision, it becomes almost certain that the assembly will make the correct choice. Majority rule in a large assembly makes it almost infallible.

Condorcet's argument, known as the "jury theorem" (henceforth, CJT), states the following. Assume that there exists some correct decision for a political community, $D = C$. Let $p = \Pr\{D = C\}$ be the uniform probability that an individual votes for the correct decision. Let P_n be the probability that a majority, $m = (n+1)/2$, of an assembly of size n, votes for the correct decision, so that $P_n = \Pr(D = C) > n/2)$. The jury theorem asserts that if $p > 1/2$ then (i) $P_n > p$, and (ii) $P_n \to 1$ as $n \to \infty$.

---

[4] On the relation between Condorcet and Rousseau, see the exchange between Grofman and Feld (1988 and 1989) with Estlund and with Waldron (Estlund, Waldron, Grofman, and Feld 1989), and below.

[5] While no mechanism of aggregation guarantees to generate a unique social choice, a unique welfare maximum can exist over cardinal preferences or with interpersonal comparisons. See Sen 1995 and Roemer 1996a.

Computation shows that the convergence is quite rapid: with $p = 0.55$, $P_{399} = 0.98$.

The intuition underlying this theorem relies on the stylized situation of a jury, facing a decision to convict or acquit someone charged with a crime. Presumably there is some true underlying state of affairs (guilty or not guilty) and the jury wants only to administer justice. Each juror has the same information and each can reason equally well. The probability that a majority (any combination of members that adds to a majority) will make the correct decision is then greater than the probability that each member would make it independently.

This theorem can be extended in several ways. Grofman, Owen, and Feld (1983) generalized it to a situation in which individual probabilities are not the same. They showed that when the individual probabilities are symmetrically distributed with the mean $\bar{p} > 1/2$, CJT still holds and the convergence is still rapid. Their theorem implies that collective competence may increase with the size of the assembly even if increasing the size lowers the average individual competence. Hence, democracy – collective decision-making by voting – is likely to yield decisions superior to those made by any single individual, even if the dictator is exceptionally wise. Since, as we have already seen, an assembly of the size $n = 399$ in which the average individual has only a 0.55 chance of voting correctly has a 0.98 of making a correct decision by majority rule, only a dictator with $p_i > 0.98$ would do better, and there may be no one in the population who is that wise. Hence, more stupid voters are likely to reach better decisions than a few wise ones.[6]

The Condorcet jury theorem and its extensions appear to provide powerful arguments in favor of rationality of democracy. At least when information is costless,[7] large assemblies deciding by a simple majority rule out-perform each individual deciding separately, a random individual making the decision for all, or an oligarchy. Hence, the normative implication of the CJT is that, if there exists one correct decision for all – that is, if the democratic process is purely "epistemic," just a search for the truth – and if individuals are endowed with reason, in the precise

[6] The CJT is based on the assumption that each individual or the average individual has enough "reason" that his or her probability of voting correctly is greater than one half. This seems to be a safe assumption but Waldron (Estlund, Waldron, Grofman, and Feld 1989) offered several arguments that we should not be sanguine about it. In fact, careful statements of this theorem make it explicit that when $p < 1/2$, $P_n < p$ and $P_n \to 0$ as $n \to \infty$. Hence, collective decision-making accentuates individual propensities both in the good and the bad direction. If individuals are more likely to vote against a correct decision, then, as Karl Pearson remarked, "... it is safer to entrust business, if it must be so, to one stupid person, than to a committee of fools" (cited by Berg 1993: 4).

[7] Sah and Stiglitz (1988) consider the costs of information, "project evaluation" in their language.

sense that each is more predisposed to adopt than to reject a socially beneficial project, then democracy is better than alternative ways of making decisions.

But what is it that the Condorcet process aggregates? The normative force of CJT arises from the result that, if $p > 1/2$, $P_n > p$, that is, the probability that an assembly of size n will adopt the correct decision by a simple majority rule is larger than p. But what is p? If it is indeed the probability of *voting* correctly, then it has no consequence beyond the voting process which results in P_n: it provides no counterfactual since it is relevant only when decisions are made collectively, by voting.[8] The statement "If each individual voted independently, . . ." makes no sense. Ladha's (1992) proof of CJT is revealing in this regard: he compares the expected value of the collective decision, nP_n, to the expected value of successes when each individual makes decisions independently, np. But voting to do something collectively and doing something independently is not the same, and it need have the same probability.

Assume that the decision is such that it can be made either by each individual separately or jointly by a vote.[9] If individuals were to make decisions in a decentralized way, each deciding what to do, the collectivity would arrive at a situation that would be strictly inferior to a state of the world that could be attained if individuals voted and the decision reached by the vote were coercively enforced. Suppose that each individual decides independently whether to vaccinate him or herself against a contagious disease, where vaccination has some positive probability of triggering the illness. Each individual would prefer not to vaccinate herself if all others (or some number of others) did, and the result would be that no one would vaccinate and the disease would be widespread. Yet if individuals vote whether to impose compulsory vaccination, they unanimously decide to do so and, in the centralized equilibrium, few people suffer from the disease. They are coerced to vaccinate for their own good.

To put it generally (Runciman and Sen 1965), whenever the structure of interests in society is such that the equilibrium in dominant strategies is inefficient, the cooperative solution is not a stable aggregation of individual interests. This solution represents the collective interest and individuals will vote for it if they expect that it would be enforced, so that others will not defect. Yet this solution is the result of mapping the

---

[8] One could interpret p as the probability that a randomly chosen dictator would make the correct decision. This interpretation cannot be sustained, however, in the presence of externalities.

[9] Note that Grofman and Owen (1986: 94) define p as the probability of "*choosing* that alternative which is the preferred choice with respect to some single designated criterion by which alternatives are evaluated" (italics supplied).

collective outcome on individual *votes* but not individual *interests*, which is the point of Estlund and of Waldron (Estlund, Waldron, Grofman, and Feld 1989). Hence, the CJT does not solve the problem of aggregation of interests, only of votes. The collective decision does identify a common interest, but this common interest is not an aggregate of individual interests, for the very reason we vote is to authorize coercing all or some individuals to do what they do not want to do. As Kelsen (1988 [1929]: 23) argues, this collective decision identifies not the *volonté generale* but a *volonté étatique*: the will to exercise rule, to coerce. To cite Dunn (1996b: 29), "democracy is one (very broadly defined) form of being ruled. . . . It is not, and cannot be, an alternative to being ruled."

But the problem in identifying a common interest is not limited to strategic interdependence that requires that cooperation be coercively enforced. If that were all, one could still sensibly claim that there is some common interest by which individuals are united, in so far as that unless this interest is made to prevail, the outcome would be collectively suboptimal: one reading of Rousseau's (1984 [1762]: 66) assumption that "If there were not some point in which all interests agree, no society could exist." The real issue is that interests of different individuals, and groups, may be in conflict (Schmitt 1988: 13).

The difference between the jury and the electorate is that while the jury is faced with an issue which has one answer which is correct for all individuals, different decisions may be correct for different voters. Suppose citizens vote on one issue, taxes. Then some people inevitably gain and some lose from any course of action a government chooses. This difference led Black (1958: 163) to conclude that the CJT was irrelevant for the theory of elections:

Now whether there is much or little to be said in favor of a theory of juries arrived at in this way, there seems to be nothing in favor of a theory of elections that adopts this approach. When a judge, say, declares an accused person to be either guilty or innocent, it would be possible to conceive of a test which, in principle at least, would be capable of telling us whether his judgment had been right or wrong. But in the case of elections, no such test is conceivable; and the phrase "the probability of correctness of a voter's opinion" seems to be without definite meaning.

Miller (1986) set himself to save the CJT from this criticism. He abandoned the assumption that there exists a unique "correct decision" for all individuals, and defined the correct decision for each voter as the decision that promotes her interests. Hence, p_i is now the probability that an individual votes in favor of his or her interests. Miller then defined the correct decision for the collectivity as the decision that would result under majority vote if everyone was certain to vote correctly. If $p > 1/2$ is the same for all voters, the CJT extends immediately: majority interest is likely to prevail, for a sufficiently large assembly the probability that it would prevail is greater than the competence of individual voters, and it increases in n, although the convergence is slower. There is, however, one important difference between the electorate and the jury theorems: while the probability that the majority interest prevails is always greater than the proportion of voters voting for the majority position, this probability need not be greater than the proportion of voters voting correctly (in support of their interests) when n is small.

Miller's is no longer an "epistemic" theory (Cohen 1986; Coleman 1989): when the minority loses, it is not because it is less well informed about the common good but because its interests are in conflict with interests of the majority. Collective decision-making may favor majority interests but the majority interest is not the common interest.[10] Miller's solution is clearly unsatisfactory: promoting the interest of the majority is not the same as furthering the interest of all the members of a political community. Grofman and Feld did not do any better in their response to Estlund and Waldron (Estlund, Waldron, Grofman, and Feld 1989): all they could say is that sometimes a common interest does exist. Hence, Black's point stands: the "correctness" of collective decisions seems to be without definite meaning when this decision consists of an imposition of one interest over another.

This conclusion will be challenged by those who believe that conflicts of interests can be overcome by a public discussion about normative reasons, "deliberation": a view in which, to cite Sieyès, politics "is not a question of a democratic election, but of proposing, listening, concerting, changing one's opinion, in order to form in common a common will" (cited by Elster 1998: 3). Yet Cohen (1997) admits that there is nothing that guarantees that deliberation, even if it satisfies all of his (1989 and 1997) stipulations, will lead to a consensus about the common good. Manin (1987) concluded that while deliberation leads to the broadest agreement possible at a particular time, it stops there, leaving conflicts unresolved; and perhaps conceptions of the common good of two groups educated to believe that their interests conflict are more divergent that those based on fragmented "wanton" desires, to use a term of Hirschman (1985). After all, this was precisely Marxists'

---

[10] Majority victory may maximize the sum of individual utilities (Dahl 1989: 143) but this sum is not increasing in welfare of each individual when there is a conflict of interest. It is not the maximum of a social welfare function.

understanding of the deliberative process: that it leads to recognizing class identity and the irreconcilability of class interests.

Thus, while I conclude that democratic decisions cannot be in general expected to be rational, this is not a deficiency of the method – making collective decisions by voting – but of the underlying structure of interests. When individual interests are harmonious to the point that individual decisions generate no externalities or when they are compatible to the point that there exists one collective interest that everyone wants to be coercively enforced, democracy generates rational decisions and does it better than alternative systems. If the everyday life of democracy consists of perpetual bickering among quarrelsome politicians, it is because interests are at stake, and interests are often in conflict.

Representation[11]

Governments are representative if they do what is best for the people, act in the best interests of at least a majority of citizens. There are four possible reasons why governments would represent interests of the people:

(1) Because only those persons who are public-spirited offer themselves for public service and they remain uncorrupted by power while in office.

(2) Because, while individuals who offer themselves for public service differ in their motivations and in their competence – some candidates for office are selfless and competent and others are rascals or potential rascals – citizens use their vote effectively to select good candidates, who remain dedicated to the public service while holding office.

(3) Because, while anyone who holds office may want to pursue some interests or values different from and costly to the people, citizens use their vote effectively to threaten those who would stray too far from the path of virtue with being thrown out of office and not being able to enjoy its fruits any longer.

(4) Because separate powers of government check and balance each other in such a way that, together, they end up acting in people's best interest.

The first hypothesis should not be dismissed. Many persons who seek public office want to serve the public and probably some remain dedicated to the public service while in power. If I do not consider this

---

[11] This section is based on joint work with Bernard Manin and Susan Stokes. See Manin, Przeworski, and Stokes 1996.

possibility, it is because this way of securing representation is not distinctive of democracy. Dictators can be also representative: if they know and if they seek to do what people want, nothing prevents them from doing it. The connection between democracy and representation cannot depend on luck. A central claim of democratic theory is that democracy offers mechanisms that systematically cause governments to be representative.

This claim is widespread: "representation," or its cognates, is frequently treated as quintessential, if not definitional, for democracy. Thus Dahl (1971: 1) observes that "a key characteristic of a democracy is the continued responsiveness of the government to the preferences of its citizens"; Riker (1965: 31) asserts that "democracy is a form of government in which the rulers are fully responsible to the ruled"; while Schmitter and Karl (1991: 76) maintain that "modern political democracy is a system of governance in which rulers are held accountable for their actions in the public realm by citizens. . . ."

Yet representation is problematic.[12] Politicians may have goals, interests, or values of their own and they may know things and undertake actions that citizens cannot observe or can monitor only at a prohibitive cost. Politicians may be willing to do anything to be (re)elected, they may seek private gain from holding public office, or they may have some well-meaning objectives that nevertheless differ from those of citizens. If they have such motivations, they will want to do things which informed citizens would not have wanted them to do. Conversely, people may be poor judges of their own interests, and politicians, knowing what is best for the public, may still act in ways that citizens do not appreciate.

There are three, and only three, ways of assessing whether or not a government is representative, in the sense that it acts in the best interest of the public: (1) if the people (or at least a majority of them; see below) has a will, then the government is representative if it implements this will; (2) if no such will exists or at least if it cannot be expressed as a

---

[12] Representation entails two distinct principal–agent relations: between citizens as principals and elected politicians as agents and between politicians as principals and non-elected bureaucrats as agents. Yet citizens' control over the bureaucracy can be only indirect, since democratic institutions contain no mechanisms that would allow citizens to sanction directly legal actions of bureaucrats. Citizens can at most consider the performance of the bureaucracy when they sanction the behavior of elected politicians. As Dunn and Uhr (1993: 2) suggest, we do not even seem to know how to think about principal–agent relations involved in controlling bureaucrats: "it is by no means clear what place executive officials are meant to play as representatives of the people. Are they agents of the government or of the people? If of the former, are they primarily responsible to the executive which employs them, or the legislature which funds them?" Hence, while the bureaucracy is supposed to be responsive to citizens, it is accountable at most to politicians. I focus, therefore, on the relation between citizens and elected politicians.

mandate, but individuals are best judges of their interests, then a government is representative if it satisfies *ex post* evaluations of its actions, as evidenced by its re-election; (3) if elections neither express a prior will nor testify ex post to the quality of government actions, representation remains a matter of educated, but inevitably contestable, judgments of informed observers.

For all its power and subtlety, Pitkin's analysis of representation is incoherent. She assumes that "normally a man's wishes and what is good for him will coincide" (1967: 156). Yet at the same time she claims both that "the represented have no will on most issues, and the duty of the representative is to do what *is* best for them, not what they latently want" (163; italics supplied) and that the incumbent's "reelection is not absolute proof that he is a good representative; it proves at most that voters think so" (165).

But if neither voters' prospective instructions nor their retrospective evaluations can be taken as criteria of whether or not the government pursues citizens' best interests, then how can we judge if the government was representative? If people do know what is good for them, then either compliance with their prospective will or the verdict based on their retrospective evaluations must be taken as informative about the quality of governments' actions. What *is* best for the represented must be what they *say* is best, either prospectively or retrospectively.

But what if people do not know what is best for them?[13] Let us reverse the assumptions of the principal–agent model altogether. Suppose that voters are concerned only with the change of their welfare during a particular term of office, while the representatives care also about the future, say the present value by the end of the term of future welfare. People are willing to re-elect a government that cuts all the trees in the country as long as they live on champagne while there are any trees left, while the government, having no interests of its own, wants only to do what people "ought to want" (Pitkin 1967: 162). Now a bad government cares about being re-elected and caters to voters' myopia, while a good government valiantly goes to defeat by turning the country into a national park. As Schumpeter (1942: 256) observed, "If results that prove in the long run satisfactory to the people at large are made the test of government *for* the people, then government *by* the people, as conceived by the classical doctrine of democracy, would often fail to meet it."

Yet the question remains: if not the people, then who is to judge what *is* best for them? This is not a rhetorical question. Stigler (1975) thought

[13] For arguments that individual preferences are not the best standard by which to evaluate collective welfare, see several essays in Sen and Williams 1982.

it was economists (obviously of his persuasion); declaring that President Salvador Allende of Chile was "elected due to the irresponsibility of the people," Henry Kissinger must have thought it was Henry Kissinger; and I think all of us scholars with political commitments make similar judgments. Moreover, these judgments can be informed: if we have views about what people "ought to want" and if we have theories about consequences of government policies, we can arrive at informed judgments about them. But we will arrive at different judgments, for we are "people," participants rather than impartial observers.

With these terminological preliminaries, let us examine the link between elections and representation. In one view of elections, their role in inducing representation is prospective; in the second view, it is retrospective. In the prospective view, parties or candidates make policy proposals during elections and explain how these policies would affect citizens' welfare; citizens decide which of these proposals they want to be implemented, and governments implement them. Thus, elections emulate the direct assembly and the winning platform becomes the "mandate" for the government to pursue. In the retrospective view, elections serve to hold governments accountable for the results of their past actions. Anticipating retrospective judgments of voters, governments choose policies and emit messages which in their best judgment will be positively evaluated by citizens by the time of the next election. Accountability works through the anticipation by governments of retrospective evaluations of citizens (Downs 1957; Mayhew 1974; Fiorina 1981; Manin 1995).

The mandate conception of representation is widespread: scholars, journalists, and ordinary citizens rely on it as if it were axiomatic. Keeler (1993), for example, explains the major policy reforms introduced by Reagan, Thatcher, and Mitterrand as follows: their respective countries faced economic crises, voters wanted change and expressed this desire at the polls, the respective governments implemented their mandates. Yet we need to ask two questions: (1) Would voters always want governments to implement mandates? (2) Can they punish governments that betray them?

If both voters and politicians are perfectly informed, then politicians offer and voters vote for platforms that maximize their welfare. If exogenous conditions unfold according to anticipations, then voters want victorious politicians to adhere to the mandate. And if politicians have proposed policies which they actually prefer, they will adhere. This model seems to account well for policy formation in Western Europe (Klingeman, Hofferbert, and Budge 1994) as well as in the United States (Miller and Stokes 1966; Page and Shapiro 1992; Stimson,

Mackuen, and Erikson 1995). One should not be surprised it does. Representation is not problematic when politicians have policy preferences, voters vote for a platform the implementation of which maximizes their welfare, and exogenous conditions do not change.

Yet if voters are not perfectly informed, they cannot be sure that implementing the mandate is best for them. Not only may people be afraid of their own passions but, if they are rationally ignorant, they must know that they do not know. As Lippman (1956) wrote about citizens, "Their duty is to fill the office and not to direct the office-holder," and Schumpeter (1942) admonished voters that they "must understand that, once they elected an individual, political action is his business not theirs. This means that they must refrain from instructing him what he is to do...." Hence, citizens may want to give the government some latitude to govern and evaluate government's actions at election times. When the government announces that the objective conditions are not what they were anticipated to be, voters are not sure if implementing the mandate is still in their best interest (see Stokes 1996 and 1997 on "policy switches"); and if implementing the mandate is not the best the government can do, then the threat of punishing incumbents who deviate from it is not credible. Voters may not like governments that betray promises, but they will not punish politicians who made them better off by deviating from them, and politicians must know that they can escape punishment for deviating from the mandate.

While various considerations may encourage adherence to electoral promises, a striking feature of democratic institutions, highlighted by Manin (1995), is that politicians are not compelled to abide by their platform in any democratic system. In no existing democracy are representatives subject to binding instructions. No national-level democratic constitution allows for recall. While provisions for impeachment and procedures for withdrawing confidence are common, they are never targeted at the betrayal of promises. Binding national referenda based on citizens' initiative are found only in Switzerland and, in more restrictive forms, in Italy and Argentina. Hence, once citizens elect representatives, they have no institutional devices to force them to adhere to promises. And electoral terms tend to be long, on average 3.8 years for legislatures and 4.9 years for presidents (Cheibub and Przeworski 1996).[14] Voters can punish politicians who betray mandates only at the time of the next election, after the effects of such a betrayal have been experienced, and since such retrospective judgments are inevitably tainted by the outcomes to which deviations from mandates have led

---

[14] Unless indicated otherwise, statistics refer to all democracies in the world between 1950 and 1990.

and by the mere passage of time, citizens cannot enforce the adherence to mandates *per se*.

Yet even if citizens are unable to control governments prospectively, they may be able to do so retrospectively, if they can force governments to account for the outcomes of their past actions. Governments are "accountable" if citizens can *discern* whether governments are acting in their best interest and *sanction* them appropriately, so that those incumbents who act in the best interest of citizens win re-election and those who do not lose them.

Politicians seeking private gains maximize the present value of the future flow of some rents, which are costly to citizens. Governments then have a one-electoral-period utility function that increases in current rents but also in the probability of re-election, which is, in turn, a decreasing function of rents. Citizens set up a mechanism that forces politicians to trade off extracting rents and losing office or not extracting rents and staying in office. To induce representation, citizens choose a voting rule that (1) meets politicians' participation ("self-selection") constraint, that is, makes it at least minimally attractive for people who have other opportunities to want to be (re)elected, and (2) meets the incentive compatibility constraint, that is, makes it in the interest of politicians to do what citizens would want them to do. As Hamilton observed, "There are few men who would not feel ... zeal in the discharge of a duty ... when they were permitted to entertain a hope of *obtaining by meriting*, a continuance of them. This position will not be disputed as long as it is admitted that the desire of reward is one of the strongest incentives of human conduct; or that the best security for the fidelity of mankind is to make their interest coincide with their duty" (Madison 1982 [1788]: Paper 72: 470).

The standard explanation of how accountability induces representation relies on "retrospective voting." In this model, citizens set some standard of performance to evaluate governments: they decide to vote for the incumbent if their income increased by at least 4 percent during the term, if streets are safe, or if the country qualifies for the finals of the World Cup. They decide to vote against the incumbent if these criteria are not fulfilled. In turn, the government, wanting to be re-elected and knowing the citizens' decision rule, does whatever possible to minimally satisfy these criteria.

To illustrate what is entailed, examine a simple model of policy choice. Suppose that the conditions under which governments operate can be "good" or "bad." Such conditions may include the contents of state coffers or the negotiating posture of international financial institutions. Governments decide whether to implement policy A which is

Table 2.1. *Payoff structure*

		Government	
		Implement A	Implement B
Conditions	"Good"	1,5	3,3
	"Bad"	3,1	1,3

better for citizens when conditions are good, or policy B, which is better when conditions are bad. Finally, assume that re-election gives a bonus $V > 2$ to the incumbent. Suppose that the structure of payoffs is as shown in table 2.1 (the first number in each pair are government rents and the second number citizens' welfare).

Voters announce the following retrospective rule: "We will vote to re-elect if we get at least 5 when conditions are good and at least 3 when conditions are bad; otherwise we will throw the rascals out." Incumbent politicians compare the value to them of pursuing the policy best for voters, which gives them the rent of 1 now plus a future bonus of $V > 2$, with the rents they can extract by going down to defeat, worth a 3, and always act in the best interest of the public. Thus Key (1966), Fiorina (1981),[15] Ferejohn (1986), Grossman and Noh (1990), and others all argue that retrospective voting is sufficient to enforce representation.[16]

But citizens often do not know whether conditions are good or bad. After all, the negotiating posture of the IMF is not something people observe, while the contents of state coffers are often deliberately obscured by the outgoing government,[17] and if voters are not sure about

[15] Fiorina (1981: 11): "Given political actors who fervently desire to retain their positions and who carefully anticipate public reaction to their records as a means to that end, a retrospective voting electorate will enforce electoral accountability, albeit in an *ex post*, not an *ex ante*, sense."

[16] Note that incumbents never lose elections in the full information equilibrium. Since in fact 162 out of 300 incumbent prime ministers and six out of fourteen incumbent presidents went to defeat whenever they presented themselves for re-election (Cheibub and Przeworski 1996), this is clearly not a reasonable conclusion.

[17] One of the peculiarities of the principal–agent relations between citizens and governments is that the principals authorize the agents to decide which rules the principals should obey and to coerce the principals to obey them (Moe 1991), and these rules include those that regulate the principals' access to information about the action of agents. Stokes (1996) cites the controversy about the true amount of public deficit in Ecuador in 1988, Bresser Pereira (1992) reports that he was told that Brazil's foreign reserves were down to nothing only when he met President Sarney after having accepted the nomination for the Ministry of Finance. Perhaps the most flagrant recent manipulation of accounting conventions occurred in France, which helped itself to Maastricht by moving some of the surplus of a state-owned firm fund to the general budget.

conditions (or about the effect of policies on outcomes), they can no longer infer whether the government acted in their best interest from observing the outcomes alone. They are in a quandary. If they set the voting rule as " 'Yes' if at least 3," they will allow governments to extract excessive rents under good conditions: they will get 3 whether conditions are in fact bad or good. In turn, if they set it as " 'No' unless at least 5," the government will have no chance to be re-elected if conditions are in fact bad and will be induced to seek excessive rents. If they do not know what the conditions are, voters can try to guess which to do but they are unable to control politicians under some conditions. Retrospective voting does not enforce representation when voters are not fully informed.[18]

Thus, neither prospective nor retrospective voting ensures that governments will be induced to promote best interests of citizens. And the voters' predicament is compounded even further because they have only one instrument – the vote – with which to achieve two targets: elect a good government and create incentives for the elected government to behave well. Madison's prescription – "The aim of every political constitution is, or ought to be, first to obtain for rulers men who possess most wisdom to discern, and most virtue to pursue, the common good of the society; and in the next place, to take the most effectual precautions for keeping them virtuous whilst they continue to hold their public trust" – hides a dilemma (Madison 1982 [1788]: Paper 57: 370). If voters use the vote to choose good governments, they must weaken the power of incentives offered to the incumbents, thus tolerating higher rents. Voters who use the vote prospectively as well as retrospectively are not irrational: if politicians are not all the same, it is better to have good ones in office. But the prospective use of the vote is costly in terms of control over the incumbents.

And what if citizens are heterogeneous, if they have conflicting interests? Note first that we are back to the conceptual drawing board. References to "people," "individuals," "citizens," "voters" no longer suffice. Now "representation" means at most acting in the best interest of a majority, some majority, rather than a minority, any minority. Suppose again that informed citizens vote on one issue, linear taxes, and the majority rule equilibrium calls for a major redistribution from the

---

[18] I used to think that the existence of an opposition is sufficient to inform voters. But predictable speech is uninformative (Austen-Smith 1990). If the government is acting in self-interest, it will offer a self-serving explanation, while the opposition, wanting to defeat the incumbent, will contest it. Since this is what voters expect both the incumbent and the opposition to do, their messages will not be credible.

rich to the poor. The government is then representative if it effectuates such a redistribution, that is, if its actions hurt a minority.[19]

One function of constitutions is to limit majority rule (see essays in Elster and Slagstad 1988). But, while the distinction is not unambiguous, constitutions protect at most rights, not interests. Between the democratic authorization of the majority to pursue its interests and the constitutional protection of rights, space is left for the majority to exploit the minority. Either elections are simply irrelevant or they do authorize the majority to exploit the minority, albeit within the constitutional limits. The only defense of the minority is rebellion and the only constraint on the majority is the threat of it,[20] and if this is true, then under the assumptions of the retrospective voting model there are two classes of equilibria: (1) if the government can satisfy the retrospective judgments of a majority without violating the constitutional limits or provoking a rebellion, it will do so by exploiting the minority and, if there is any slack, also extracting surplus rents from the majority, and (2) if either of these constraints bites, the government will, within the legal limits, dedicate itself to pursuing interests of its own or its minority cronies.

Thus, if people are not perfectly informed and if they are not homogeneous, governments may either favor interests of some majority (not necessarily the one that elected them) as well as their own at the expense of a minority, or they may pursue their own interests or values at the expense of everyone.

---

[19] True, governments rarely admit that their actions hurt anyone. President Salvador Allende's declaration that "I am not the President of all the Chileans" was a blunder. Edward Heath seems to have been the only politician in recent times who openly declared that he represents class interests, and he was promptly removed from office by his colleagues. Yet elections are partisan, and the differences between parties are not only epistemic: if they were, why would we repeatedly observe an association between class positions and the vote? Thus, every few years we are treated to the same spectacle: politicians campaign in elections appealing to partisan interests, only so that the elected government could claim that it represents everyone.

[20] Guinier (1994: 77) claims that a transient majority is constrained in its actions by the prospect that it may become a minority. This could be true if (1) because the current majority is afraid that the future majority would use the instruments of power it creates against it, the current majority delegates some of its powers to third parties (bureaucracies, courts) or (2) because "do unto others as you would have them do onto you" is an equilibrium of the repeated game. Yet she is correct that, short of constitutional limits, nothing stops a majority from exploiting a permanent minority. Consociational arrangements do limit majority rule in the presence of permanent minorities, but they are adopted where the minorities would rebel in the presence of a pure majority rule.

Equality

Does equality in the political realm lead to equality in the economic realm? The answer to this question is obvious: around 1990, the income of an average Belgian in the top quintile was 4.4 times higher than that of one in the bottom quintile, the income of a wealthy American was 9.8 times higher than that of a poor one, and the income of an average Brazilian in the top 20 percent was 26.3 times higher than of one in the bottom 20 percent. The Gini index in countries that enjoyed democratic regimes for at least ten years ranged from 25.91 in Spain (at expenditure basis; Finland had 26.11 on income basis) to 59.60 in Brazil (income basis).[21] So the only puzzle is why the poor, equipped with the right to vote, do not take it away from the rich.

Note that during the first half of the nineteenth century almost everyone expected they would. Conservatives agreed with socialists that democracy, specifically universal suffrage and the freedom to form unions, must threaten property. The Scottish philosopher James Mackintosh predicted in 1818 that if the "laborious classes" gain franchise, "a permanent animosity between opinion and property must be the consequence" (cited in Collini, Winch, and Burrow, 1983: 98). David Ricardo was prepared to extend suffrage only "to that part of them [the people] which cannot be supposed to have an interest in overturning the right to property" (*ibid.*: 107). Thomas Macaulay in his speech on the Chartists in 1842 (1900: 263) pictured universal suffrage as "the end of property and thus of all civilization." Eight years later, Karl Marx expressed the same conviction that private property and universal suffrage are incompatible (1952 [1850]: 62). According to his analysis, democracy inevitably "unchains the class struggle": the poor use democracy to expropriate the riches; the rich are threatened and subvert democracy, typically by "abdicating" political power to the permanently organized armed forces. As a result, either capitalism or democracy crumbles. The combination of democracy and capitalism is thus an inherently unstable form of organization of society, "only the political form of revolution of bourgeois society and not its conservative form of life" (1934: 18), "only a spasmodic, exceptional state of things ... impossible as the normal form of society" (1971: 198).

Moreover, this is what most people around the world still expect. The first connotation of "democracy" among most survey respondents in Latin America and Eastern Europe is "social and economic equality": in Chile, 59 percent of respondents expected that democracy would

---

[21] These numbers are taken from Deininger and Squire 1996. Income-based measures make the distribution appear less egalitarian than expenditure-based.

attenuate social inequalities (Alaminos 1991), while in Eastern Europe the proportion associating democracy with social equality ranged from 61 percent in Czechoslovakia to 88 percent in Bulgaria (Bruszt and Simon 1991).

There are good reasons they should. Take the median-voter model: each individual is characterized by an endowment of labor or capital, and we can rank all individuals from the poorest to the richest. Individuals vote on the rate of tax to be imposed on incomes generated by supplying these endowments to production. The funds generated by this tax are either equally distributed to all individuals or spent to produce public goods equally valued by all individuals. Once the tax rate is voted on, individuals maximize utility by deciding in a decentralized way how much of their endowments to supply. The median-voter theorem asserts that, when some technical conditions hold, there exists a unique majority rule equilibrium, this equilibrium is the choice of the voter with the median preference, and the voter with the median preference is the one with median income. And when the distribution of incomes is downward skewed, as it always is, majority rule equilibrium is associated with a complete equality of post-fisc (tax and transfer) incomes.

Explanations why this does not happen abound. There were three traditional Marxist explanations (Przeworski 1986): (1) *False consciousness*. Workers and other poor people do not know what is good for them, in some versions because of "ideological domination," in turn rendered possible by the private ownership of the means of ideological production; (2) *Betrayal*. Workers and other poor people are repeatedly betrayed by their leadership, which becomes coopted; (3) *Repression*. Democracy operates only as long as it does not generate outcomes adverse to the interests of the bourgeoisie; if it does, the bourgeoisie seeks recourse to force. Yet the working class has been neither a perpetual dupe nor a chronic sucker nor a passive victim: workers did organize in unions and in many countries as political parties; these organizations have had political projects of their own; they chose strategies and pursued them to victories as well as defeats.

More recent explanations claim that the private ownership of capital limits the range of outcomes that can ensue from the democratic process. According to this argument, dubbed by Przeworski and Wallerstein (1988) "structural dependence of the state on capital," the state, regardless who occupies its heights, elected by whom and with what intentions, is constrained in any capitalist economy by the fact that crucial economic decisions – those affecting employment and investment – are a private prerogative (Block 1977; Lindblom 1977). The argument goes as follows:

(1) Even if state policies are binding, private economic agents always enjoy some discretion in their decisions. They may be legally prohibited not to engage in some actions, say producing PCBs; they may be forced to allocate a part of their income to collective consumption; or they may be contingently subsidized for some decisions, say for investing. Yet private ownership implies that agents preserve some decisional latitude: most importantly, firms decide whether to employ and to invest, while households decide whether to supply labor services.

(2) If private agents make decisions to maximize utility and if whatever generates utility is affected by state policy, then so will be the decisions of these agents. Examples abound: income tax makes saving less attractive, insurance makes individuals more likely to take risks, import licenses affect firm size, etc. The degree of sensitivity of individual decisions to the policies depends on the specific policy instruments. Hence, policy instruments are characterized by specific elasticities of supply of productive inputs. Policies are "neutral" when they do not affect the supply of factors.

(3) If the realization of the objectives of the state depends for whatever reasons on the outcome of decentralized decisions, then any government must anticipate the effect of policies on these decisions when choosing the optimal policy. The state is constrained in choosing policies by the effect of these policies on private decisions. In particular, if redistribution of incomes downwards results in lowering total output, the optimal policy of an egalitarian government stops well short of equality.

(4) The limitation imposed by private ownership of productive endowments has consequences reaching far beyond the distribution of income. When collective decisions must anticipate their effect on the supply of productive resources, the collectivity cannot reach all the allocations of resources that are feasible given these resources. Whether people want equality, justice, or beauty, they cannot collectively will to implement these goals while fully utilizing the available resources. Thus, private ownership imposes a constraint on "popular sovereignty."

For an application of this argument, return to the median-voter model. If decentralized decisions are sensitive to the tax rate, that is, if taxes generate deadweight losses, informed voters will anticipate this effect and the majority rule equilibrium will stop short of equality. (The most general treatment of this topic is by Aumann and Kurz 1977.) Since perfect equality can be achieved only at the cost of reducing total output, citizens anticipate this constraint when they vote, and the result is that they vote for tax rates that leave a fair degree of inequality. Similar models were developed with regard to investment decisions of firms by van der Ploeg (1982), Przeworski and Wallerstein (1988), and Barro (1990).

One can cite alternative formulations but the general logic is the same. Whenever private agents respond in a decentralized way to state policies, the policy choice, and the actual allocation of resources and distribution of incomes, are constrained by private decisions. The constraining power of agents with different endowments depends on the magnitude of these endowments and the elasticity with which they are supplied.

Yet while this explanation is certainly plausible, I am not convinced it is true. For one, the evidence concerning the magnitude of deadweight losses tends to be inconclusive: the estimates range from astronomical to minimal.[22] Second, since at least on paper policy instruments differ in their effect on factor supply, the puzzle is why governments would ever use inefficient ways of redistributing incomes (Becker 1976 and 1985; Przeworski and Wallerstein 1988). Perhaps the Right has succeeded in convincing poor voters that deadweight losses are larger than they in fact are. Or perhaps right-wing governments deliberately opt for inefficient ways of redistribution to protect their constituency from egalitarian pressures. In either case, the mechanism that stops democracy from redistributing incomes is no longer economic, but either ideological or political.

Yet one more explanation has been recently offered by Roemer (1996b). In his story the redistributive moderation of left-wing parties is due to the multidimensionality of the issue space in which voters locate themselves: left-wing parties are afraid of repelling by their economic program voters who may be attracted to them on other grounds, say anti-clericalism. Whether this is a better or a sufficient explanation, I do not know.

That democracy is compatible with a fair degree of inequality is obvious; why it is so remains perplexing.

In defense of minimalism

It thus seems that choosing rulers by elections does not assure either rationality, or representation, or equality. Moreover, I am inclined to

---

[22] Browning and Johnson (1984) calculated that the marginal deadweight loss of taxation in the United States is $9.31: an additional dollar in taxes would lower the total output by this amount. Laffont and Tirole (1994) take $1.30 as the ballpark number for the shadow price of public funds. Yet many econometric studies – too many to be cited – find no effect of minimum wages on employment, of wages and taxes on labor supply of full-age males, or of tax rates on savings.

expect that similar analyses would lead to negative results with regard to several other normatively desirable and politically desired criteria. Roemer (1996a), for one, concluded that there are no reasons to expect that voting would lead to an implementation of any criteria of justice. Przeworski and Limongi (1997a) discovered that average economic performance is not better in systems with contested elections than under various species of dictatorship. So it seems that a minimalist conception of democracy is just that: minimalist.

These findings may be less weighty than they appear. After all, I have treated elections in isolation from several institutional features that characterize modern democracies, in particular, separation of powers, with the attendant mechanisms of checks and balances, as well as constitutionalism. Perhaps if I had provided a richer institutional description, we would have arrived at different conclusions: Persson, Roland, and Tabelini (1996), for example, developed a model in which separation of powers assures that governments are representative even when voters are ill-informed.[23] Moreover, rationality, representation, and equality are matters of degree: perhaps many decisions about matters of common interest are rational, perhaps most governments seek to do what they think is best for the public, perhaps the observed degree of inequality is largely a result of efforts rather than of luck. I am happy to accept these possibilities. Conversely, nothing I said should prevent us from embracing the Churchillian view that democracy is more rational, more representative, and more egalitarian than dictatorship *tout court* or its various species.

Yet suppose this is all there is to democracy: that rulers are elected. Is it little? It depends on the point of departure.[24] If one begins with a vision of a basic harmony of interests, a common good to be discovered and agreed to by a rational deliberation, and to be represented as the view of the informed majority, the fact that rulers are elected is of no particular significance. Voting is just a time-saving expedient (Buchanan and Tullock 1962) and majority rule is just a technically convenient way of identifying what everyone would or should have agreed to. Yet if the point of departure is that in any society there are conflicts, of values and of interests, electing rulers appears nothing short of miraculous.

Let us put the consensualist view of democracy where it belongs – in the Museum of Eighteenth-century Thought – and observe that all societies are ridden with economic, cultural, or moral conflicts. True, as the modernization theory (notably Coser 1959) emphasized, these

---

[23] Their model is less than persuasive, however, since it leaves no room for political parties, which can serve as a mechanism of collusion between powers.
[24] Shapiro (1996: 82) also takes this position.

conflicts can be "cross-cutting": they need not pit class against class or religion against religion. They can be attenuated by an "overlapping consensus": consensus about practicalities compatible with differences of values (Rawls 1993). They may be also moderated by public discussion of both normative and technical reasons, although, as I have argued above, deliberation is a two-edged sword, for it may lead just to solidifying conflicting views. Yet in the end, when all the coalitions have been formed, the practical consensus has been elaborated, and all arguments have been exhausted, conflicts remain.

My defense of the minimalist conception proceeds in two steps. I take it as obvious that we want to avoid bloodshed, resolving conflicts through violence.[25] Starting with this assumption, I first argue that the mere possibility of being able to change governments can avoid violence. Secondly, I argue that being able to do it by voting has consequences of its own.

Popper's defense of democracy is that it allows us to get rid of governments peacefully. But why should we care about changing governments?[26] My answer is that the very prospect that governments may change can result in a peaceful regulation of conflicts. To see this argument in its starkest form, assume that governments are selected by a toss of a, not necessarily fair, coin: "heads" mean that the incumbents should remain in office, "tails" that they should leave. Thus, a reading of the toss designates "winners" and "losers." This designation is an *instruction* what the winners and the losers should and should not do: the winners should move into a White or Pink House or perhaps even a *palacio*; while there they can take everything up to the constitutional constraint for themselves and their supporters, and they should toss the same coin again when their term is up. The losers should not move into the House and should accept getting not more than whatever is left.

Note that when the authorization to rule is determined by a lottery, citizens have no electoral sanction, prospective or retrospective, and the incumbents have no electoral incentives to behave well while in office. Since electing governments by a lottery makes their chances of survival independent of their conduct, there are no reasons to expect that governments act in a representative fashion because they want to earn re-election: any link between elections and representation is severed.

Yet the very prospect that governments would alternate may induce the conflicting political forces to comply with the rules rather than engage in violence, for the following reason. Although the losers would

---

[25] I am not arguing against Locke that violence is never justified, just that a system that systematically avoids it is preferable to one that does not.

[26] I want to thank Ignacio Sanchez-Cuenca for posing this question.

be better off in the short run rebelling rather than accepting the outcome of the current round, if they have a sufficient chance to win and a sufficiently large payoff in the future rounds, they are better off continuing to comply with the verdict of the coin toss rather than fighting for power. Similarly, while the winners would be better off in the short run not tossing the coin again, they may be better off in the long run peacefully leaving office rather than provoking violent resistance to their usurpation of power. Regulating conflicts by a coin toss is then a self-enforcing equilibrium (Przeworski 1991: chap. 1). Bloodshed is avoided by the mere fact that, à la Aristotle, the political forces expect to take turns.

Suppose first that the winners of the coin toss get some predetermined part of the pie, $1/2 < x < 1$, while losers get the rest.[27] Winners decide at each time whether to hold elections at the next time and losers whether to accept defeat or to rebel. If democracy is repeated indefinitely from $t = 0$ on, the winner at $t = 0$ expects to get $D_W = x + V_W(e,x)$ and the loser at $t = 0$ expects to get $D_L = (1-x) + V_L(1-e,x)$, where V stands for the present value of continuing under democracy beyond the current round, e is the probability the current incumbent will win the next toss. Let "democratic equilibrium" stand for a pair of strategies in which the current winners always hold tosses if they expect losers to comply and the current losers always comply if they expect the winners to hold tosses. Then such an equilibrium exists if everyone is better off under democracy than under rebellion: if $D_W > R_W$ and $D_L > R_L$, where R stands for the expected values of violent conflict for each of the two parties.

Moreover, the prospect of alternation may induce moderation while in office. Suppose that the current incumbent can either manipulate the probability, e, of being re-elected or can decide what share of the pie, $x \in [0,1]$, to take, or both. There are some initial values $\{e(0),x(0)\}$; at $t = 1$ the coin is tossed and it designates winners and losers. Whoever is the winner now chooses $\{e(1),x(1)\}$: the rules for this round, etc. Hence, rules are not given *ex ante*: the incumbent manipulates them at will. Yet there are conditions under which a democratic equilibrium exists in which the incumbents do not grab everything. If the cost of rebellion is sufficiently high for both, each incumbent will prefer to moderate its behavior while in office under democracy rather than provoke a rebellion by the current loser.

As Hardin (1989: 113) puts it, "for the constitutional case, the ultimate source [of stability] is the internal costs of collective action for

---

[27] This analysis is based on joint work with James Fearon, still in progress.

re-coordination or, in Caesar's word, *mutiny*." Yet if the threat of mutiny were the only incentive to moderation, why would we ever adopt procedures that subject control over the exercise of rule to a lottery? If the relevant political actors knew what would happen as the result of an open conflict, they could just agree to a distribution that would have resulted from an open confrontation. Instead of a coin toss deciding who gets what, the distribution would be fixed to reflect the strength the conflicting political forces could muster in an open confrontation, x for one, (1–x) for the other. So why do we have democracy: an agreement to toss a coin with probabilities e and (1–e)?

The reason, in my view, is that it would be impossible to write a dictatorial contract that would specify every contingent state of nature. In turn, leaving the residual control – control over issues not explicitly regulated by contract – to the dictator would generate increasing returns to power and undermine the contract. Endowed with residual control, the dictator could not commit itself not to use the advantage to undermine the strength of the adversaries in an open conflict. Hence, to avoid violence, the conflicting political forces adopt the following device: agree over those issues that can be specified and allow the residual control to alternate according to specified probabilities. In this sense, the constitution specifies x, the limits on incumbents, and e, their chances in electoral competition, but a random device decides who holds residual control.

Yet we do not use random devices; we vote. What difference does that make?

Voting is an imposition of a will over a will. When a decision is reached by voting, some people must submit to an opinion different from theirs or to a decision contrary to their interest.[28] Voting authorizes compulsion. It empowers governments, our rulers, to keep people in jail,[29] sometimes even to take their life, to seize money from some and give it to others, to regulate private behavior of consenting adults. Voting generates winners and losers, and it authorizes the winners to impose their will, even if within constraints, on the losers. This is what "ruling" is. Bobbio's (1984: 93) parenthetical addition bares a crucial implication of the Schumpeterian definition: "by 'democratic system'," Bobbio says, "I mean one in which supreme power (supreme in so far as it alone is authorized to use force as a last resort) is exerted in the name of and on behalf of the people by virtue of the procedure of elections."

---

[28] This sentence is a paraphrase of Condorcet (1986 [1785]: 22): "il s'agit, dans une loi qui n'a pas été votée unanimement, de soumettre des hommes à une opinion qui n'est pas la leur, ou à une décision qu'ils croient contraire à leur intérêt."

[29] Indeed, the oldest democracy in the world is also one that keeps more people in jail than any other country in the world.

It is voting that authorizes coercion, not reasons behind it. *Pace* Cohen (1997: 5), who claims that the participants "are prepared to cooperate in accordance with the results of such discussion, treating those results as authoritative," it is the result of voting, not of discussion, that authorizes governments to govern, to compel. Deliberation may lead to a decision that is reasoned: it may illuminate the reasons a decision is or should not be taken. Further, these reasons may guide the implementation of the decision, the actions of the government. But if all the reasons have been exhausted and yet there is no unanimity, some people must act against their reasons. They are coerced to do so, and the authorization to coerce them is derived from counting heads, the sheer force of numbers, not from the validity of reasons.

What difference, then, does it make that we vote? One answer to this question is that the right to vote imposes an obligation to respect the results of voting. In this view, democracy persists because people see it as their duty to obey outcomes resulting from a decision process in which they voluntarily participated. Democracy is legitimate in the sense that people are ready to accept decisions of as yet undetermined content, as long as they can participate in the making of these decisions. I do not find this view persuasive, however, either normatively or positively. Clearly, this is not the place to enter into a discussion of a central topic of political theory (Dunn 1996a: chap. 4) but I stand with Kelsen (1998 [1929]: 21) when he observes that "The purely negative assumption that no individual counts more than any other does not permit to deduce the positive principle that the will of the majority should prevail," and I know no evidence to the effect that participation induces compliance.

Yet I think that voting does induce compliance, through a different mechanism. Voting constitutes "flexing muscles": a reading of chances in the eventual war. If all men are equally strong (or armed) then the distribution of vote is a proxy for the outcome of war. Referring to Herodotus, Bryce (1921: 25–6) announces that he uses the concept of democracy "in its old and strict sense, as denoting a government in which the will of the majority of qualified citizens rules, taking qualified citizens to constitute the great bulk of the inhabitants, say, roughly three-fourths, *so that physical force of the citizens coincides (broadly speaking) with their voting power*" (italics supplied). Condorcet claims that this was the reason for adopting majority rule: for the good of peace and general welfare, it was necessary to place authority where lies the force.[30] Clearly, once physical force diverges from sheer numbers, when

---

[30] "Lorsque l'usage de soumettre tous les individus à la volonté du plus grand nombre, s'introduisit dans les sociétes, et que les hommes convinrent de regarder la décision de

the ability to wage war becomes professionalized and technical, voting no longer provides a reading of chances in a violent conflict. But voting does reveal information about passions, values, and interests. If elections are a peaceful substitute for rebellion (Hampton 1994), it is because they inform everyone who would mutiny and against what. They inform the losers – "Here is the distribution of force: if you disobey the instructions conveyed by the results of the election, I will be more likely to beat you than you will be able to beat me in a violent confrontation" – and the winners – "If you do not hold elections again or if you grab too much, I will be able to put up a forbidding resistance." Dictatorships do not generate this information; they need secret police to find out. In democracies, even if voting does not reveal a unique collective will, it does indicate limits to rule. Why else would we interpret participation as an indication of legitimacy, why would we be concerned about support for extremist parties?

In the end, the miracle of democracy is that conflicting political forces obey the results of voting. People who have guns obey those without them. Incumbents risk their control of governmental offices by holding elections. Losers wait for their chance to win office. Conflicts are regulated, processed according to rules, and thus limited. This is not consensus, yet not mayhem either. Just limited conflict; conflict without killing. Ballots are "paper stones," as Engels once observed.

Yet this miracle does not work under all conditions.[31] The expected life of democracy in a country with per capita income under $1,000 is about eight years.[32] Between $1,001 and $2,000, an average democracy can expect to endure eighteen years. But above $6,000, democracies last forever. Indeed, no democracy ever fell, regardless of everything else, in a country with a per capita income higher than that of Argentina in 1976: $6,055. Thus Lipset (1959: 46) was undoubtedly correct when he argued that "The more well-to-do a country, the greater the chance that it will sustain democracy."

Several other factors affect the survival of democracies but they all pale in comparison to per capita income. Two are particularly relevant. First, it turns out that democracies are more likely to fall when one party controls a large share (more than two-thirds) of seats in the legislature.

la pluralité comme la volonté de tous, ils n'adoptèrent pas cette méthode comme un moyen d'éviter l'erreur et de se conduire d'après des décisions fondées sur la vérité: mais ils trouvèrent que, pour le bien de la paix et l'utilité générale, *il falloit placer l'autorité où etoit la force*" (Condorcet 1986 [1785]: 11; italics supplied).

[31] The forthcoming paragraphs are based on Przeworski, Alvarez, Cheibub, and Limongi 1996, and Przeworski and Limongi 1997b.

[32] Expected life is the inverse of the probability of dying. The income numbers are in purchasing power parity international dollars of 1985.

Secondly, democracies are most stable when the heads of governments change not too infrequently, more often than once every five years (although not as often as less than every two years). Thus, democracy is more likely to survive when no single force dominates politics completely and permanently.

Finally, the stability of democracies does depend on their particular institutional arrangements: parliamentary democracies are much more durable than pure presidential ones. The expected life of democracy under presidentialism is twenty-one years, while under parliamentarism it is seventy-two years. Presidential systems are less stable under any distribution of seats; indeed, they are less stable whatever variable is controlled for. The most likely reason presidential democracies are more fragile than parliamentary ones is that presidents rarely change because they are defeated in elections. Most of them leave office because they are obligated to do so by constitutionally imposed term limits. In turn, whenever incumbent presidents can run and do, two out of three win re-election (Cheibub and Przeworski 1996). Presidentialism thus appears to give an excessive advantage to incumbents when they are legally permitted to run for re-election and, in turn, to prevent the incumbents from exploiting this advantage, it obligates them to leave office whether or not voters want them to stay.

Here then are three facts: (1) democracies are more likely to survive in wealthy countries; (2) they are more likely to last when no single political force dominates; and (3) they are more likely to endure when voters can choose rulers through elections. And these facts add up: democracy lasts when it offers an opportunity to the conflicting forces to advance their interests within the institutional framework.

In the end then, the Popperian posture is not sufficient, because democracy endures only under some conditions. Elections alone are not sufficient for conflicts to be resolved through elections. And while some of these conditions are economic, others are political and institutional. Thus, a minimalist conception of democracy does not alleviate the need for thinking about institutional design. In the end, the "quality of democracy," to use the currently fashionable phrase, does matter for its very survival. But my point is not that democracy can be, needs to be, improved, but that it would be worth defending even if it could not be.

REFERENCES

Alaminos, Antonio. 1991. *Chile: transición political y sociedad.* Madrid: Centro de Investigaciones Sociologicas.

Arrow, Kenneth A. 1951. *Social Choice and Individual Values*. New York: Wiley.

Aumann, Robert J. and Mordecai Kurz. 1977. "Power and taxes." *Econometrica* 45: 1137–61.

Austen-Smith, David. 1990. "Credible debate equilibria." *Social Choice and Welfare* 7: 75–93.

Barro, Robert J. 1990. "Government spending in a simple model of endogenous growth." *Journal of Political Economy* 98: 103–25.

Becker, Gary S. 1976. "Comment (on Peltzman)." *Journal of Law and Economics* 1: 245–8.

   1983. "A theory of competition among interest groups for political influence." *Quarterly Journal of Economics* 98: 371–400.

Berg, Sven. 1993. "Condorcet's jury theorems, dependency among jurors." *Social Choice and Welfare* 10: 87–95.

Black, Duncan. 1958. *The Theory of Committees and Elections*. Cambridge: Cambridge University Press.

Block, Fred. 1977. "The ruling class does not rule: notes on the Marxist theory of the state." *Socialist Revolution* 33: 6–28.

Bobbio, Norberto. 1984. *The Future of Democracy*. Minneapolis: University of Minnesota Press.

Bresser Pereira, Luiz Carlos. 1992. "Contra a corrente no Ministério da Fazenda." *Revista Brasileira de Ciências Sociais* 19: 530.

Browning, Edgar K. and William R. Johnson. 1984. "The trade-off between equality and efficiency." *Journal of Political Economy* 92: 175–203.

Bruszt, László and János Simon. 1991. "Political culture, political and economical orientations in Central and Eastern Europe during the transition to democracy" (ms). Budapest: Erasmus Foundation for Democracy.

Bryce, James. 1921. *Modern Democracies*. New York: Macmillan.

Buchanan, James and Gordon Tullock. 1962. *The Calculus of Consent: Logical Foundations of Constitutional Democracy*. Ann Arbor: University of Michigan Press.

Cheibub, Jose Antonio and Adam Przeworski. 1996. "Democracy, elections, and accountability for economic outcomes." Revised paper presented at the Conference on Democracy and Accountability, New York University, 27–9 April.

Cohen, Joshua. 1986. "An epistemic conception of democracy." *Ethics* 97: 26–38.

   1989. "The economic basis of deliberative democracy." *Social Philosophy & Policy* 6: 25–50.

   1993. "Moral pluralism and political consensus." In David Copp, Jean Hampton, and John Roemer (eds.), *The Idea of Democracy*, pp. 270–91. Cambridge: Cambridge University Press.

   1997. "Procedure and substance in deliberative democracy." In Jon Elster (ed.), *Democratic Deliberation*. New York: Cambridge University Press.

Coleman, Jules. 1989. "Rationality and the justification of democracy." In Geoffrey Brennan and Loren E. Lomasky (eds.), *Politics and Process*, pp. 194–220. New York: Cambridge University Press.

Collini, Stefan, Donald Winch, and John Burrow. 1983. *That Noble Science of Politics*. Cambridge: Cambridge University Press.

Condorcet. 1986 (1785). "Essai sur l'application de l'analyse a la probabilité des décisions rendues a la pluralité des voix." In *Sur les élections et autres textes.* Textes choisis et revus par Olivier de Bernon. Paris: Fayard.

Coser, Lewis. 1959. *The Functions of Social Conflict.* Glencoe: Free Press.

Dahl, Robert. 1971. *Polyarchy: Participation and Opposition.* New Haven: Yale University Press.

 1989. *Democracy and Its Critics.* New Haven: Yale University Press.

Deininger, Klaus and Lyn Squire. 1996. "A new data set measuring income inequality." *The World Bank Economic Review* 10: 565–92.

Downs, Anthony. 1957. *An Economic Theory of Democracy.* New York: Harper and Row.

Dunn, Delmer D. and John Uhr. 1993. "Accountability and responsibility in modern democratic governments." Paper presented at the Annual Meeting of the American Political Science Association, Washington, DC, 2–5 September.

Dunn, John. 1996a. *The History of Political Theory and other Essays.* Cambridge: Cambridge University Press.

 1996b. "Situating democratic political accountability." Revised paper presented at the Conference on Democracy and Accountability, New York University, 27–9 April.

Elster, Jon. 1998. "Introduction." In Jon Elster (ed.), *Deliberative Democracy.* New York: Cambridge University Press.

Elster, Jon and Rune Slagstand. 1988. *Constitutionalism and Democracy.* Cambridge: Cambridge University Press.

Estlund, David, Jeremy Waldron, Bernard Grofman, and Scott Feld. 1989. "Democratic theory and the public interest: Condorcet and Rousseau revisited." *American Political Science Review* 83: 1317–40.

Ferejohn, John. 1986. "Incumbent performance and electoral control". *Public Choice* 50: 5–25.

Fiorina, Morris P. 1981. *Retrospective Voting in American National Elections.* New Haven: Yale University Press.

Grofman, Bernard and Guillermo Owen (eds.), 1986. *Information Pooling and Group Decision Making.* Greenwich, CT: JAI Press.

Grofman, Bernard, Guillermo Owen, and Scott Feld. 1983. "Thirteen theorems in search of the truth." *Theory and Decision* 15: 261–78.

Grofman, Bernard and Scott Feld. 1989. "Rousseau's general will: a Condorcetian perspective." *American Political Science Review* 82: 567–76.

Grossman, Herschel I. and Suk Jae Noh. 1990. "A theory of kleptocracy with probabilistic survival and reputation." *Economics and Politics* 2: 157–71.

Guinier, Lani. 1994. *The Tyranny of the Majority: Fundamental Fairness in Representative Democracy.* New York: The Free Press.

Hampton, Jean. 1994. "Democracy and the rule of law." In Ian Shapiro (ed.), *NOMOS XXXVI: The Rule of Law,* pp. 13–45.

Hardin, Russell. 1989. "Why a constitution?" In Bernard Grofman and Donald Wittman (eds.), *The Federalist Papers and the New Institutionalism,* pp. 100–20. New York: Agathon Press.

Hirschman, Albert. 1985. "Against parsimony: three ways of complicating some categories of economic discourse." *Economics and Philosophy* 1: 7–21.

Keeler, John T. S. 1993. "Opening the window for reform: mandates, crises, and extraordinary decision-making." *Comparative Political Studies* 25: 433–86.

Kelsen, Hans. 1988 (1929). *La Démocratie. Sa Nature–Sa Valeur*. Paris: Economica.

Key, V. O., Jr. 1966. *The Responsible Electorate*. New York: Vintage.

Klingeman, Hans-Dieter, Richard I. Hofferbert, and Ian Budge. 1994. *Parties, Policies, and Democracy*. Boulder, CO: Westview Press.

Ladha, Krishna K. 1992. "The Condorcet jury theorem, free speech, and correlated votes." *American Journal of Political Science* 36: 617–34.

Laffont, Jean-Jacques and Jean Tirole. 1994. *A Theory of Incentives in Procurement and Regulation*. Cambridge, MA: MIT Press.

Lindblom, Charles. 1977. *Politics and Markets*. New York: Basic Books.

Lippmann, Walter. 1956. *The Public Philosophy*. New York: Mentor Books.

Lipset, Seymour Martin. 1959. "Some social requisites of democracy: economic development and political legitimacy." *American Political Science Review* 53: 69–105.

Macaulay, Thomas B. 1900. *Complete Writings*, vol. 17. Boston and New York: Houghton-Mifflin.

Madison, James. 1982 (1788). *The Federalist Papers by Alexander Hamilton, James Madison and John Jay*. Edited by Gary Wills. New York: Bantam Books.

Manin, Bernard. 1987. "On legitimacy and political deliberation." *Political Theory* 15: 338–68.

1995. *Principes du gouvernement représentatif*. Paris: Calmann-Lévy.

Manin, Bernard, Adam Przeworski, and Susan C. Stokes. 1996. "Can citizens control representatives through elections?" Revised paper presented at the Conference on Democracy and Accountability, New York University, 27–9 April.

Marx, Karl. 1934. *The Eighteenth Brumaire of Louis Bonaparte*. Moscow: Progress Publishers.

1952 [1850]. *Class Struggles in France, 1848 to 1850*. Moscow: Progress Publishers.

1971. *Writings on the Paris Commune*. Edited by H. Draper. New York: International Publishers.

Mayhew, David R. 1974. *Congress: The Electoral Connection*. New Haven: Yale University Press.

Miller, Nicolas R. 1986. "Information, electorates, and democracy: some extensions and interpretations of the Condorcet jury theorem." In Bernard Grofman and Guillermo Owen (eds.), *Information Pooling and Group Decision Making*. Greenwich, CT: JAI Press.

Miller, Warren E. and Donald E. Stokes. 1966. "Constituency influence in Congress." In Angus Campbell, Philip E. Converse, Warren E. Miller, and Donald E. Stokes (eds.), *Elections and the Political Order*, pp. 351–73. New York: Wiley.

Moe, Terry M. 1991. "Political institutions: the neglected side of the story." *Journal of Law, Economics, and Organization* 6: 213–53.

Page, Benjamin J. and Robert Y. Shapiro. 1992. *The Rational Public: Fifty Years of Trends in Americans' Policy Preferences.* Chicago: University of Chicago Press.

Paldam, Martin. 1991. "How robust is the vote function? A study of seventeen nations over four decades." In Helmuth Northop, Michael S. Lewis-Beck, and Jean-Dominique Lafay (eds.), *Economics and Politics: The Calculus of Support,* pp. 9–31. Ann Arbor: University of Michigan Press.

Persson, Torsten, Gerard Roland, and Guido Tabelini. 1996. "Separation of powers and accountability: towards a formal approach to comparative politics." Discussion Paper No. 1475. London: Centre for Economic Policy Research.

Pitkin, Hanna F. 1967. *The Concept of Representation.* Berkeley: University of California Press.

Ploeg, Rick van der. 1982. "Government policy, real wage resistance and the resolution of conflict." *European Economic Review* 19: 181–212.

Popper, Karl. 1962. *The Open Society and Its Enemies.* London: Routledge and Kegan Paul.

Powell, Jr, G. Bingham and Guy D. Whitten. 1993. "A cross-national analysis of economic voting: taking account of the political context." *American Journal of Political Science* 37: 391–414.

Przeworski, Adam. 1986. *Capitalism and Social Democracy.* Cambridge: Cambridge University Press.

1991. *Democracy and the Market.* New York: Cambridge University Press.

Przeworski, Adam, Mike Alvarez, Jose Antonio Cheibub, and Fernando Limongi. 1996. "What makes democracies endure?" *Journal of Democracy* 7: 39–55.

Przeworski, Adam and Fernando Limongi. 1997a. "Modernization: theories and facts." *World Politics* 49: 155–83.

1997b. "Development and democracy." In Alex Hadenius (ed.), *Democracy's Victory and Crisis.* Cambridge: Cambridge University Press.

Przeworski, Adam and Michael Wallerstein. 1988. "Structural dependence of the state on capital." *American Political Science Review* 82: 12–29.

Rawls, John. 1993. "The domain of the political and overlapping consensus." In David Copp, Jean Hampton, and John E. Roemer (eds.), *The Idea of Democracy.* Cambridge: Cambridge University Press.

Riker, William. 1965. *Democracy in America* (2nd edn). New York: Macmillan.

Roemer, John E. 1996a. *Theories of Distributive Justice.* Cambridge, MA: Harvard University Press.

1996b. "Why the poor do not expropriate the rich in democracies: a new explanation." Working Paper #95–04. Department of Economics, University of California, Davis.

Rousseau, Jean-Jacques. 1984 (1762). *Of the Social Contract.* Translated by Charles M. Sherover. New York: Harper & Row.

Runciman, W. G. and Amartya K. Sen. 1965. "Games, justice, and the general will." *Mind* 74: 554–62.

Sah, Raj and E. Joseph Stiglitz. 1988. "Committees, hierarchies and polyarchies." *The Economic Journal* 98: 451–70.

Schmitt, Carl. 1988. *The Crisis of Parliamentary Democracy.* Cambridge, MA: MIT Press.

Schmitter, Philippe and Terry Lynn Karl. 1991. "What democracy is ... and what it is not". *Journal of Democracy* 2: 75–88.

Schumpeter, Joseph A. 1942. *Capitalism, Socialism, and Democracy.* New York: Harper & Brothers.

Sen, Amartya. 1995. "Rationality and social choice." *American Economic Review* 85: 1–25.

Sen, Amartya and Bernard Williams (eds.). 1982. *Utilitarianism and Beyond.* New York: Cambridge University Press.

Shapiro, Ian. 1996. *Democracy's Place.* Ithaca: Cornell University Press.

Skinner, Quentin. 1973. "The empirical theorists of democracy and their critics: a plague on both houses." *Political Theory* 1: 287–306.

Stigler, George J. 1975. *The Citizen and the State: Essays on Regulation.* Chicago: University of Chicago Press.

Stimson, James A., Michael B. Mackuen, and Robert S. Erikson. 1995. "Dynamic representation." *American Political Science Review* 89: 543–65.

Stokes, Susan C. 1996. "Accountability and policy switches." Paper presented at the Conference on Democracy and Accountability, New York University, 27–9 April.

1997. "Democratic accountability and policy change: economic policy in Fujimori's Peru." *Comparative Politics* 29: 209–26.

Weffort, Francisco. 1992. *Qual Democracia?* Sao Paulo: Companhia das Letras.

3   Does democracy engender justice?

John E. Roemer

1   Keeping the terms straight

Does, or might, democracy engender justice? Whether this question is interesting depends, of course, on the definitions we adopt of democracy and justice. I begin by arguing for particular definitions.

An analogy is perhaps useful. In the 1960s and 1970s, an intellectual habit developed, on the left, of defining socialism as the confluence of all good things. If an actual country did not exhibit all good things, it could not, therefore, be socialist. For example, because socialism requires internationalism (a good thing), if two countries go to war with each other, at least one must not be socialist (e.g., the Sino-Soviet split, or the Sino-Vietnam war). This definition of socialism was not useful, I contend, for social science. A useful definition of socialism is one that defines it as a set of institutions and practices (public ownership of the means of production, planning, etc.); then the social scientist can inquire into the laws of motion of a socialist society, and perhaps deduce whether all good things would, or might, come about within it.

There is, today, a similar habit of idealizing democracy, that is, of defining it to consist in all good things. Let me quote, as an example, from a recent paper of Karl Klare:

There is a chance to imagine and put in place a new, postliberal form of democracy, one that is more egalitarian, participatory, and environmentally sensitive; a type of democracy that is feminist in inspiration and design, and committed to ending racial hierarchy and injustice. Postliberal democracy would aim to multiply and enrich the opportunities for participation, extending them beyond the electoral arena to the administrative process, and to "private spheres" such as the workplace and family. New linkages could be configured between social, economic, and political life – for example between work and family – allowing more diverse possibilities for human self-realization and, in particular, allowing new roles and possibilities for women. The economic order could be made more solidaristic and participatory. New, nonhierarchical relationships between ethnic, racial, and religious groups could be fashioned, building a celebration of cultural diversity into social and political institutions. (Klare 1994: 310)

Table 3.1

	Procedural	end-state
Impartiality	Rawls (1971)	Utilitarianism
	Barry (1995)	Equal welfare
Mutual advantage	Gauthier ?	Gauthier (1986)

I contend that this conception of democracy is not useful to the social scientist. What Klare is really discussing is a just society, not a (merely) democratic one.

We must, I believe, insist upon a division of labor between the concepts of democracy and justice for the initially posed question to be interesting. Democracy should be defined as a set of institutions and practices whose intention is to implement a certain kind of equal participation of citizens in the political process. Justice, on the other hand, consists in a set of relations among persons, and between persons and goods, in a society. With this division of labor, the initial question becomes a scientific one: will a given set of institutions and practices bring about the particular set of relationships that justice requires?

2   Kinds of justice and democracy

Species of justice can be classified along (at least) two dimensions: whether the concept is procedural or end state, and whether it is one of impartiality or mutual advantage. The first distinction is due to Nozick (1974), and the second to Barry (1989). Table 3.1 illustrates the four possibilities.

Gauthier argues clearly the Hobbesian view that justice is brought about by a set of rules enabling each to seek his best advantage without disabling others from seeking theirs, and he deduces an end state, namely the Kalai–Smorodinsky solution of the bargaining problem. Rawls conceives of justice as fairness, or impartiality, and argues that justice regulates only the basic structure of social institutions. (Some might see the difference principle as an end-state principle, but Rawls seems to believe that the difference principle regulates how institutions are constructed, not how actual resource allocations are made.) Barry (1995) argues for justice as impartiality, but insists that justice only requires certain procedures be followed: justice, at least in Barry's 1995 volume, does not entail particular resource allocations. What is required is that the resource allocation be arrived at by forms of political argument, and resolution, that satisfy certain criteria. Utilitarianism (maximizing the sum of utilities) and equal welfare can both claim to be impartial, and they surely prescribe end states. Nozick's view of justice does not fall neatly in this table; it is surely procedural, but neither impartial nor mutual advantage.

Perhaps the least demanding definition of democracy is Adam Przeworski's: a system is democratic if it conducts elections and the losers are not thrown in jail. Though spare, this definition is, according to what I have said, of the right kind. I would happily admit a larger set of criteria as necessary for democracy, institutional criteria designed to permit and encourage equal political participation, or equal opportunity for political participation, among the citizenry. These criteria should be stated in institutional terms. For example, it would be admissible to say that democracy requires a system of one-man-one-vote, where electoral districts must satisfy demographic characteristics a, b, and c, and winners are decided according to such-and-such a procedure; it would not be admissible to say that democracy requires a system of equal political participation. The basic point is that democracy should be defined in such a way that only a graduate student in political science, rather than a seasoned philosopher, is required to classify regimes as democratic or not.

One account of democracy that, in my view, requires too much is called deliberative democracy. Joshua Cohen provides a recent statement:

A deliberative conception of democracy puts public reasoning at the center of political justification . . . . [In such a discussion citizens] are *reasonable* in that they aim to defend and criticize institutions and programs in terms of considerations that others, as free and equal, have *reason to accept*, given the fact of reasonable pluralism and on the assumption that those others are themselves reasonable. (Cohen 1996: 19–21)

Now compare Cohen's definition of deliberative democracy with Thomas Scanlon's definition of contractualism, a species of justice as impartiality. According to Scanlon, a society is just precisely when it is governed by a set of rules that meet a certain stipulation.

An act is wrong if its performance under the circumstances would be disallowed under any system of rules for the general regulation of behavior which no one could reasonably reject as a basis for informed, unforced general agreement. (Scanlon 1982: 110)

And further:

According to contractualism, the source of motivation that is directly triggered by a belief that an action is wrong is the desire to be able to justify one's actions to others on grounds that they could not reasonably reject (reasonably, that is, given the desire to find principles which others similarly motivated could not reasonably reject). (Scanlon 1982: 116)

It is difficult to distinguish Cohen's deliberative democracy from Scanlon's contractarian justice. Were one to accept Cohen's account of democracy and Scanlon's characterization of justice then, trivially, the former would entail the latter.

Having now set the methodological ground rules, let me muse about the possibility that democracy engender the various kinds of justice classified in table 3.1. I think the easiest deduction is that democracy may well be able to bring about justice in the southwest corner. For democracy is, first of all, a system in which competing interest groups form parties to fight, according to the rules of the political game, for their interests. The "procedures" may well be approximated by a set of rules and institutions, and the outcome of the political process would then qualify, assuming those institutions are used and rules followed, as the resolution of the struggle for advantage by these groups.

I am convinced by Barry (1995), however, that justice must be conceived of as impartiality, not mutual advantage, and hence it is only the top row of table 3.1 that is salient for me. I shall discuss the northeast corner of the table in section 4. This leaves the northwest corner of table 3.1, to which I now proceed.

3   Can democracy engender justice which is procedural and impartial?

Brian Barry (1995), who has written most extensively on the concept of justice as impartial and procedural, takes Scanlon's (1982 and 1988) contractarian proposal as a generic instance of the kind. Scanlon's contractarian proposal differs from Rawls's in two ways: there is no veil of ignorance, which, as in Rawls, forces individuals in the contractarian setting to be impartial, and individuals are motivated not only by their own personal aims, but by a desire to seek agreement, on "reasonable" terms, with others who are similarly motivated.

The nub of the question (of this section's title) seems to me to be the following: why should democracy, a set of institutions and rules designed to regulate political competition among interest groups with conflicting aims, produce "a desire to seek agreement, on reasonable terms, with others who are similarly motivated"? To be somewhat more careful, we need not, in fact, demonstrate that democracy would produce a citizenry characterized by that desire, but only something weaker: that democracy will or would produce a set of social agreements (policies) that *would* have been produced by a citizenry motivated by such a desire. This distinction is, I think, important, for as I will argue, it is far easier to demonstrate the revised claim than the claim posed, in interrogative form, in the first sentence of this paragraph.

The Scanlonian idea is that a just set of rules and institutions is one that comes about when a citizenry, whose members are each motivated by a desire to seek agreement under certain conditions, meet in a contractarian situation. I am proposing that a set of rules and institutions is just (according to the impartial construal) if one can demonstrate that it *would* have come about in such a contractarian situation, even if it, in fact, did not – it could, to take a slightly preposterous case, have been imposed by an omniscient dictator. Now, in reality, the simplest proof that a set of rules and institutions could have come about in a particular way is to observe that it did come about that way. But this kind of demonstration, though sufficient, is not necessary. When Barry, for instance, argues that justice as impartiality cannot entail certain specific practices, such as discrimination against homosexuals, he is arguing in the conditional manner: the proof consists in saying that *were* a citizenry to seek agreement under the stipulated conditions, they could not possibly come to a policy of discrimination against homosexuals. From this Barry concludes that non-discrimination against persons on the basis of sexual preference is a necessary condition of justice as impartiality.

I will argue that democracy (in the minimalist, Przeworskian sense) may well produce a set of policies that could have come about from a citizenry engaging in the Scanlonian contractarian situation, under the proper cooperative motivation to seek agreement, even though that will not transpire because citizens actually have those motivations. The argument proceeds from what is, I think, a quite robust empirical truth: in the advanced democracies, policies are never advocated by saying that their purpose is to enhance the welfare of a small interest group at the expense of others. Even if the real intention of advocates of some policy is to advance the interests of only a small group, and if the consequence will be a cost to many others, those advocates expound some form of the "rising-tide-lifts-all-boats" argument. Arguments for such policies are couched in universalistic terms that, I will argue, no person can reasonably reject.

How can this be possible – how, that is, can two opposite policies (raise taxes or reduce taxes) each be couched in terms that no reasonable person could reject? The answer is that the effects of a policy always depend upon the values of certain parameters of the economy and/or human behavior, and, as these values are often difficult to estimate, it is not unreasonable to believe, given the uncertainty of the true parameter values, that either of two opposite policies could have widely beneficial effects. For example, the Republican Party argues for reducing capital gains taxes not on the basis that such a reduction would increase the wealth of the rich, but because it would increase investment which would raise employment and the welfare of the working class. The critical parameter value here is the investment elasticity with respect to the tax rate. Democrats argue that increasing the minimum wage would not lower employment, and would make working people better off: the critical parameter here is the elasticity of the demand for labor by certain kinds of firms with respect to the wage.

Now one might protest, against my claim, that many of these political arguments are not ones that reasonable individuals should accept, individuals who (hypothetically) are motivated by a desire to reach an agreement with others on reasonable terms. I disagree. Experts disagree about the values of the parameters in question. How can an ordinary citizen have more privileged information? Given the conflicting testimony of experts, it would seem that the typical citizen cannot reasonably reject *any* proposed policy. When the phase of political argument is over, and the phase of choosing the policy occurs (say, with a vote), many citizens (or legislators) will not vote for one policy or another on the basis of which will be better for the general welfare, but on the basis of self-interest (or the interest of their constituents or principals). But this, I claim, is not germane to evaluating whether the conditional contractarian procedures have been met. What is germane is that arguments for the competing policies have been put forth which no reasonable person could reject.[1] Whether voters actually vote on the basis of what they think will be good for the general welfare is irrelevant.

Why should it be that arguments in a democracy are always posed with a universalistic appeal? I believe there are two main reasons. First, it will generally be the case that there is a large spectrum of citizens (on the continuum of socio-economic traits) who are genuinely undecided about which policy is best for them, and because they form a spectrum,

---

[1] Perhaps some elaboration is required here. I am saying that one can represent, schematically, the typical political argument as between two positions that claim that a certain economic parameter, given our knowledge, most likely has a value of x, on the one hand, or y, on the other. (The Republicans say x, the Democrats say y.) More generally, one position says that the likely value of the parameter is characterized by a probability distribution F, on a certain interval, and the other says the probability distribution is really G. Each side marshals expert opinion to bolster its claim. Now, one might say, since some experts say F is the right distribution, that a reasonable person could reject the claim that G is. Hence, not both policies must be accepted as reasonable by a citizen. In fact, neither policy need be accepted as reasonable by a citizen, by this argument. I am rejecting this claim, and saying that, if experts disagree, then no reasonable person can fail to be skeptical; hence, no reasonable person can reject either proposed policy.

arguments that have a universal appeal to self-interest stand the best chance of recruiting the largest number of them. Second, there will, generally, be a large set of citizens who will not, or believe they will not, be affected by the policy in question, and these citizens tend to vote sociotropically (if they vote) – that is, for the policy they think will be best for the citizenry at large. To appeal to these voters also requires making universalistic arguments. I do not wish to imply these are the only reasons: for instance, there is evidence that even people who will be affected by policies vote not on the basis of self-interest, but socio-tropically. I do not think one needs to invoke this less robust observation to make the point.

To sum up, I have argued that democracies produce political arguments for policies of a universalistic nature. The last step consists in noting that this is precisely the kind of argument that would have to be made *were* the citizenry to be characterized by a desire to seek agreement among reasonable persons. In other words, actual democracies approximate, and slightly amended ones would approximate even better, the Scanlonian requirement for implementing justice as impartiality. To repeat the one slightly subtle move in this argument, I have nowhere argued that citizens in democracies will actually come to be characterized as having that Scanlonian desire.

It will not escape the reader's attention that the kind of justice I have been saying democracy can bring about is only procedural, not end-state. In particular, the distribution of economic welfare might be highly unequal. An egalitarian, therefore, would have good cause to reject the northwest corner of the table as the right conception of justice, if she buys my argument, or, to be somewhat more careful, to reject Scanlon's particular concretization of procedural, impartial justice. Indeed, the possibly non-egalitarian nature of Scanlonian justice, if I am correct, follows from the way I fleshed out the plastic term "reasonable," and that highly unequal distributions of resources might follow from my way of fleshing out what "reasonable" means followed from a fact about the world, namely, the difficulty in knowing, with a high degree of certainty, the values of parameters of economic processes and human nature. In short, I am afraid that the Scanlon–Cohen move generates a conception of justice with only weak implications with respect to resource allocation and the distribution of economic welfare.

4   Democracy and impartial, end-state justice

I shall not investigate the general question one could pose here, but a special case: must democracy eventually generate justice conceived of as equality of condition among citizens? I cannot here digress to the intensely interesting, and controversial, issue of precisely what condition should be equalized under an egalitarian construal of justice. I will, however, take it that the various candidates for the equalisandum would all imply a much more egalitarian distribution of income than we observe in almost all countries today.[2]

I have already argued that democratic arguments take a universalistic form. The question is whether, over time, the constraint to argue universalistically will force democratically chosen policies to be increasingly egalitarian in their effects. There are, evidently, arguments for and against.

I begin with two arguments in favor. The first is that, with the development of social science (economics, psychology, sociology), experts will not credibly be able to differ significantly in the values they assign to the critical parameters of the socio-economic mechanism. All experts will converge to something near the true values of these parameters. Therefore, any policy which can credibly claim to increase the welfare of all must, in fact, do so. Now just because a policy increases the welfare of all does not mean it creates more equality of condition – it could create less. So I must make a stronger argument, that policies with universalistic appeal must claim to distribute benefits fairly, where fairness entails a decreasing inequality of condition. To argue that the conception of fairness will come to entail ever-increasing equality of condition is a major undertaking, and it is not one I can pursue here. I say, then, that the first argument would go by establishing three premises: (1) that democratic arguments are posed universalistically, (2) that, due to the development of social science, experts will not credibly be able to disagree a great deal about the values of parameters in the economic mechanism, and (3) that conceptions of fairness entail, or will come to entail, increasing equality of condition[3] (for instance, that condition might be "opportunity for the good life").

The second argument is that the general population will become increasingly well educated as economic development continues, which will force political parties/candidates to be less demagogic, and stick

---

[2] I take equality of income to be the salient equality, not equality of wealth. Unequal wealths should be significant, for an egalitarian, only if they generate unequal incomes, or unequal streams of lifetime income. If a society were characterized by unequal wealths, but those wealths never generated unequal streams of income, an egalitarian should have no complaint. This is not an absurd thing to imagine: there might be returns to scale in wealth holding, so that a small fraction of people should hold all the wealth, but the income stream from those holdings might be distributed in an egalitarian manner.

[3] I do not claim (3) is true, but that it is a premise of this argument.

closer to the truth. Essentially, this argument substitutes "the increased sophistication of the citizenry" for "the development of social science" above.

I proceed to present several arguments against. The first concerns the multidimensionality of electoral politics. It is commonly observed that the relevant issue space of electoral politics in the advanced democracies is (at least) two-dimensional (see Laver and Hunt 1992; Kitschelt 1994; Poole and Rosenthal 1991). One issue, characteristically, concerns redistribution, and the other concerns "values" – what Kitschelt calls the "authoritarian–libertarian" axis. It might not be far-fetched to say that the second issue reflects a good part of what makes up different religious views in the population. If most societies will always be characterized by a spectrum of religious views, or of views concerning what constitutes the good, then it is not unreasonable to think that electoral politics will always, in those societies, be multi-issued.

In a recent paper (Roemer 1998b), I study the nature of electoral equilibrium when there are two parties, which represent different constituencies in the population, competing on a two-dimensional issue space. Call the first party Labour: it has pro-redistribution, libertarian preferences; call the second party Conservative: it has anti-redistribution, authoritarian preferences. The citizenry have preferences whose ideal points cover the issue space (that is, there are voters with all possible ideal points in the two-dimensional issue space), but the distribution of such ideal points (voters) can be very general. A political equilibrium consists of a pair of platforms, each of which announces the two-dimensional policy that a party will seek to implement, if it wins the election, and which together constitute an equilibrium in the voting game.[4] I prove the following:

If the non-redistributive issue is sufficiently important to voters, and if condition * holds, then, in electoral equilibrium, the Labour party (and, a fortiori, the Conservative party) will announce a platform with very little redistribution (i.e., low tax rates). This holds even when a large majority of the population desire a high degree of redistribution.

Condition * : The mean wealth of the cohort of voters who hold the median view on the authority–liberty issue is greater than the mean wealth in the population as a whole.

The particular form of condition * is not important here: what is salient is that that condition, which is a characteristic of the distribution of voter preferences, is not bizarre or improbable. (In fact, I have calculated, from voter survey data, that condition * in fact holds in the

---

[4] Indeed, the result I shall describe holds for several definitions of equilibrium.

United States, and Great Britain, where various construals of the authority–liberty issue are taken.) So, if my model of electoral politics is correct, then the above theorem could provide an explanation for why the British Labour Party (and perhaps the US Democratic Party) takes a relatively conservative position on redistribution.

The general result, of which I have reported an instance, which I am confident is quite robust (even though the instance I report is associated with a particular model of electoral politics), is that when politics are multidimensional, there is little reason to think that political equilibrium will entail a high degree of redistribution, in a polity which is character-ized by a significant variation in preferences on other, non-distributive issues. In fact, the countries where we do see a high degree of redistribu-tion (the Nordic countries) are characterized by a rare homogeneity on the "values" issue, due to the great degree of religious, ethnic, and linguistic homogeneity of their polities. (How does this play itself out in my model of electoral politics? If there is something approximating universal agreement on the values issue, then that issue will not become a political issue, and electoral competition will be uni-dimensional, where redistribution is the sole issue. In that case, if the two parties represent "poor" and "rich" voters [i.e., are pro- and anti-redistribu-tion], then the pro-redistribution party wins, as long as median wealth is less than mean wealth, a fact which is true in every country in the world.)

So I claim that, in societies which are heterogeneous in regard to preferences on non-economic issues, the democratic process may well not produce (i.e., should condition * hold) considerable redistribution, which is to say, it will not tend to produce equality of condition. The key premise, here, is the heterogeneity of values, and I note that such heterogeneity is a key assumption of the Rawls–Cohen–Barry formu-lation of the problem of justice (in Cohen's case, of deliberative democ-racy). It is, indeed, this heterogeneity which motivates the central issue for these authors, whether or not the definition of justice they propose is indeed neutral with respect to heterogeneous conceptions of the good (see Rawls 1993).

Finally, the electoral equilibrium I have been discussing satisfies, it seems to me, the conditions of procedural, impartial justice. That citizens vote according to their own preferences, as they do in my model, does not violate Barry's requirements of impartiality.

The argument just given assumes that citizens' preferences are self-regarding. Recently, Piketty (1995) has produced a fascinating argu-ment showing that, even should voters be other-regarding in their preferences, and care about the unluckiest in society, democratic political equilibrium will not necessarily entail a great deal of redistribution from the rich to the poor. Thus, Piketty's argument shows that, even should citizens have internalized a Rawlsian kind of view, many may well not vote for redistributive policies.

In Piketty's multiperiod model, an individual will receive either a high (H) or low (L) income in a given period. The income she receives is a random variable, with a mean that depends positively on the effort she invested in the economic process: say her income will be $a\theta + \epsilon$, where θ is her effort, a is a positive number, and ϵ is a random variable with mean zero. If the number a is very small, then receiving a large income is mainly a matter of luck, while if a is large, it is mainly a matter of having expended effort. The key assumption of the model is that individuals do not know the true value of a, that is, of the key parameter in the economic process. They form beliefs about the value of a from their own experience. Thus, for example, if an individual exerts high effort and receives a high income, he tends to think that a is large and the effect of luck is small. Individuals update their beliefs about the value of a each period in the Bayesian manner, given their own historical experience. No individual can see the efforts expended by others, so his inferences are taken solely from his own experience.

Piketty shows that, if individuals begin with a spectrum of beliefs about the value of a, and they *rationally update* their beliefs over time, choosing their effort optimally each period, given their current beliefs about the importance of effort in the income-producing process, then the society will converge to having different beliefs about the value of a. Individuals who think a is large are "right-wing" (i.e., think high income is largely a matter of working hard), while individuals who think a is small are "left-wing" (i.e., think income is largely a matter of luck).

The electoral issue this society faces is how much redistribution there should be from those with H incomes to those with L incomes. Citizens are other-regarding in this sense: they will vote for redistribution if they think those with L incomes have those incomes largely in consequence of bad luck, and they will vote against redistribution if they think L incomes are a consequence of not having expended effort. Thus, "right-wing" people vote against redistribution, and "left-wingers" for redistribution. Because, in general, the stationary set of beliefs can entail having an arbitrary distribution of left-wing and right-wing voters, there is no assurance that politics will produce highly redistributive policies.

The important premises of Piketty's argument are that: (1) the relationship between effort and income is stochastic and obscure, (2) individuals form beliefs in a rational way, and (3) they are other-regarding, rather than self-interested. The argument produces the unhappy result of possibly low redistribution even when there are no right-wing parties or media trying to twist the facts, and even when voters are other-regarding. Piketty's model is an instance of the general argument I made earlier: that, when parameters of the economic mechanism are obscure, it is possible that reasonable people will reach very different views as to their values. Piketty's model is, in one sense, more damaging to the prognosis of equality in a Scanlonian world than my earlier example, for the sharply differing views citizens come to have about economic parameters are not due to their having listened to experts who had, themselves, different ideological (or class) positions.[5]

5   Conclusion

The reader will note that the arguments in the last two sections depend upon subsets of these three features of society: that there is considerable uncertainty about the (true) values of economic parameters, that there are heterogeneous conceptions of the good (values), and that there is a considerable spectrum of incomes or wealth before the degree of redistribution is chosen by the democratic process. I argued, in section 3, that it might well be possible for democracy to engender the kind of procedural, impartial justice that has been most recently elaborated by Barry (1995), and is advocated as well by Scanlon (1982 and 1988), Rawls (1971 and 1993) and Cohen (1996). But my conclusion was that the sufficient conditions for just procedures that these authors propose are incapable of guaranteeing the kind of equality of condition that they prize. In section 4, I asked whether democracy would indeed tend to deliver that kind of equality of condition; the two arguments I offered in favor of such a conclusion both depended upon the elimination of uncertainty about the values of economic parameters.

I take the last two arguments in section 4, against concluding that democracy entails equality of condition, to be instances of a general phenomenon, that the kinds of uncertainty and heterogeneity postulated in this section's first sentence push against democracy's engendering justice conceived of as equality of economic condition. I do think, however, that the two pro arguments offered in section 4 have some weight, and that, consequently, advanced democracies will, over time,

---

[5] One might argue against the salience of Piketty's model for our purposes, because it assumes that citizens can observe only their own effort. Thus, conditions of "full information" would require that citizens know the response of income to effort *generally* in society. But I say this would be to assume away the central problem, that economic parameters are, because of the complexity of the economic mechanism, obscure. Piketty's model captures that obscurity by the particular assumption that individuals observe only their own effort.

come to be characterized by more equality of economic condition than they currently have. My conjecture is that that degree of equality will be considerably less than present-day theorists of equality of condition (Sen 1980; Dworkin 1981; Arneson 1989; G. A. Cohen 1989; Roemer 1998a) think of as necessary for distributive justice.

REFERENCES

Arneson, Richard. 1989. "Equality and equality of opportunity for welfare." *Philosophical Studies* 56: 77–93.
Barry, Brian. 1989. *Theories of Justice.* Berkeley: University of California Press.
    1995. *Justice as Impartiality.* Oxford: Clarendon Press.
Cohen, G. A. 1989. "On the currency of egalitarian justice." *Ethics* 99: 906–44.
Cohen, Joshua. 1996. *Liberty, Equality, Democracy.* Cambridge, MA: Dept of Political Science, MIT (xeroxed).
Dworkin, Ronald. 1981. "What is equality? Part 2: Equality of resources." *Philosophy & Public Affairs* 10: 283–345.
Gauthier, David. 1986. *Morals by Agreement.* Oxford: Oxford University Press.
Kitschelt, Herbert. 1994. *The Transformation of European Social Democracy.* New York: Cambridge University Press.
Klare, Karl. 1994. "Legal theory and democratic reconstruction: reflections on 1989." In G. S. Alexander and G. Skapska (eds.), *A Fourth Way?* New York and London: Routledge.
Laver, Michael and W. B. Hunt. 1992. *Policy and Party Competition.* London: Routledge and Kegan Paul.
Nozick, Robert. 1974. *Anarchy, State, and Utopia.* New York: Basic Books.
Piketty, Thomas. 1995. "Social mobility and redistributive politics." *Quarterly Journal of Economics* 110: 551–84.
Poole, Kenneth and Howard Rosenthal. 1991. "Patterns of Congressional voting." *American Journal of Political Science* 35: 228–78.
Rawls, John. 1971. *A Theory of Justice.* Cambridge, MA: Harvard University Press.
    1993. *Political Liberalism.* New York: Columbia University Press.
Roemer, John E. 1998a. *Equality of Opportunity.* Cambridge, MA: Harvard University Press.
    1998b. "Why the poor do not expropriate the rich: an old argument in new garb." *Journal of Public Economics* 70: 399–424.
Scanlon, Thomas. 1982. "Contractualism and utilitarianism." In Amartya Sen and Bernard Williams (eds.), *Utilitarianism and Beyond.* Cambridge: Cambridge University Press.
    1988. "Levels of moral thinking." In D. Seanor and N. Fotion (eds.), *Hare and Critics.* Oxford: Clarendon Press.
Sen, Amartya. 1980. "Equality of what?" In S. McMurrin (ed.), *The Tanner Lectures on Human Values.* Vol. I. Salt Lake City: University of Utah Press.

4   Democracy and other goods[1]

Partha Dasgupta and Eric Maskin

1   The democratic process

In his masterly affirmation of the democratic ideal, Dahl (1989) observes that "effective participation by citizens" and "voting equality among citizens" have often been taken to be the two features that embody the idea of democratic process. But he argues that any association which governs itself by them alone should be regarded as conforming to the ideal in a narrow sense only (108–11). Dahl then shows that there is a third requirement – "enlightened understanding" – which, when added to the two, defines a full procedural democracy with respect to its agenda and in relation to its demos (people). He writes (111–12):

democracy has usually been conceived as a system in which rule by the people makes it more likely that the people will get what it wants, or what it believes is best, than alternative systems like guardianship in which an elite determines what is best. But to know what it wants, or what is best, the people must be enlightened, at least to some degree … [Thus] each citizen ought to have adequate and equal opportunities for discovering and validating … the choice on the matter to be decided that would best serve the citizen's interests.

Dahl then shows that even this is not enough. He adds a fourth requirement (1989: 112–14), that citizens must have the exclusive opportunity to decide how matters are to be placed on the agenda of those matters that are to be decided by means of the democratic process. Moreover, final control of the agenda by citizens, Dahl argues, presupposes that citizens are qualified to decide (1) which matters do or do not require binding decisions; (2) of those that do, which matters they are qualified to decide for themselves as a collective; and (3) the terms on which they delegate authority.

Taken together, the four criteria define *representative democracy*, with clearly established limits on the agenda over which collective decisions

[1] Research support from the Beijer International Institute of Ecological Economics, Stockholm, is gratefully acknowledged.

are to be made. This means that the possible centrality in the political lexicon of individual rights (such as non-interference by others on matters in the private domain) is consonant with the democratic ideal.

Dahl then proves that even this would not suffice. He adds a fifth requirement, concerning inclusion (119–31), that "the demos must include all adult members of the association except transients and persons proved to be mentally defective." He concludes that, if democracy is the ideal, the five criteria, taken together, are the standard by which political processes ought to be judged.

In this chapter we will take it that the five requirements of an ideal democratic process are uncontroversial. Our aim is to build on these ideas by presenting several findings that have emerged, since Dahl's book was published, on both the theory and practice of democracy. We present them here in the belief that they add to our understanding of the strengths and limitations of the democratic ideal.

Section 2 will be concerned with decision rules for translating individual values (or preferences) into collective choice. We will call them "voting rules." Dahl's five requirements do not specify the voting rule that best reflects the democratic ideal. We should not expect it to be otherwise, for Arrow's classic formulation of the idea of democratic voting rules showed how wide a range such rules could in principle encompass (Arrow 1963 [1951]). Dahl suggests, however, that the rule that has historically been regarded as appropriate to the democratic process is the majority rule; and he observes:

virtually everyone assumes that democracy requires majority rule in the weak sense that support by a majority ought to be *necessary* to passing a law. But ordinarily supporters of majority rule mean it in a much stronger sense. In this stronger sense, majority rule means that majority support ought to be not only necessary but also *sufficient* for enacting laws. (Dahl 1989: 135 [emphasis in the original])

But as Dahl himself notes, even the term "majority" rule is not unambiguous: it refers to a family of voting rules, for example, that the alternative to be chosen is the one that wins over all others by a simple majority, or that if an alternative is to win outright, it should not be beaten by any other by more than one-third of the number of voters (hence the term, two-thirds-majority rule), and so on. Dahl (1989, especially chap. 10) marshals a powerful case for majority rules in general, but gives particular attention to the simple majority rule. He recognizes that all such rules are subject to potential deficiencies, for example, that cycles exist in which no majority preference can be established; but, then, *all* democratic decisions rules that satisfy the conditions enunciated in Arrow's famous impossibility theorem (Arrow

1963 [1951]) suffer from such problems. Bergson (1976) observed that representative democracy as, say, reflected in "democratic-one-man-rule," can violate one of Arrow's conditions (the "independence of irrelevant alternatives") – but Bergson also noted that this does not make representative democracy immune to Arrow's problem.

Among democratic voting rules, the simple majority rule (we will call *this* the majority rule) has a particularly strong intuitive appeal. May (1952) offered an axiomatic account of where that appeal lies. In section 2 we present a new defense of majority rule, one which complements May's finding. We show that, among all voting rules satisfying a set of intuitively appealing conditions that have been much studied in the literature, majority rule is immune to cycles (i.e., the rule is transitive) on the largest domain of configurations of individual preferences, and is the unique such rule. To put it briefly, majority rule is robust.

Section 2 identifies the attraction of majority rule as an expression of the democratic decision-making process. In the remainder of the chapter we explore a number of instrumental virtues of democracy. In section 3 we develop the third of Dahl's five criteria, namely "enlightened understanding," quoted above. We argue that limited knowledge and asymmetric information among members of a demos do not merely call out for the creation of opportunities among people to acquire more information, they also provide an instrumental justification for democracy. It has been said that democracy is the worst system of government, except for the other systems of government. Incomplete and asymmetric information among members of a demos provide an explanation for why the epithet is true. We argue this by appealing to recent findings on the management of local common-property resources among rural communities in poor countries. These empirical findings reveal, in particular, the instrumental value of local participatory democracy. Related to this, political scientists have drawn attention to the positive influence civic engagement can have on government performance in democratic societies (Putnam 1993; Cohen and Rogers 1995). Their argument is that government accountability requires collective action. But collective action requires coordination; more fundamentally, it requires that people trust one another *to* coordinate. Civic engagement creates trust by reducing the uncertainties each party harbours about others' predilections and dispositions. Contrariwise, an absence of such engagement makes trust that much harder to build. In an interesting, suggestive paper, Seabright (1997) has provided both analytical and empirical support for this reasoning by showing that trust can indeed be "habit forming."

In section 4 we focus on representative democracy and the

concomitant idea of political competition. As Shapiro and Hacker-Cordón note above, the idea of political competition was central to Schumpeter's reformulation of the concept of democracy (Schumpeter 1942). The thought is that political democracy and civil liberties together are a means by which government can be made accountable; but the view is often questioned for poor countries, for it is not uncommon to hear the suggestion that citizens of poor countries cannot afford such luxuries as civil and political rights, that they are inimical to economic development. A natural question to then ask is if there is in fact a conflict in poor countries between economic development and political and civil liberties. In section 5 we look at some evidence and arrive at a tentative, and what we think is an encouraging, finding on this.

Democracy is all things to all people. As Shapiro and Hacker-Cordón also observe above, if democrats expect much of democracy, democracy all too often disappoints. The recent empirical findings we report in this paper suggest that, happily, democracy is more consonant with other social goods than critics of democracy are inclined to believe.

2   The reach of the majority rule

The rules that transform individual values into collective choice differ widely across countries. In his classic work, Arrow (1963 [1951]) offered a particular axiomatization of democratic rules and showed that they cannot always be "coherent"; that is, no voting rule satisfying a particular set of democratic criteria is transitive if the domain of individual values (or preferences) is unrestricted.[2] This means that, unless restrictions are placed on the domain, every such voting rule can be relied upon to generate cycles for some configurations of preferences. The most famous illustration of this remains the Condorcet cycle, generated by the majority rule.

To illustrate the Condorcet cycle, consider three voters, who rank three alternatives (labelled x, y, z) as, respectively, "x over y over z," "y over z over x," and "z over x over y." Simple majority rule is intransitive under this configuration of preferences. To confirm this, note that, since two of the voters prefer x to y, simple majority rule requires that x be ranked over y; likewise, since two of the voters prefer y to z, the rule requires that y be ranked over z. By transitivity, x should be ranked over z. But since two of the voters prefer z to x, the rule requires that z be ranked over x, which is a contradiction.

Why is majority rule, nevertheless, intuitively appealing? It is because

---

[2] We are using "values" and "preferences" interchangeably here because their distinction plays no role in what follows.

the rule, especially when applied to choices over political candidates, possesses several compelling properties. First, it satisfies the Pareto principle: if all voters prefer alternative x to alternative y, the rule ranks x over y. Secondly, it is anonymous: the rule treats all voters symmetrically in the sense that the ranking is independent of voters' labels. Anonymity, therefore, captures the second of Dahl's five criteria: voting equality among citizens. And thirdly, majority rule satisfies neutrality: its ranking over any pair of alternatives depends only on the pattern of voters' preferences over the pair, not on the alternatives' labels.

Neutrality is symmetry with respect to alternatives. In the context of representative democracy, neutrality is a natural requirement of a voting rule: it prohibits procedural discrimination against candidates. Rules that violate neutrality have built into them preconceived rankings, for example, favouring the status quo. If preconceived social rankings are to be avoided, neutrality is the condition that can ensure its avoidance.

But majority rule is not the only voting rule satisfying anonymity, neutrality, and the Pareto principle; there is a vast array of others (e.g., the two-thirds-majority rule; and the Pareto-extension rule, wherein two alternatives are considered to be socially indifferent unless *all* voters prefer one to the other). However, all are subject to Arrow's stricture, that is, each will generate cycles for some configurations of preferences.

In this context, Dasgupta and Maskin (1998) have constructed a new defense of majority rule when the number of voters is large. They have shown that, among all voting rules that satisfy anonymity, neutrality, and the Pareto principle, majority rule is immune to cycles (i.e. it is transitive) on the largest domain of individual preferences; moreover, it is the unique such rule. To be precise, they have shown that if, for some domain of individual preferences, a voting rule satisfying anonymity, neutrality, and the Pareto principle is transitive, then so is majority rule transitive on this domain. Moreover, unless a voting rule is itself the majority rule, there exists some domain of individual preferences on which majority rule is transitive, but the voting rule in question is not. The result captures the sense in which majority rule is robust.[3]

To obtain an understanding of the result, let us return to the Condorcet example. Imagine that there are three voters and three alternatives {x,y,z}. Imagine also that the voters can have strict

---

[3] Maskin (1995) explored the robustness of majority rule for the case of a finite number of voters. He proved that it is robust when the number of voters is odd. But the oddness restriction is discomfiting. It is invoked to avoid pathologies that arise when, for example, exactly half the population prefers x to y and the other half prefers y to x. In large organizations such knife-edge cases are unlikely to occur. In order to formalize this idea, Dasgupta and Maskin (1998) have studied the case where the number of voters is a continuum.

preferences only. It then follows that there are in all six possible preference orderings for each voter: [x,y,z], [y,z,x], [z,x,y], [x,z,y], [z,y,x], [y,x,z].[4] It will be noticed that there are now two possible Condorcet cycles, one generated from the first triple {[x,y,z], [y,z,x], [z,x,y]}, another from the second triple {[x,z,y], [z,y,x], [y,x,z]}. It is an easy matter to show that majority rule is transitive on a domain of preference profiles if, and only if, for all triples of alternatives {x,y,z}, one of the orderings {[x,y,z], [y,z,x], [z,x,y]} and one of the orderings {[x,z,y], [z,y,x], [y,x,z]} are absent from the domain; Condorcet cycles are thereby avoided. It is also possible to show that for any other voting rule satisfying anonymity, neutrality, and the Pareto principle to be transitive on a domain of preference profiles, a greater number of preference orderings must be absent from the domain.

In order to illustrate this, consider for example the two-thirds-majority rule. It can be shown (Dasgupta and Maskin 1998) that this rule is transitive on a domain of preference profiles if, and only if, for any triple {x,y,z}, there exists a member, say, x, such that for all preference orderings in the domain, x is either the best, or the worst, or strictly in between y and z. This means that at least four of the six possible strict orderings {[x,y,z], [y,z,x], [z,x,y], [x,z,y], [z,y,x], [y,x,z]} must be omitted from the domain (two from the first group of three, and two from the second group of three).

As another example, consider the plurality rule, wherein candidate x wins over candidate y if and only if the number of voters who rank x over all other candidates exceeds the number of voters who rank y over all other candidates. It can be shown (Dasgupta and Maskin 1998) that this rule is transitive on a domain of preference profiles if, and only if, for any triple {x,y,z}, there exists a member, say, x, such that for all preference orderings in the domain, x is either the best or the worst. This again means that at least four of the six possible strict orderings {[x,y,z], [y,z,x], [z,x,y], [x,z,y], [z,y,x], [y,x,z]} must be omitted from the domain (two from the first group of three, and two from the second group of three).[5]

These considerations bear on the character of voting rules. In recent years, though, the spheres in which democracy ought to be practised have received greater attention. Of particular interest are findings on the management of local common-property resources. We turn to this.

---

[4] In writing [x,y,z] we mean that x is ranked over y and y is ranked over z, and so on.
[5] We may conclude, therefore, that the plurality rule is transitive on a still smaller domain of individal preferences than the two-thirds-majority rule.

3   Local democracy and the local commons

Garrett Hardin's famous statement on the fate of common-property resources (Hardin 1968), that they erode because people "free-ride" on others and, so, consume them in excess, was telling for such globally mobile resources as the atmosphere and the open seas. But Hardin's essay has often misled people into thinking that the "tragedy of the commons" is also an apt metaphor for geographically localized common-property resources, such as ponds, streams, woodlands and local forests, threshing grounds, swinden fallows, and grazing fields. The theory of games taught us some time ago that the local commons can in principle be managed efficiently by the users themselves, that there is no obvious need for some agency external to the community of users (e.g., the state) to assume a regulatory role, nor a need for privatising the commons (Dasgupta and Heal 1979: chap. 3). A large body of recent evidence confirms the theory's prediction: members of local communities have often cooperated in protecting their commons from excessive use.[6]

Why should we expect such a marked difference between the fates of local and global common-property resources? One reason is that individual use is more easily observable by others when the resource is not spread out spatially, which means that it is easier to prevent people from free-riding on the local commons. (Contrast the use of a village tube-well with the littering of streets in a metropolis; or cattle-grazing in the village commons with deforestation on mountainous terrains.) However, bargaining, enforcement, and information costs also play a role in the relative efficacy of the various rules that can in principle be invoked for sharing the benefits and burdens associated with an efficient use of common-property resources. Thus, it matters whether the users know one another (contrast a village grazing ground with ocean fisheries); it matters whether increased mobility makes future encounters among group members more uncertain (contrast a traditional village with a modern metropolis); and it matters whether population pressure leads bargaining costs to exceed the benefits of cooperation. The confirmation of theory by current evidence on the fate of different categories of common-property resources has been one of the most pleasing features of modern economic analysis. Since much of the evidence comes from poor countries, we will concentrate on them.

[6] There is now a large empirical literature recording both the successes and failures of common-property resource management. Chopra, Kadekodi, and Murty (1989), Feeney et al. (1990), Ostrom (1990 and 1996), Baland and Platteau (1996: chaps. 10–13), and Netting (1997) offer good reviews of the findings.

Are common-property resources extensive in poor countries? As a proportion of total assets, their presence ranges widely across ecological zones. In India they appear to be most prominent in arid regions, mountain regions, and unirrigated areas; they are least prominent in humid regions and river valleys (Agarwal and Narayan 1989). There is, of course, an economic explanation for this, based on the common human desire to pool risks. An almost immediate empirical corollary is that income inequalities are less where common-property resources are more prominent. However, aggregate income is a different matter, and it is the arid and mountain regions and unirrigated areas that are the poorest. This needs to be borne in mind when government policy is devised. As may be expected, even within dry regions, dependence on common-property resources declines with increasing wealth across households.[7]

Jodha (1986) used data from over eighty villages in twenty-one dry districts from six tropical states in India to estimate that, among poor families, the proportion of income based directly on the local commons is for the most part in the range 15–25 percent (see also Jodha 1995). This is a substantial proportion. Moreover, as sources of income, they are often complementary to private-property resources, which are, in the main, labor, milch and draft animals, cultivated land and crops, agricultural tools (e.g., ploughs, harrows, levellers, and hoes), fodder-cutting and rope-making machines, and seeds. Common-property resources also provide the rural poor with partial protection in times of unusual economic stress. For landless people they may be the only non-human asset at their disposal. A number of resources (such as fuelwood and water, berries and nuts, medicinal herbs, resin, and gum) are the responsibility of women and children.

A similar picture emerges from Hecht, Anderson, and May (1988), who describe in rich detail the importance of the extraction of babassu products among the landless in the Brazilian state of Maranhão. The support such extraction activity offers the poorest of the poor, most especially the women among them, is striking. These extractive products are an important source of cash income in the period between agricultural-crop harvests.[8]

Typically, the local commons are not open for use to all: they are not "open access" resources. In most cases they are open only to those

---

[7] For further discussion of this link, see Dasgupta and Mäler (1991). In his work on South Indian villages, Seabright (1997) has shown that cooperatives (that are not necessarily connected with the management of local commons) are more prevalent in the drier districts.

[8] For a similar picture in the West African forest zone, see Falconer (1990).

having historical rights, through kinship ties, community membership, and so forth. Social capital, viewed as a complex of interpersonal networks, is telling in this context: it hints at the basis upon which cooperation has traditionally been built.[9]

Communal management of the local commons is not restricted to poor countries. In summarizing his findings on the management of the local commons in the Swiss Alpine forests, Netting (1997) reported that the elected village council marked equivalent shares of standing timber for cutting, and community members drew lots for these shares. Punishment was meted out to those who took more than their share. In the summer, cattle owners could graze only as many beasts on the communal alp as they fed from their own supply of hay during the preceding winter. Thus the total number of animals was kept roughly in line with the fodder potential of all village irrigated meadows, but individual owners of larger hay lands had the right to graze more cows on the commons.

Thus far the prevalence of local common-property resources. As we noted earlier, the empirical literature has also confirmed that resource users in many instances cooperate, often through not-undemocratic means, to ensure that the resource base is not eroded. Attempts have also been made by social scientists to explain observed asymmetries in the distribution of benefits and burdens of cooperation in terms of underlying differences in the circumstances of the various parties. For example, in her study of collectively managed irrigation systems in Nepal, Ostrom (1996) has explained observed differences in benefits and burdens among users (e.g., who gets how much water from the canal system and who is responsible for which maintenance task) in terms of such facts as that some farmers are head-enders, while others are tail-enders. Ostrom (1990) has also tried to explain why cooperation has failed to get off the ground where it did not get established, and why cooperation broke down in a number of cases where it did break down.

There are a number of curious implications of modern game theory that have also been useful in interpreting evidence. In a summary of her research findings on local irrigation in Nepal, Ostrom (1996) notes that systems that had been improved by the construction of permanent headworks were in worse repair, delivered substantially less water to the tail-end than to the head-end of the systems, and had lower agricultural productivity than the temporary headworks made of stone, trees, and

---

[9] See Coleman (1990) and Putnam (1993). Cohen and Rogers (1995) have developed these ideas further by studying certain features of local communitarian activities, in particular their role in fostering democratic institutions. Dasgupta (1997) contains an economist's account of the notion of social capital.

mud that had been constructed and managed by the farmers themselves.

Ostrom has an explanation for this. She suggests that, unless it is accompanied by countermeasures, the construction of permanent headworks alters the relative bargaining positions of the head- and tail-enders, resulting in so reduced a flow of benefits to the latter group that they have little incentive to help repair and maintain the headworks, something the head-enders on their own cannot do. Head-enders gain from the permanent structures, but the tail-enders lose disproportionately. She also notes that traditional farm-managed systems sustained greater equality in the allocation of water than modern systems managed by such external agencies as the government and foreign donors.

Wade (1988) has also conducted an empirical investigation of community-based allocation rules over water and the use of grazing land. Forty-one South Indian villages were studied, and it was found, for example, that downstream villages had an elaborate set of rules, enforced by fines, for regulating the use of water from irrigation canals. Most villages had similar arrangements for the use of grazing land. In an earlier work on the Kuna tribe in the Panama, Howe (1986) described the intricate set of social sanctions that are imposed upon those who violate norms of behavior designed to protect their source of fresh water. Behavior dictated by social norms could seem incongruent with the democratic ideal, but the theory of repeated games has shown that there can be a close connection between the two. Social norms can be viewed as self-enforcing behavioural strategies. Even if a resource allocation rule among members of a community were chosen democratically, there would be a problem of enforcement. Norms are a way the rule could be enforced without the community having to rely on the coercive powers of a higher authority (e.g., the state).[10]

This said, it is important to caution against romanticizing communitarian arrangements over the use of the local commons. Beteille (1983), for example, contains examples of how access is often restricted to the privileged (e.g., high-caste Hindus in India). Rampant inequities exist in rural community practices. We are laying stress upon the fact that the local commons are often not unmanaged; we are not suggesting that they are invariably managed efficiently, nor that they are inevitably managed in ways that involve an equitable distribution of benefits and burdens. Good management of the commons requires more than mere

[10] Fudenberg and Maskin (1986) contains a general proof of the proposition.

local participation; it needs enlightened government engagement as well.

Not surprisingly, information about the ecology of the local commons is usually in the hands of those who, historically, have made use of them. This means that, as a general rule, decisions regarding the local commons ought to be left in the hands of the users themselves. It forms one reason why it is so important that local democracy be encouraged to flourish in rural communities of poor countries. The local commons will almost certainly remain the single source of vital complementary and insurance goods for poor people for a long time to come. One of the duties of the state is to help develop rural infrastructure and markets for credit and insurance, each of which could be expected to lessen the community's reliance on the commons. However, there is little case for centralized command and control over the use of the commons; quite the contrary, there is a case for helping the growth of local democracy. As women are often the ones to work on the commons, they would be expected to know much about the ecological processes upon which their communities depend, so an important task for the state is to help women participate in the democratic process. More generally, the state is obliged to ensure that local decision-making is made in an open way. It would help prevent the economically powerful among rural communities from usurping control over such decisions. This tension – the simultaneous need for increased decentralization of rural decision-making, and for state involvement in ensuring that the seat of local decisions is not usurped by the powerful – poses the central dilemma in the political economy of rural poverty. Civic engagement, local democracy, income security, and environmental protection would appear to be tied to each other.[11]

4   Representative democracy and political competition

At a village level, participatory democracy may well work. There are problems with it at a more extensive level, which political theorists have long noted. The case Dahl (1989) makes is, consequently, for representative democracy. But no discussion of representative democracy, however brief, can get off the ground without an acknowledgment of the instrumental worth of political competition.

Competition in the political sphere not only enables citizens to shop among contenders to govern, it also enables them to shop for ideas on governance. Pluralism in the political domain is akin to competition in

[11] See Esman and Uphoff (1984) and Ghai and Vivian (1992) for case studies on the effectiveness of local democracy for rural development.

the market-place. Competition is desirable even in an unchanging environment: it discourages inefficiency. Competition is necessary to keep incumbents from slacking.[12]

Under changing circumstances and the birth and growth of new ideas, the argument for political competition is, possibly, even stronger. It is not merely personal dictatorships that are likely to be a harbinger of disaster in the long run. Even party systems, unless disciplined by political competition, are prone to ossification. Admittedly, even single-party systems can field competition, as members vie with one another for control of the party apparatus. But for a political party to be definable, there must be something fixed on its agenda, at least in the short to medium term; it would not be a party otherwise. For this reason single-party systems seem unable to field the spectrum of ideas political democracies can. Moreover, the judiciary is often unable to act independently of the legislative and executive branches of government under a single-party system. Over time this proves corrosive, stifling, and ultimately oppressive. Political competition enables citizens in the long run to change their portfolio of risks, much as they can in financial markets.[13]

Unless they can be held accountable by independent bodies at every level, however, even democratically elected governments are not immune to the commands of powerful groups. But authoritarian regimes in general, and dictatorships in particular, are a different species. Except possibly in emergencies, they can be expected to be inefficient, because among other things they have little incentive to encourage the production, dissemination, and use of information. Moreover, even seemingly benign authoritarian regimes turn nasty when economic circumstances run into awkward corners, or when citizens (often minorities) seek changes in their social and political situation, or begin demanding patterns of goods not currently obtainable in the economy, or, more generally, demand changes in the resource-allocation mechanism currently in operation.

Admittedly, authoritarian regimes can leave citizens alone to pursue their lives. Authoritarian governments have also been known to provide a good environment for economic activity. But a commonly held belief that benevolent authoritarianism is a sure-fire route to sustained economic betterment is a belief in an incongruent object: sustained

---

[12] Besley and Coate (1997) have developed a formal model in which political competition provides the necessary mechanism for representative democracy to yield an efficient outcome.

[13] Dixit (1996) and Myerson (1997) offer good accounts of what is currently understood about political competition subject to transaction costs.

benevolent authoritarianism. Pointing to economies that have achieved significant economic progress under authoritarian regimes is no guide to political action. Citizens cannot will wise authoritarianism into existence, nor can they remove an authoritarian regime readily if the political leadership proves to be unsound. A central problem with authoritarianism is its lack of incentives for error-correction, a point that has repeatedly been made by advocates of liberal democracies.

From this it does not, of course, follow that political democracy guarantees progress, nor that it propels economic growth or promotes substantial equality in well-being. In fact it guarantees none of these things. What political pluralism does, when it is allied to a commitment on the part of citizens that good government must protect and promote civil and political liberties, is to encourage the creation of a social and economic environment where citizens have a chance to thrive. Of course, if civic order and general civic responsibility have broken down, there is no prescription to be had, either one way or the other. It is hard to know what prescriptions one can conceive at this moment for Rwanda, Somalia, or the Sudan.

These brief remarks have been deliberately speculative. They are certainly not uncontroversial, most especially, perhaps, in the context of poor countries. So in the following section we will look at some statistical evidence.

5   Democracy and human development: some evidence

Is democracy associated with human development? For example, is growth in national income per head, or increases in life expectancy at birth and the infant survival rate, or improvements in literacy, greater in countries where citizens enjoy less curtailed civil and political liberties?

The case-by-case approach to such questions has enjoyed a long tradition, but it is often so case-specific that it is difficult to draw a general picture from the studies. An alternative is to conduct statistical analyses of cross-country data;[14] but the limitations of statistical analysis are often noted by social scientists, many of whom find them mechanical, bloodless, and lacking in the kind of insights that only micro-historical studies can offer. There is something in this, but it is also good to recognize their strength. Statistical analyses should be seen as complements to the case studies of nations and regions. Their strength lies in that we avoid getting enmeshed in historical details, which can

---

[14] Taylor and Jodice (1983) contains studies based on time series.

mesmerize us into thinking that whatever happens to be the case has had a certain inevitability about it.

The study of cross-country statistics is also frequently criticized on grounds that figures for such indices as national income, the literacy rate, and life expectancy at birth are well known to be defective. To give an example, for several sets of countries the available data are not quite comparable: not only were they not collected in the same year, the methods deployed for collecting them were not the same. In the extreme, some of the data reflect not much more than interpolations on data collected in neighbouring countries. All this provides an argument for being careful in designing their analysis (for example, making only ordinal comparisons, so as to nullify systematic biases; see below), it is not a reason for assuming a coy posture and pretending that cross-country statistics have nothing to offer.[15]

A further criticism of cross-country statistical inquiries into the links between civil and political liberties, on the one hand, and improvements in the standard of living, on the other, has been that they have often arrived at contradictory results. But it is as well to check the methodologies deployed in such studies before worrying whether their answers tally. Numerical indices of civil and political liberties have no cardinal significance, they make only ordinal sense. However, a number of published studies have ignored this and run linear regressions between indices of freedom and measures of the living standard. That the findings in such studies are not consonant with those that make use only of ordinal information is no reason to think that the latter are uninformative.

In an early statistical inquiry, Dasgupta (1990) explored possible links between political and civil liberties and changes in the standard of living. The study was restricted to poor countries. Only ordinal information was used and no attempt was made to search for causality in the relationships that emerged. In the remainder of this section we will summarize the findings.

The sample consisted of countries where, in 1970, real national income per head was less than $1,500 at 1980 international dollars. There were fifty-one such countries with populations in excess of 1 million (Summers and Heston 1988). The period under observation was the decade of the 1970s. Table 4.1 summarizes the data.[16]

The first column of Table 4.1 presents the average of the 1970 and 1980 figures for real national income per head. We will use this average as reference, rather than income per head at some given year during the

[15] World Bank (1991) contains a good discussion of the limitations of international statistics.
[16] The account here is taken from Dasgupta (1990) and (1993).

Table 4.1. *Improvements in living standards*

	Y	ΔY	E	ΔE	M	ΔM	L	ΔL	R1	R2
Bangladesh	499.0	17.9	45.0	8.6	140.0	0.0	22.0	4.0	4.9	4.2
Benin	552.5	6.5	40.0	17.5	155.0	21.4	5.0	23.0	7.0	6.3
Bolivia	1383.0	23.6	46.0	11.8	153.0	16.1	39.0	24.0	5.6	4.1
Botswana	1179.0	67.7	50.0	16.7	101.0	25.3	41.0	**	2.1	3.1
Burundi	324.0	5.7	45.0	2.9	137.0	8.7	14.0	11.0	7.0	6.4
Cameroon	789.0	24.5	49.0	12.9	126.0	17.2	19.0	**	6.1	4.4
CAR	499.0	4.7	42.0	13.2	153.0	7.0	7.0	26.0	7.0	7.0
Chad	409.5	24.2	38.0	9.5	171.0	14.9	6.0	9.0	6.4	6.4
China	1315.5	60.0	59.0	38.1	69.0	47.5	43.0	26.0	6.7	6.7
Congo	986.5	1.1	51.0	13.8	98.0	17.0	16.0	**	5.9	6.1
Ecuador	2005.0	85.8	58.0	22.7	100.0	27.8	68.0	13.0	6.4	3.7
Egypt	833.0	48.3	51.0	24.1	158.0	33.8	26.0	18.0	5.6	4.7
Ethiopia	333.0	4.7	43.0	2.7	158.0	2.0	4.0	11.0	6.3	6.1
Gambia	561.0	1.8	36.0	9.1	185.0	14.9	**	**	2.0	2.0
Ghana	494.5	25.9	49.0	9.7	110.0	10.0	27.0	**	6.6	5.1
Haiti	623.0	26.5	48.0	12.5	162.0	19.7	15.0	8.0	6.4	6.0
Honduras	1001.0	16.0	53.0	25.9	115.0	26.7	45.0	15.0	6.1	3.0
India	595.0	6.6	48.0	18.8	139.0	24.8	28.0	8.0	2.1	3.3
Indonesia	811.0	90.2	47.0	18.2	121.0	14.4	39.0	23.0	5.0	5.0
Jordan	1653.0	32.7	55.0	28.0	90.0	40.0	32.0	38.0	6.0	6.0
Kenya	607.0	19.9	50.0	16.7	102.0	20.7	20.0	27.0	5.0	4.6
Korea	1779.0	99.2	60.0	35.0	51.0	46.3	71.0	22.0	4.9	5.6
Lesotho	527.0	92.8	49.0	9.7	134.0	14.5	**	**	5.3	3.9
Liberia	694.0	4.0	47.0	15.2	124.0	21.1	9.0	16.0	6.0	4.3
Madagascar	631.0	12.5	45.0	17.1	183.0	21.4	**	**	5.1	4.4
Malawi	359.0	38.5	40.0	10.0	193.0	13.1	**	**	6.9	6.0
Mali	336.5	12.3	40.0	10.0	204.0	10.3	2.0	8.0	7.0	6.6

Table 4.1. (*Cont.*)

	Y	ΔY	E	ΔE	M	ΔM	L	ΔL	R1	R2
Mauritania	573.0	1.1	39.0	9.8	166.0	15.4	5.0	12.0	5.9	6.0
Mauritius	1254.5	44.8	62.4	17.0	61.4	31.5	**	**	2.7	2.3
Morocco	1037.5	36.9	52.0	17.9	128.0	22.0	14.0	14.0	4.6	4.4
Nepal	498.0	3.2	41.6	9.1	157.4	10.3	9.0	10.0	6.0	5.0
Niger	421.0	10.0	38.0	9.5	170.0	12.5	1.0	9.0	6.7	6.0
Nigeria	727.0	30.8	44.0	11.1	158.0	27.0	15.0	19.0	5.7	4.0
Pakistan	893.0	24.1	46.0	8.8	142.0	13.6	15.0	9.0	4.3	4.9
Paraguay	1584.0	66.4	65.0	6.7	59.0	24.5	75.0	9.0	4.9	5.4
Philippines	1322.5	41.8	57.0	17.4	66.0	25.0	72.0	3.0	4.9	5.1
Rwanda	323.5	41.4	48.0	9.4	135.0	6.4	16.0	34.0	6.9	5.3
Senegal	752.0	2.1	43.0	5.4	164.0	11.0	6.0	4.0	5.6	4.4
Sierra Leone	485.5	11.5	34.0	8.7	197.0	13.4	7.0	8.0	5.6	5.0
Somalia	394.5	11.0	40.0	10.0	158.0	8.8	2.0	58.0	7.0	6.4
Sri Lanka	1108.5	17.8	64.0	25.0	52.0	42.9	75.0	10.0	2.0	3.0
Sudan	667.5	-4.5	42.0	10.5	149.0	18.7	13.0	19.0	5.9	5.7
Swaziland	911.0	45.2	46.1	16.5	145.2	8.7	**	**	5.7	3.9
Tanzania	318.0	24.7	45.0	14.3	132.0	10.7	10.0	69.0	6.0	6.0
Thailand	1378.5	59.4	58.0	18.2	73.0	34.9	68.0	18.0	5.4	4.1
Tunisia	1460.5	71.5	53.9	24.9	127.2	30.2	16.0	46.0	6.0	5.0
Uganda	304.5	27.0	47.0	3.0	117.0	3.7	25.0	27.0	7.0	7.0
Yemen	742.0	81.6	38.6	10.4	187.8	13.6	3.0	18.0	7.0	7.0
Zaire	291.0	37.4	45.0	11.4	131.0	16.5	31.0	24.0	7.0	6.1
Zambia	752.5	9.3	46.5	10.7	106.0	16.3	29.0	15.0	5.0	4.9
Zimbabwe	870.0	14.8	50.5	15.3	96.2	16.0	39.0	30.0	5.9	5.0

Y: gross national income per head in US$; average of 1970 and 1980 values at 1980 international prices

ΔY: percentage change in Y over the decade 1970–80

E: life expectancy at birth in 1970

ΔE: life expectancy improvement index = $\dfrac{\text{(life expectancy at birth in 1980 – life expectancy in 1970)} \times 100}{\text{(80 – life expectancy at birth in 1970)}}$

M: infant mortality rate per thousand infants in 1970

ΔM: infant mortality improvement index = $\dfrac{\text{(infant mortality rate in 1970 – infant mortality rate in 1980)} \times 100}{\text{(infant mortality rate – 10)}}$

L: percentage adult literacy rate in 1960

ΔL: adult literacy rate improvement index = (adult literacy rate in 1980 – adult literacy rate in 1960)

R1: political rights index, averaged over 1973–9 (decreasing with increasing liberty)

R2: civil rights index, averaged over 1973–9 (decreasing with increasing liberty)

Abbreviations: CAR (Central African Republic).

Source: Dasgupta (1993: table 5.4).

decade, because growth rates differed across countries during the period. One common measure of economic performance is the percentage change in real income per head. This is provided in column (2). It will be noticed that an astonishing fifteen of the fifty-one countries experienced a *decline* in real income per head during the 1970s.

Column (3) records life expectancy at birth in 1970. We need to construct a measure of the change in this index over the decade. This is a delicate matter. Equal increments are possibly of less and less ethical worth as life expectancy rises to sixty-five or seventy years and more. But we are measuring performance here. So it would seem that it becomes more commendable if, with increasing life expectancy, the index were to rise at the margin. The idea here is that it becomes more difficult to increase life expectancy as life expectancy itself rises. A simple index capturing this feature is the ratio of the increase in life expectancy to the shortfall of the base-year life expectancy from some target, say eighty years. Column (4) of the table gives this index of improvement over the period 1970–80 for fifty-one countries. All but two countries, Rwanda and Uganda, recorded an improvement.

Column (5) provides infant mortality rates in 1970. Construction of an index of improvement in these poses a similar problem. The ethical issues here are, no doubt, different from those concerning increases in life expectancy at birth. But we are trying to record performance in this field. A figure of 10 per 1,000 for the infant mortality rate is about as low as it is reasonable for poor countries to aspire to for a long time to come. So we take the index of improvement to be the ratio of the decline in the infant mortality rate over the period in question (1970–80) to the base-year infant mortality rate minus ten. All countries in our sample have shown an improvement in infant survival rates. Column (6) presents values for this index of improvement.

Column (7) presents literacy rates. Now, construction of an index of improvements in literacy rates does not pose problems of the kind we face in connection with life expectancy at birth and infant survival rates. It is not immediately clear why it should be a lot less or a lot more difficult to increase the literacy rate when people are more literate; except, that is, near 0 and 100 percent. This suggests that we should simply measure increases in adult literacy rates if we want to measure net improvements in this field. The net increase in literacy rates is provided in column (8). It will be noticed that all countries recorded an improvement.[17]

[17] The coverage here is smaller. Figures for adult literacy rate are not available for a number of countries. The period of coverage is also different from that of the other columns: 1960–80.

Table 4.2. *Correlation matrix of indicators of improvements in living standards*

ΔY	.5883$^{(*}$					
ΔE	.6578$^{(*}$	.4113$^{(*}$				
ΔM	.7546$^{(*}$	.4129$^{(*}$	.7917$^{(*}$			
ΔL	−.0308	.0660	.2710$^{(*}$	.0631		
R1	.5187$^{(*}$	.2956$^{(*}$	.2383$^{(*}$	.4058$^{(*}$	−.3769$^{(*}$	
R2	.4493$^{(*}$	.2776$^{(*}$	.2788$^{(*}$	.3730$^{(*}$	−.2806$^{(*}$	.7290$^{(*}$
	Y	ΔY	ΔE	ΔM	ΔL	R1

Note: $^{(*}$ indicates that a correlation is significant at a 5% level. The correlations are based on 51 observations, except that those for the changes in adult literacy, ΔL, are based on 42 observations.

Source: Dasgupta (1993: table 5.5).

Columns (9) and (10) present indices of political and civil rights in the sample of countries, averaged over the period 1973–9 (Taylor and Jodice 1983: tables 2.1 and 2.2). The indices range from 1 to 7, where 1 is the highest level for both political and civil rights. Even a glance at the two columns tells us that, for the most part, political and civil liberties have been scarce goods in poor countries. There are exceptions, of course, most notably Botswana, the Gambia, India, Mauritius, and Sri Lanka, but, statistically, poor countries during the 1970s had very poor records on political and civil rights, a matter to which we will return.

We will now study rank orders. Table 4.2 consists of the twenty-one (Spearman) rank correlation coefficients associated with the six columns of figures we are studying, namely, real national income per head and its percentage growth; improvements in life expectancy at birth, infant survival rates, and adult literacy rates; and the extent of political and civil rights enjoyed by citizens. The correlation matrix tells us that:

1. Political and civil rights are positively and significantly correlated with real national income per head and its growth, with improvements in infant survival rates, and with increases in life expectancy at birth. (The level of significance is 6.6 percent for growth in real income per head. Each of the other figures is at a level of significance less than 5 percent.)
2. Real national income per head and its growth are positively and significantly correlated, and they in turn are positively and significantly correlated with improvements in life expectancy at birth and infant survival rates.
3. Improvements in life expectancy at birth and infant survival rates are, not surprisingly, highly correlated.

4. Political and civil rights are not the same, but they are strongly correlated.
5. Increases in the adult literacy rate are not related systematically to incomes per head, or to their growth, or to infant survival rates. They are positively and significantly correlated with improvements in life expectancy at birth, but they are negatively and significantly correlated with political and civil liberties.

These observations suggest that literacy stands somewhat apart from other "goods." It does not appear to be driven with the three other measures of the living standard being studied here. Furthermore, regimes that had bad records in political and civil rights were associated with good performances in this field. We have no explanation for this, but it is difficult to resist speculating on the matter. One possibility is that literacy was used by a number of states in the sample to promote the acceptance of established order. This would seem plausible in rural communities, where the classroom provides a relatively cheap means of assembling the young and propagating the wisdom and courage of the political leadership. Education in this case would be a vehicle for ensuring conformity, not critical thinking.

Do these findings tally with those others that are based on ordinal measures? Barro (1996) is one of the few subsequent studies to have taken the ordinal nature of political- and civil-rights indices seriously.[18] His sample contains 100 countries, and he finds that middle-level democracy (as measured by the same indices of political civil liberties as the ones here) is more favourable for growth in living standards than low levels. This is consonant with the findings we have reported here.

Of course, the correlation observed in the data does not imply causation. Each of the indices would in any case be "endogenous" in any general political theory. For example, it is most probable that democracy is correlated with some omitted feature (e.g., the extent to which the rule of law is exercised and rights to property are secured) that enhances growth in national income per head, or life expectancy at birth. We should also bear in mind that indices of political and civil liberties can change dramatically in a nation, following a *coup d'état*, a rebellion, an election, or whatever; and as a six-year average index (the period 1973–9) has been used for them in table 4.2, we must be careful in interpreting the statistical results.[19] Subject to these obvious cautions, what the evidence seems to be telling us is that, statistically speaking, of

---

[18] But only in the second half of the article. The first half was devoted to running linear regressions.
[19] As a matter of fact, though, changes in political and civil liberties indices over the period 1973–9 were slight for most countries in the sample.

the fifty-one poor countries on observation, those whose citizens enjoyed greater political and civil liberties also experienced larger improvements in life expectancy at birth, real income per head, and infant survival rates. The argument that democracy is a luxury poor countries cannot afford is belied by our data. This seems to us to be eminently worth knowing.

REFERENCES

Arrow, Kenneth J. 1963 [1951]. *Social Choice and Individual Values*. New York: John Wiley.
Baland, J.-M. and J.-P. Platteau. 1996. *Halting Degradation of Natural Resources: Is There a Role for Rural Communities?* Oxford: Clarendon Press.
Barro, R. J. 1996. "Democracy and growth." *Journal of Economic Growth* 1: 1–27.
Bergson, A. 1976. "Social choice and welfare economics under representative government." *Journal of Public Economics* 6: 171–90.
Besley, T. and S. Coate. 1997. "An economic model of representative democracy." *Quarterly Journal of Economics* 112: 85–114.
Beteille, André (ed.). 1983. *Equality and Inequality: Theory and Practice*. Delhi: Oxford University Press.
Chopra, K., G. K. Kadekodi, and M. N. Murty. 1989. *Participatory Development: People and Common Property Resources*. New Delhi: Sage.
Cohen, J. and J. Rogers. 1995. "Secondary associations and democratic governance." In J. Cohen, J. Rogers, *et al.* (eds.), *Associations and Democracy*. London: Verso.
Coleman, J. 1990. *Foundations of Social Theory*. Cambridge, MA: Harvard University Press.
Dahl, Robert. 1989. *Democracy and Its Critics*. New Haven: Yale University Press.
Dasgupta, Partha. 1990. "Well-being and the extent of its realization in poor countries." *Economic Journal* 100 (Supplement): 1–32.
1993. *An Inquiry into Well-Being and Destitution*. Oxford: Clarendon Press.
1998. "Economic development and the idea of social capital." Mimeo., Faculty of Economics, University of Cambridge.
Dasgupta, Partha and Geoffrey M. Heal. 1979. *Economic Theory and Exhaustible Resources*. Cambridge: Cambridge University Press.
Dasgupta, Partha and K.-G. Mäler. 1991. "The environment and emerging development issues." *Proceedings of the World Bank Annual Conference on Development Economics 1990* (Supplement to the *World Bank Economic Review* and the *World Bank Research Observer*), pp. 101–32.
Dasgupta, Partha and Eric Maskin. 1998. "On the robustness of majority rule." Mimeo., Faculty of Economics, University of Cambridge.
Dixit, Avinash. 1996. *The Making of Economic Policy: A Transaction-cost Politics Perspective*. Cambridge, MA: MIT Press.
Esman, M. J. and N. T. Uphoff. 1984. *Local Organizations: Intermediaries in Rural Development*. Ithaca: Cornell University Press.
Falconer, J. 1990. *The Major Significance of "Minor" Forest Products*. Rome: Food and Agriculture Organization.

Feeny, D. *et al.* 1990. "The tragedy of the commons: twenty-two years later." *Human Ecology* 18: 1–19.

Fudenberg, D. and Eric Maskin. 1986. "The folk theorem in repeated games with discounting and with incomplete information." *Econometrica* 54: 533–54.

Ghai, D. and J. M. Vivian (eds.), 1992. *Grassroots Environmental Action: People's Participation in Sustainable Development.* London: Routledge.

Hardin, Garrett. 1968. "The tragedy of the commons." *Science* 162: 1243–8.

Hecht, S., A. B. Anderson and P. May. 1988. "The subsidy from nature: shifting cultivation, successional palm forests and rural development." *Human Organization* 47: 25–35.

Howe, J. 1986. *The Kuna Gathering.* Austin: University of Texas Press.

Jodha, N. S. 1986. "Common property resources and the rural poor." *Economic and Political Weekly.* 21: 1169–81.

  1995. "Common property resources and the environmental context: role of biophysical versus social stress." *Economic and Political Weekly* 30: 3278–83.

Maskin, Eric. 1995. "Majority rule, social welfare functions, and game forms." In K. Basu, P. K. Pattanaik, and K. Suzumura (eds.), *Choice, Welfare and Development.* Oxford: Clarendon Press.

May, K. 1952. "A set of necessary and sufficient conditions for simple majority decisions." *Econometrica* 10: 680–4.

Myerson, R. 1997. "Economic analysis of political institutions: an introduction." In D. Kreps and K. Wallis (eds.), *Advances in Economic Analysis and Econometrics.* Cambridge: Cambridge University Press.

Netting, R. McC. 1997. "Unequal commoners and uncommon equity: property and community among smallholder farmers." *The Ecologist* 27: 28–33.

Ostrom, E. 1990. *Governing the Commons: The Evolution of Institutions for Collective Action.* Cambridge: Cambridge University Press.

  1996. "Incentives, rules of the game, and development." *Proceedings of the Annual World Bank Conference on Development Economics 1995* (Supplement to the *World Bank Economic Review* and the *World Bank Research Observer*): pp. 207–34.

Putnam, R. D., with R. Leonardi and R. Y. Nanetti. 1993. *Making Democracy Work: Civic Traditions in Modern Italy.* Princeton, NJ: Princeton University Press.

Schumpeter, J. 1942. *Capitalism, Socialism and Democracy.* New York: Harper.

Seabright, P. 1997. "Is cooperation habit-forming?" In P. Dasgupta and K.-G. Mäler (eds.), *The Environment and Emerging Development Issues.* Oxford: Clarendon Press.

Summers, R. and A. Heston. 1988. "A new set of international comparisons of real product and prices: estimates for 130 countries, 1950–1985." *Review of Income and Wealth* 34.

Taylor, C. L. and D. A. Jodice. 1983. *World Handbook of Political and Social Indicators,* Vol. I. New Haven: Yale University Press.

Wade, R. 1988. *Village Republics: Economic Conditions for Collective Action in South India.* Cambridge: Cambridge University Press.

World Bank. 1991. *World Development Report.* New York: Oxford University report.

Part II

Beyond minimalism

5 Democracy and development: a complex relationship

Pranab Bardhan

Introduction

Most of us, ardent democrats all, would like to believe that democracy is not merely good in itself, it is also valuable in enhancing the process of development. Of course, if we take a suitably broad concept of development to incorporate general well-being of the population at large, including some basic civil and political freedoms, a democracy which ensures these freedoms is, almost by definition, more conducive to development on these counts than a non-democratic regime. We may, however, choose to look at freedoms as potentially instrumental to development, as is usually the case in the large empirical literature that aims at finding a statistical correlation between some measure of democracy and some measure of a narrower concept of development (that does not include those freedoms as an intrinsic part of the nature of development itself).

I have in general found this empirical literature rather unhelpful and unpersuasive. It is unhelpful because usually it does not confirm a causal process and the results often go every which way. Even the three *surveys* of the empirical literature that I have seen come out with three different conclusions: one by Sirowy and Inkeles (1991) is supportive of a negative relationship between democracy and development; one by Campos (1994) is of a generally positive relationship; and the one by Przeworski and Limongi (1993) is agnostic ("we do not know whether democracy fosters or hinders economic growth").[1] The empirical literature is generally unpersuasive because many of the studies are beset with serious methodological problems (such as endogeneity of political regimes to economic performance, selection bias, etc.), as Przeworski and Limongi carefully point out, and problems of data quality. For these and other reasons I am not a great fan of cross-country regressions, even

---

[1] In their more recent empirical work Przeworski and Limongi (1997) conclude that political regimes do not differ in their impact on the growth of per capita incomes, if we treat population growth as endogenous to the regime.

93

though the easy availability in recent years of "cleaned-up" international datasets and of the hardware and software for statistical processing have made them a favorite pastime for many of my colleagues in the profession.

In this paper I shall use the more old-fashioned methods of comparative-institutional analysis to understand the mechanisms through which democracy may help or hinder the process of development, occasionally drawing upon the contrasting development experience in largely authoritarian East Asia and democratic South Asia in the 1960s, 1970s and 1980s. Everyone, of course, knows that over these three decades average economic performance, both in terms of per capita income growth and broader indicators such as the human development index, has been substantially better in the former region than in the latter (this is also the case in the bilateral comparison of the two largest countries in the world, one in the former region and one in the latter: China and India). Yet it is possible to argue that authoritarianism may be neither necessary nor sufficient for fostering the institutional mechanisms behind the differential economic performance; it is the purpose of this paper to begin to probe the relationship (or the lack of it) between these mechanisms and the nature of political regime, in a way that may not be apparent from a simple cross-country aggregative statistical correlation.

We should also mention that although in my subsequent analysis I shall not try to define democracy with any great precision, it is useful to keep a distinction between three aspects of democracy: one relates to some basic minimum civil and political rights enjoyed by citizens, another to some procedures of accountability in day-to-day administration under some overarching constitutional rules of the game, and another to periodic exercises in electoral representativeness. These aspects are of varying strength in different democracies, particularly in the few developing countries where democracy has been sustained over some period. On the other hand, a few authoritarian countries may display some degree of administrative accountability at certain levels of government, and may also have periodic renewals through acclamatory or referendum-style elections.

State autonomy and development

It is a staple of the new institutional economics and the law and economics literature that a basic precondition of development is a minimum legal and contractual structure and a set of well-defined and enforced property rights; the general presumption in this literature is that democracy is better suited to provide this environment. But I agree with Przeworski and Limongi (1993) when they say that "the idea that democracy protects property rights is a recent invention, and we think a far-fetched one." If the majority are poor, and the democratic processes work, the property rights of the rich minority may always be under a threat. Of course, democracy may be ideologically more hospitable to a rule of law, but it is the predictability rather than legal accountability that is really at stake here, and it is not always clear that an authoritarian regime cannot provide a framework for a predictable set of contracts. Over much of the last three decades, for example, the first family in Indonesia or the KMT leadership in Taiwan has provided a reasonably predictable and durable (even though corrupt) contractual environment for private business to thrive, without the procedural formalities of a democracy. On the other hand, in some democratic regimes, in spite of the existence of an admirable legal-contractual structure on paper, the courts (and the administrative arbitration machinery) are hopelessly clogged and, under the circumstances, the businessman values his connection with a durable politician much more than the legal niceties. The durability of a politician may vary wildly from one democracy to another (in one the incumbent legislator may have the edge, as in the United States; in another the electorate may be more inclined to "throw the rascals out" with regular frequency, as in India), and also from an authoritarian regime to another (one may be more *coup*-prone than another).

It should also be pointed out that the rule of law that a democracy is supposed to uphold does not by itself preclude that the laws themselves may not be conducive to development. Even in some of the richest democracies of the world while the *enforcement* of laws may be better and subject to less corruption and arbitrariness than in developing countries, the process of *enactment* of those laws is subject to an enormous amount of influence peddling for contributions to campaign finance and other perquisites for legislators. Over time this problem has got worse in most democracies, as elections have become frightfully expensive. When policies to be legislated are up for sale to the highest contributor to the campaign fund, development projects may not win out (the policy decision in the budget may go in favor of buying one more military aircraft rather than 100 rural health clinics), and it is not much consolation to be told that the policies thus legislated will be implemented well by the bureaucracy and the court system under a democracy. Of course, in an open polity there may be more avenues for mobilizing public pressure against covert (but not always illegal) sales of public policy.

Not all cases of public pressure that democracy facilitates help development, either. Democracies may be particularly susceptible to populist pressures for immediate consumption, unproductive subsidies, autarchic trade policies, and other particularistic demands that may hamper long-run investment and growth. On the other hand, authoritarian rulers who may have the capacity to resist such pressures may instead be self-aggrandizing, plundering the surplus of the economy. In fact, historically, authoritarian regimes come in different kinds, some deriving their legitimacy from providing order and stability (like that of Franco in Spain or, more recently, SLORC in Myanmar), some from rapid growth (such as Park Chung Hee in South Korea). Sah (1991) has argued that authoritarian regimes exhibit a larger variance in economic performance than democracies.

The East Asian success story in development over the 1960s, 1970s, and 1980s has convinced many that some degree of insulation of the bureaucracy, in charge of formulating long-run development policies and guiding their implementation, from the ravages of short-run pork-barrel politics is important; the role played by powerful semi-autonomous technocratic organizations such as the Economic Planning Bureau in South Korea and the Industrial Development Bureau in Taiwan clearly points in this direction.[2] It is claimed that authoritarianism made it less difficult for the regimes in East Asia to sustain this insulation. Of course, one can point out that authoritarianism is neither necessary (even in East Asia, postwar Japan has successfully insulated parts of the bureaucracy without giving up on democracy), nor sufficient (even in East Asia, the dictatorship of Marcos in the Philippines is an obvious counterexample, not to speak of authoritarian regimes in many other parts of the world) for such insulation.

Among the enabling conditions for insulation in East Asia, Evans (1995) emphasizes the Weberian characteristics of internal organization of the state, such as highly selective meritocratic recruitment and long-term career rewards for members of the bureaucracy. Such Weberian characteristics are present to a reasonable degree in the upper echelons of the Indian civil service, but over time the democratic political process has eroded some of the insulation. This is evident particularly in political decisions on transfers of civil servants: powerful politicians who cannot sack you can make life unpleasant by getting you transferred to undesirable jobs and locations. In Latin America in general the appointments in the bureaucracy are more often matters of political patronage. Geddes

---

[2] It is interesting to note, however, that contrary to one of the articles of faith among macroeconomists, the central banks in East Asia (including those in Japan) never enjoyed much insulation. Yet this lack of autonomy does not seem to have interfered with their following a generally rather conservative monetary policy, at least until recently. (The same is true for India.)

(1994), in an analysis of the obstacles to building state capacity in Latin America, shows how in the recent history of that continent the political leaders have frequently faced a dilemma between their own need for immediate political survival, buying political support with patronage in appointments to economic management positions, and their longer-run collective interests in economic performance and regime stability. In India, as well, administrative appointments outside the main civil service, such as those to the boards of public sector corporations particularly in provincial governments, are often used as political sine-cures to keep clamouring factions happy.

A more disturbing sign of politicization of the internal organization of the government in a democracy is indicated by the systematic erosion of the institutional independence of the police and the criminal justice system that is slowly creeping through some states of North India in a way that is familiar from Sicilian politics under the Christian Demo-crats. A significant number of elected politicians in these states are crime bosses or their accomplices, who have figured out that, once elected on a ruling party ticket, they can neutralize the police who will not press or pursue the criminal charges against them with any alacrity. Given their organizational and financial resources these bosses have an edge over other politicians in winning elections, and the poor are often dedicated voters for them, as they nurse their local constituency assidu-ously even as they loot from the system in general. Another example of the exposure of the administrative system to the marauding forces of populist politics is provided by the widespread presumption among the borrowers (both rich and poor) from government-owned or controlled credit institutions in many countries that they can default on loans with impunity, as the politicians who have to depend on their votes cannot afford to let bank officials be too harsh with them. This has been one of the major reasons for the massive failures of state intervention in credit in developing countries.

In the recent literature on the role of the state in economic develop-ment[3] the issue of insulation or autonomy of the state has been formulated in terms of the notion of the ability to credibly precommit familiar from industrial economics. The ruler in a "strong" state[4] is

---

[3] See, for example, Bardhan 1990 and 1997 and Rodrik 1992.

[4] In any empirical exercise to explain growth performance in terms of state "strength" in this sense, one has to be careful to avoid a selection bias. It is quite possible that economies in their most successful phases have less political conflict (most groups are doing well without political exertion, and the few losing groups are bribed) and therefore their governments have an appearance of "strength"; their commitments are not challenged or reversed by political action. This is an important issue that needs to be examined with detailed historical data. The determined way the South Korean state had

taken to be a Stackelberg leader: he maximizes his objective function subject to the reaction function of the ruled and in this process internalizes the economic costs of his impositions in accordance with that reaction function. In contrast, one can say that the "weak" state is a Stackelberg follower; it cannot commit to a particular policy and merely reacts to the independent actions of the private actors such as special interest groups. Thus it is easy to see that, compared to the strong state, the weak state will have too much of undesirable interventions (creating distortions in the process of generating rent for lobbying groups) and, by the same logic, will have too little of the desirable interventions[5] (as may be necessary in the case of all kinds of market failures or the more general case of coordination failures), since the state does not take into account or internalize the effects of its own policies.

Elster has argued that to be credible and effective, precommitment requires democracy. The promises of a ruler are much more credible if there is a well-established procedure for throwing the ruler out of office for failure to keep those promises. "To be effective, power must be divided" (Elster 1994). This is a central theme of much of the recent work on constitutional political economy. Similarly, North and Weingast (1989) have cited the historical case of the Glorious Revolution in England in 1688, which by strengthening political institutions that constrained the king enhanced his commitment to securing private property rights and thus fostered economic growth.

I am not fully convinced by this argument. Democracy is neither necessary nor sufficient for effective precommitments. Let me illustrate this in the context of development by taking the case of infant-industry protection, which has been popular in developing countries, as it was in the early stages of industrialization in the US and Germany. At the time when such protection against foreign competition is usually initiated, by the very nature of the argument for temporary protection, it is granted for a short period until the industrial infant can stand on its own feet. But in most countries infant-industry protection inevitably runs up against the time-inconsistency problem. When the initial period of protection is about to expire, political pressures for its renewal become inexorable, and in this way the infant industry soon degenerates into a geriatric protection lobby. Given the concentration and visibility of

---

handled various macroeconomic crises, say, in the 1970s (the two oil shocks, massive foreign debt, inflation, etc.) suggests to me that the Korean state's "strength" was not just a reflection of the success of the economy.

[5] While our distinction between the strong and the weak state is thus qualitatively similar to the distinction Olson (1993) has drawn between the ruler as a "stationary bandit" and as a "roving bandit," he overlooks the case where the latter may have too little of desirable interventions.

benefits from the perpetuation of this protection and the diffuseness of its costs, there is little organized popular pressure in a democracy against it. No conniving leader faces dismissal on this ground, making constitutional provisions for throwing out the ruler largely irrelevant here. Thus well-established procedures of democracy are not sufficient for credible commitments.

The most successful cases of infant-industry protection in recent history have taken place under some of the authoritarian regimes of East Asia, particularly Taiwan and South Korea. There have been some remarkable instances in these regimes of the government holding steadfastly to its promise of withdrawing protection from an industry after the lapse of a preannounced duration, letting the industry sink or swim in international competition.[6] Democracy was not necessary to establish credibility of commitment. In fact there is evidence now that with the recent advent of democracy in these countries, some of the earlier commitments of their governments have become weaker (as, for example, in the case of the promised withdrawal of protection of small manufacturing enterprises against competition from the *chaebols* in South Korea).

If market competition in general, and international competition in particular, is important in the development process, as a disciplining factor on productive efficiency and as an inducement to cost and quality consciousness, it is necessary to examine the role democratic institutions play in the management of conflicts that inevitably arise from the disruptions and dislocations in social and economic life that market competition brings in its wake. It has sometimes been claimed (for example, in the Italian and Iberian fascist writings in the 1920s and 1930s, or in the postwar studies on corporatism) that the state, for the sake of such conflict management, may need to structure interest representation in society, coopting and controlling unruly elements, monitoring and containing demands so that they do not get out of hand. Such corporatist regimes usually tend toward authoritarian practices, but the latter are not strictly necessary as the history (until recently) of centralized wage bargaining in the open economies of democratic Scandinavia, or of industrial policy in the small European states about which Katzenstein (1985) has written, amply demonstrates. But the initial conditions in the latter countries were arguably rather special, and

---

[6] For an example of how the government in Taiwan imposed an import ban on VCRs in 1982 to help out two of the main domestic electronic companies, and withdrew it after barely eighteen months when they failed to shape up to meet international standards, see Wade 1990.

quite different particularly from more heterogeneous and unequal societies.

The general theory of bureaucracy suggests[7] that it is difficult to devise high-powered incentive contracts for civil servants on account of what is called a "common agency" problem (i.e., the civil servant has to be the agent of multiple principals), and under low-powered incentives for civil servants their "capture" by the special interest groups is considered very likely. To the extent an authoritarian regime provides a more unified line of command, the common agency problem may be somewhat less severe. Of course, political corruption may be larger in autocracies with centralized bribe collection ("one-stop shopping") from the interest groups by the ruling gang. Rasmusen and Ramseyer (1994) have modelled a coordination problem[8] in bribe collection in democratic polities: they use a coordination game among wealth-maximizing legislators to show that if the latter cannot coordinate their actions, the equilibrium bribe amount for "selling" private-interest statutes will be lower than in the case of an autocrat, even if the cost of corruption for the politicians under the two regimes is kept the same. In some actual democratic polities such coordination problems are reduced by committee systems, disciplined factions, and party political machines. It is reported that in postwar Japan the Liberal Democratic Party (particularly its so-called Policy Affairs Research Council, where important policies were made and payoffs were coordinated behind closed doors) has been quite successful in centralizing bribery.

Coordinated corruption may, of course, have less adverse consequences for resource allocation efficiency than uncoordinated corruption, as Shleifer and Vishny (1993) have suggested (comparing corruption in Communist Russia with that in the post-Communist years), since in the former case the bribee will internalize some of the distortionary effects of corruption. It has sometimes been suggested that corruption in countries such as South Korea may have been more in the form of lump-sum contributions to the president's campaign slush fund, without taxing economic activity at the margin, thus having least distortionary effects. The important question here, however, is how the ruler can credibly promise to keep the contributions lump-sum, and not come back again for quid pro quo deals at the margin.

The autonomy of the state has other costs in terms of economic efficiency. Bureaucratic insulation makes it difficult to attain flexibility

---

[7] See Wilson 1989, Tirole 1994, and Dixit 1995.
[8] The essential problem is due to an externality that each democratic legislator's vote potentially imposes on every other legislator, when they cannot coordinate their votes to demand a bribe which compensates them for that externality.

in dealing with changes in technical and market conditions (and may thus discourage risk taking), and also in correcting wrong decisions. This flexibility had been maintained in East Asia by fostering a dense network of ties between public officials and private entrepreneurs through deliberative councils (as in Japan or South Korea) or through the tightly knit party organization (as in Taiwan), allowing operational space for negotiating and renegotiating goals and policies, sharing information and risks, and for coordinating decisions (and mutual expectations) with remarkable speed. Such cozy government–business relations[9] are more difficult to achieve (or are politically more suspect) in societies (in South Asia, for example) that are more heterogeneous and unequal.

In many situations the state is neither a Stackelberg leader nor a Stackelberg follower. Neither the state actors nor the private interest groups usually have the power unilaterally to define the parameters of their action. Both may be strategic actors with some power to influence the terms, and the outcome of the bargaining game depends on their varying bargaining strengths in different situations. Set in a bargaining framework, one may begin to resolve a problem of motivation that afflicts much of the discussion on the relationship between authoritarianism and development. An authoritarian ruler may be better insulated and may have the capacity to resist particularistic pressures, but why would he be interested in playing a positive role in the development process? What is in it for him? To this Olson (1993) would answer that a rational autocrat, as a "stationary bandit," has an "encompassing interest" in the productivity of society as a whole and will take into account the deadweight losses from unduly onerous impositions on society's productive capacity. But in this model the power of the ruler to collect taxes or rents is invariant with respect to the policies to promote productivity.

But what if some of the latter policies increase the disagreement payoffs (and hence tilt the bargaining outcome in favor) of the ruled? As Robinson (1995) has emphasized, it may not be rational for an autocrat to carry out institutional changes that safeguard property rights, law enforcement, and other economically beneficial structures, if in the process his rent-extraction machinery has a chance of being damaged or weakened. He may not risk upsetting the current arrangement for the uncertain prospect of a share in a larger pie. For some of the "stationary bandits" in this century (the Duvaliers in Haiti, Trujillo in the Dominican Republic, Somoza in Nicaragua, Mobutu in Zaire, and so on), who

---

[9] In very recent years such cozy relations have been a source of problems in the financial sector in East Asian countries.

systematically plundered and wrecked their economies for excruciatingly long periods, this may have been a serious consideration. In contrast, in South Korea and Taiwan initial conditions were much more favorable to the ruled (with land reforms and expansion of mass education), and one of the few ways open to the dictators to secure their position was to derive their legitimacy from ambitious programs of shared economic growth (thus shifting the whole bargaining frontier outward), that would also serve nationalistic goals such as catching up with Japan and warding off the Communist threat.

Mechanisms of accountability

Democracy helps development through the accountability mechanisms it instals for limiting the abuse of executive power, and provides a system of periodic punishments for undesirable government interventions in the economy and rewards for desirable interventions. (Of course, these rewards and punishments by a politician's local constituency need not be consistent with the development goals of the economy as a whole, as in the case of the durable politician who regularly brings the "pork" home.) Accountability mechanisms are particularly important in averting disasters; in their absence, major ecological damages in the Soviet Union and Eastern Europe went on unchecked for too long. In 1959–61 China had the world's worst famine this century, which killed many millions of people, whereas post-independence India, with a much lower average availability of food for the poor than China, largely avoided such disasters. Sen (1983) has commented that Indian democracy, with its free press and vigorous opposition parties, has been politically quicker in averting sporadic threats of famines and starvation deaths; but at the same time, the Indian political system, unlike the Chinese, seems to have been unable to deal effectively with endemic hunger and malnutrition. Sometimes in a democracy it seems easier to focus political attention to dramatic disturbances in a low-level equilibrium, than to the lowness of the level itself.

Checks and balances in the allocation of control rights and standards of transparency and auditing ("institutionalized suspicion") associated with the democratic process keep gross abuses and wastes under control. If there is a public complaints mechanism in place, a democratic regime, other things remaining the same, may generate too many complaints (since the penalty for complaints is usually relatively low[10]), and thus leading to too much screening and the consequent delay of

[10] Of course, whistleblowers losing jobs are not infrequent in democratic regimes.

projects, compared to an authoritarian regime where complaints may be more risky. Of course, in many democracies public scrutiny, particularly of high officials, is constrained by laws regarding official secrecy (such as the Official Secrets Act of 1923 that the Indian government inherited from the British) and the difficulty auditors always face in disentangling malfeasance from sheer incompetence (the rules of punishment are quite different for the two, and in the case of the latter often non-existent in insulated bureaucracies). Checks and balances in a bureaucracy often involve a multiple veto power system. While this system inevitably involves delay in decision-making, it is supposed to keep corrupt officials in check. One high official in New Delhi is reported to have told a friend, "If you want me to move a file faster, I am not sure I can help you; but if you want me to stop a file I can do it immediately." This ability to "stop a file" at multiple points creates its own opportunities for corruption and makes the process more uncertain and thus costly. A multiple veto system also has an inherent bias toward rejecting too many good proposals (or what is called Type I error) and inhibiting against risk taking in general.

Of course, the type of decision-making structure in economic administration is not uniquely related to the nature of political regime; a democratic public administration may be organized as a centralized hierarchy, whereas an authoritarian ruler may choose to organize his economic administration up to a certain level as a system with parallel independent decision-makers. In a situation of highly imperfect information the desirability of even uninformed central control varies, as Bolton and Farrell (1990) show, according to the relative importance of private information and the need for coordination, which may vary from case to case. They also point, drawing from the literature on dynamic incentive contracts, to the importance of commitment constraints. If the central authority cannot commit to when or how much it will intervene in a long drawn-out process of production, individual agents' incentives may be adversely affected: they may not undertake socially desirable investments for fear of being expropriated *ex post*, or they may not disclose valuable private information for fear that the central authority might use this information against them. Going back to our earlier discussion, we may note again that authoritarianism is neither necessary nor sufficient for commitment.

In developing countries where much of the economy is in the vast informal sector and dispersed in far-flung villages and small towns, the accountability mechanisms of democracy are particularly important at the local community level. Large-scale development projects directed from above by an insulated modernizing elite are often inappropriate technologically or environmentally, and far removed from or insensitive to local community needs and concerns. Rather than involving the local people and tapping into the large reservoir of local information, ingenuity, and initiative, these projects often treat them simply as objects of the development process; they end up primarily as conduits of largesse for middlemen and contractors, and encourage widespread parasitism on the state.

There is, however, no one-to-one relationship between the strength of democracy at the national political level and that of institutions of accountability at the local level. In large parts of Northern India, for example, it is common to observe the serious problem of absenteeism of salaried teachers in village public schools and of doctors in rural public health clinics. The villagers are usually quite aware of the problem but do not have the institutional means of correcting it, as the state-funded teachers and doctors are not answerable to the villagers in the insufficiently decentralized system. On the other hand, in non-democratic China the local Communist Party officials have sometimes been quite responsive to local needs (at least as long as they are not conflicting with the Party's program), as the comparative study of two villages in China and India by Drèze and Saran (1995) shows in the context of China's far better performance in the provision of primary education at the local level. (Similar accounts are available of more effective public pressure in rural basic education and health services in Cuba compared to some of the more democratic regimes in Latin America.) There are, of course, many authoritarian countries where local accountability is completely absent and the situation is much worse than in North India.

Even in otherwise centralized bureaucracies the nature of institutional design for the delegation of implementation tasks to local-level agencies is not uniquely related to the nature of the political regime at the national level. Wade (1997) points to interesting contrasts between the mode of operation of the Korean irrigation bureaucracy (under an authoritarian regime in the recent past) and that of the Indian, and the clearly more locally effective performance of the former. The Indian canal systems are large, centralized hierarchies in charge of all functions (operations and maintenance as well as design and construction). Their ways of operation (including the promotion and transfer rules for officials, rules designed to minimize identification between the irrigation patrollers and the local farmers, and the frequent use of low-trust management and supervision methods) and source of finance (most of the irrigation department's budget comes in the form of a grant from the state treasury) are totally insensitive to the need for developing and drawing upon local "social capital." In Korea there are functionally separate organizations in the canal systems. The implementation and routine maintenance tasks are delegated to the Farmland Improvement Associations, one per catchment area, which are staffed by local part-time farmers (selected by the village chiefs), knowledgeable about changing local conditions, dependent for their salary and operational budget largely on the user fees paid by the farmers, and continually drawing upon local trust relationships.

One reason why the Indian local irrigation bureaucracy is kept at arm's length from the local farmers is the constant suspicion of the "capture" of the former by the latter. In general, local democracies are supposed to be more vulnerable to corruption than the national government. One of the central results of the literature on collective action is that small group size and proximity help collective action. Collusions are thus easier to organize and enforce in proximate groups, risks of being caught and reported are easier to manage, and the multiple interlocking social and economic relationships among the local influential people act as formidable barriers to entry into these cozy rental havens. On the other hand, if institutions of local democracy are firmly in place along with a vigorous opposition party and free press, the political process can be more transparent and the theft of funds and the sale of influence become more visible compared to the system of centralized corruption. As Crook and Manor (1994) point out, on the basis of indirect but strong evidence in the case of the state of Karnataka in South India, this may reduce the overall amount of money and resources siphoned off through corruption: even though there are more hands in the till, it is difficult for people to steal very much (in big central government projects, on the other hand, a single transaction can yield very large bribes). Ironically, on account of the increased openness and visibility of the system compared to the earlier centralized system, local people believed, often wrongly, that corruption had increased.

The "capture" problem of local democracies can have severe implications in areas with marked social and economic inequalities. There are many situations in which decentralization may leave the poor grievously exposed to the mercies of the local overlords and their malfeasance. There are certain fixed costs of organizing resistance groups or countervailing lobbies. As a result the poor may sometimes be more unorganized at the local level than at the national level where they can pool their organizing capacities. In these situations they may even be able occasionally to play pivotal roles in national coalitions and get redistributive transfers in their favor under centralized systems. In the history of the United States, for example, movements in favor of "state rights" diminishing the power of the federal government have often been interpreted as regressive, working against poor minorities. The US case also shows that in situations of inequality and decentralization of financing of local schools, etc., neighborhoods deteriorate with the secession of the rich. In developing countries, advocates of "grass-roots democracy" have to be careful about these implications for the poorest sections of the population.

Under conditions of social and economic inequality, expansion of democracy may also have ambiguous effects on collective action in management of the local commons (irrigation, forestry, fisheries, grazing land, etc.).[11] In many local communities, some rudimentary forms of cooperation on the commons have been sustained and enforced over generations by traditional authority structures. While there may have been some trace of a sharing ethic, the predominant social norm was often that of an unequal patron–client system, in which the powerful, who might enjoy disproportionate benefits from the institutions of cooperation, enforced the rules of the game and gave leadership to solidaristic efforts. As the advent of participatory politics and social upheavals erode the legitimacy of the traditional authorities, and as political and economic modernization improves the options of both "exit" and "voice" for the common people, these solidaristic ties loosen, social sanctions against defectors from pre-existing arrangements become less effective, and the old cooperative institutions sometimes crumble. There follows increased dependence on the state bureaucracy to carry out functions such as local resource management and maintenance of local public goods which were previously in the domain of locally autonomous, though hierarchical and lop-sided, organizations. Many rural communities in poor countries are now in this difficult transition period, with traditional cooperative institutions on the decline, while the new self-governing associations, based on defined rights and legal-rationalistic norms (such as regular auditing of accounts or checks and balances on arbitrary use of power) are still struggling to be born.

Problems in ethnically divided societies

Finally, there are some special problems for democracy and development when the groups that get more easily mobilized are not interest groups familiar from the Western theories of democracy, but are more in the nature of sectarian or ethnic groups. The costs of collective action

---

[11] For a formal treatment of the problem of asymmetric enforcement and exit options in the context of conservation of local common-pool resources in terms of a non-cooperative game, see Dayton-Johnson and Bardhan 1996.

are often lower with ethnic bonding and identity politics than in the case of interest group politics. Apart from being identity anchors in unsettled social and economic surroundings, ethnicity can serve, in the context of various kinds of interethnic competition, as a device to segment an expanding market, create rents, and channel the flow of rents to particular groups. As the government has become important in economic activities, and as democratic awareness spreads out in ever-widening circles, more and more mobilized groups have used ethnicity for staking a claim in the process of rent-sharing.

This takes the form, to give examples from two democratic developing countries, of highly successful demands for large "backward caste" quotas in public-sector jobs and admission to higher education in India, and of all kinds of preferential policy (including in business contracts and permits in the private sector) for the *bumiputera* in Malaysia. Politicians, faced with ethnic turmoil, are quick to adopt these policies as a low-cost populist strategy. But these policies, even when their immediate financial costs are low, may sometimes be costly in the long run. Systematic economic analysis of their efficiency effects in developing countries is rather scarce.

The standard efficiency argument against job quotas for disadvantaged groups is that it splinters the labor market, distorts allocation of labor between covered and other sectors, and may adversely affect the incentives for skill acquisition among members of the quota-protected group (as emphasized by Coate and Loury (1993)). But if group-specific dynamic externalities and "social capital" (in the form of role models, peer group effects, job market connections, etc.) are important determinants of economic success as in the models of Benabou (1996) and Durlauf (1996), preferential policies can increase efficiency by changing the way workers are sorted across occupations and firms. In addition, if employers hold negative-stereotype views about some ethnic worker productivity, and if in such cases the return to acquiring signals of ability is low or if signals are uninformative, preferential job policies for a time can help in eliminating stereotypes and thus improve incentives for skill acquisition on the part of the ethnic workers.

To the extent that preferential policies are supposed to cope with a historical handicap, their economic rationale is akin to that behind the age-old argument for infant-industry protection in early stages of development. Some disadvantaged groups need temporary protection against competition so that they can participate in learning by doing and on-the-job skill formation before catching up with the others. Some of the standard arguments against infant-industry protection are then equally applicable to preferential policies. For example, as we have noted before, the "infant," once protected, sometimes refuses to grow up; preferential policies, once adopted, are extremely difficult to reverse. The Indian constitution stipulated a specified duration for job reservation for the lowest castes and tribes; this has not merely been extended indefinitely, the principle of "reservation" has now been extended to a large number of other castes. Another argument against infant-industry protection is that even when the goal is justifiable, it may be achieved more efficiently through other policies. For example, a disadvantaged group may be helped by a preferential investment policy or development programs in a particular area where the group is concentrated or with preferential loans, scholarships, job training programs, and extension services for its members, instead of job quotas that bar qualified candidates coming from advanced groups. Such indirect policies of helping out backward groups are also less likely to generate political resentment (particularly because, in this case, the burden may be shared more evenly, whereas in the case of job quotas the redistributive burden falls on a small subset of the advanced community).

Populist pressures are not unfamiliar in authoritarian regimes, but the demands for spreading the patronage more evenly are much more difficult to resist under a democracy. To the extent democratic demands for short-run intergroup equity and for carving up the market in protected niches drown the considerations of efficiency, development suffers. But there are situations where the cause of equity also helps efficiency, and we need more empirical work on this in developing countries before we can make pronouncements on one side or the other. In particular, in situations of deep distrust among ethnic groups (which characterize many poor countries) and when the ethnic composition of the electorate militates against the basic uncertainty of electoral outcome that, as Przeworski (1991) argues, sustains democracy, forms of credible commitment to intergroup equity, even going beyond the consociational arrangements envisaged by Lijphart (1977), can help development. Rent-sharing, regional autonomy and devolution of power, and political and constitutional ways of curbing the excesses of majoritarian democracy (where some groups are in danger of being perpetually excluded from power) are extremely important for social peace and preservation of the minimum underpinnings of economic development. While democracy in general can diffuse some ethnic tensions, certain forms of democracy may be more conducive to compromise, coalition building, and coordination than other forms[12] (for example, first-past-the-post electoral rules in single-member

---

[12] For a comparative study of the electoral systems in two ethnically heterogenous countries – Sri Lanka and Malaysia – and their contrasting effects, see Horowitz 1989.

constituencies, giving the majority party a disproportionate number of seats, can be quite damaging in ethnically divided polities).

In this chapter we have tried to understand the multidimensional process by which democracy tends to affect the pace and pattern of development and find that not all of the process is pretty or wholesome. Yet I remain an incorrigible optimist for the long-run healing powers of democracy. My guarded wistfulness may be better expressed by quoting from a recent speech[13] in New York by Adam Michnik, a veteran of the Polish struggle for democracy:

Democracy is neither black nor red. Democracy is gray. . . . It chooses banality over excellence, shrewdness over nobility, empty promise over true competence . . . It is eternal imperfection, a mixture of sinfulness, saintliness and monkey business. This is why the seekers of a moral state and of a perfectly just society do not like democracy. Yet only democracy – having the capacity to question itself – also has the capacity to correct its own mistakes.

Then Michnik is reported to have ended his speech with a slight stammer: "G-G-Gray is beautiful!"

REFERENCES

Bardhan, Pranab. 1990. "Introduction to a symposium on the state and economic development." *Journal of Economic Perspectives* 4(3): 3–7.
    1997. "The political economy of development policy: an Asian perspective." In Louis Emmerij (ed.), *Economic and Social Development into the XXI Century*, pp. 273–87. Washington, DC: InterAmerican Development Bank.
Benabou, R. 1996. "Equity and efficiency in human capital investment: the local connection." *Review of Economic Studies* 63: 237–64.
Bolton, Patrick and Joseph Farrell. 1990. "Decentralization, duplication, and delay." *Journal of Political Economy* 98(4): 803–26.
Campos, Nauro. 1994. "Why does democracy foster economic development: an assessment of the empirical literature." Unpublished: University of Southern California, Los Angeles.
Coate, Stephen and Glenn Loury. 1993. "Will affirmative action policies eliminate negative stereotypes?" *American Economic Review* 83(5): 1220–40.
Crook, Richard and James Manor. 1994. "Enhancing participation and institutional performance: democratic decentralization in South Asia and West Africa." Report to Overseas Development Administration, UK.
Dayton-Johnson, Jeff and Pranab Bardhan. 1996. "Inequality and conservation on the local commons: a theoretical exercise." University of California at Berkeley Working Paper.
Dixit, Avinash. 1995. *The Making of Economic Policy: A Transaction Cost Politics Perspective*. Cambridge, MA: MIT Press.
Drèze, Jean and Mrinalini Saran. 1995. "Primary education and economic development in China and India: overview and two case studies." In

---

[13] Reported in the *New Yorker*, 9 December 1996.

K. Basu *et al.* (eds.), *Choice, Welfare and Development: A Festschrift in Honor of Amartya K. Sen*, pp. 182–241. Oxford: Clarendon Press.

Durlauf, Steve. 1996. "A theory of persistent income inequality." *Journal of Economic Growth* 1(1): 75–94.

Elster, Jon. 1994. "The impact of constitutions on economic performance." *Proceedings of the World Bank Annual Conference on Development Economics*, pp. 209–26.

Evans, Peter. 1995. *Embedded Autonomy.* Princeton: Princeton University Press.

Geddes, Barbara. 1994. *Politician's Dilemma: Building State Capacity in Latin America.* Berkeley: University of California Press.

Horowitz, Donald. 1989. "Incentives and behavior in the ethnic politics of Sri Lanka and Malaysia." Working Paper in Asian-Pacific Studies, Duke University, Durham, NC.

Katzenstein, Peter. *Small States in World Markets: Industrial Policy in Europe.* Ithaca: Cornell University Press.

Lijphart, Arendt. 1977. *Democracies in Plural Societies: A Comparative Exploration.* New Haven: Yale University Press.

North, Douglass C. and Barry R. Weingast. 1989. "Constitutions and commitment: evolution of institutions governing public choice." *Journal of Economic History*, 49: 803–32.

Olson, Mancur. 1993. "Dictatorship, democracy, and development." *American Political Science Review* 87(3): 567–75.

Przeworski, Adam. 1991. *Democracy and the Market.* New York: Cambridge University Press.

Przeworski, Adam and Fernando Limongi. 1993. "Political regimes and economic growth." *Journal of Economic Perspectives* 7(3): 51–70.
    1997. "Democracy and development." In Alex Hadenius (ed.), *Democracy's Victory and Crisis*, pp. 157–87. Cambridge: Cambridge University Press.

Rasmusen, Erik and Mark Ramseyer. 1994. "Cheap bribes and the corruption ban: a coordination game among rational legislators." *Public Choice* 78(3–4): 305–27.

Robinson, James. 1995. "Theories of bad policy." Unpublished: University of Southern California, Los Angeles.

Rodrik, Dani. 1992. "Political economy and development policy." *European Economic Review* 36: 329–36.

Sah, Raaj K. 1991. "Fallibility in human organizations and political systems." *Journal of Economic Perspectives* 5(2): 67–88.

Sen, Amartya K. 1983. "Development: Which Way Now ?" *Economic Journal*, 93: 745–62.

Shleifer, Andrei and Robert Vishny. 1993. "Corruption." *Quarterly Journal of Economics* 108(3): 599–617.

Sirowy, Larry and Alex Inkeles. 1991. "The effects of democracy on economic growth and inequality: a review." In Alex Inkeles (ed.), *On Measuring Democracy: Its Consequences and Concomitants.* New Brunswick, NJ: Transaction Publishers.

Tirole, Jean. 1994. "The internal organization of government." *Oxford Economic Papers*.

Wade, Robert. 1990. *Governing the Market: Economic Theory and the Role of the*

Government in East Asian Industrialization. Princeton: Princeton University Press.

1997. "How infrastructure agencies motivate staff: canal irrigation in India and the Republic of Korea." In Ashoka Mody (ed.), *Infrastructure Strategies in East Asia: The Untold Story,* pp. 109–30. The World Bank, Washington, DC.

Wilson, James Q. 1989. *Bureaucracy: What Government Agencies Do and Why They Do It.* New York: Basic Books.

6 Death and taxes: extractive equality and the development of democratic institutions

Margaret Levi

"No taxation without representation" is emblematic of the demand for democratic governance. This famous slogan poses a question rather than provides the answer to when and where the demand arises and to when and where it is transformed from a demand to an institutionalized practice. All states extract taxes and men, but democratic institutions take root only in some places and not in others. State building involves a wide range and variety of practices, but everywhere it includes the forging of governmental institutions capable of extracting ever more money and manpower from the population, and almost everywhere there are rebellions, evasions, and other forms of resistance. Yet democracy does not necessarily result.

An argument in some of the literature is that democracy emerges and is stable only where there is a developed economy, but even a quick glance at history suggests that development, at least according to current standards, is hardly a prerequisite for the initial establishment of legislatures, the franchise, and other democratic institutions. A more convincing claim is that democracies and certain kinds of economic development, most particularly capitalist economic development, tend to correlate, that the economic rights essential for the one are also essential for the other. However, that, too, falls down on close inspection.

Another approach offered – but not fully explored – by Douglass North (1990; see also Denzau and North 1994) is that stable democracies, as well as stable markets, rest on informal institutions, such as customs and norms, as much as on the formal institutions of legislatures, franchise, and contract enforcement. If this is true, the question is pushed one step further back: How do such norms arise? Seymour Martin Lipset, in his 1993 Presidential Address to the American Sociological Association, emphasizes the strong correlations between sustained democracy and being British or a former British colony on the one hand, and being a largely Protestant country on the other (1994: 5). Robert Putnam (1993) claims democracy is most likely to flourish where there are strong horizontal linkages created by membership in secondary associations – even where there is a strong Catholic tradition, as in Northern Italy. The determinism implied by such culturalist path dependent arguments has an initial appeal.[1] However, the long democratic traditions of France, the Netherlands, and the Scandinavian countries undermine Lipset's correlational approach, and the considerable lapses from democracy in Northern Italy and other countries (and localities) with horizontal linkages upset Putnam's claim. Certain norms and customs may well be crucial to the development of democracy, but the conditions under which they arise and flourish appear to be more complicated than the simple, if elegant, answers provided by Lipset and Putnam.

A review of the literature reveals not only how much has been written and said on the subject of the emergence and maintenance of democracy but also how little is left unsaid. A totally original thesis does not seem likely this third or so century into the discussion, nor is it realistic to presume that a re-examination of the early democracies will reveal new facts that will set in motion a whole new interpretation. What is a social scientist to do in such a circumstance?

My response is to narrow the question. Here I attempt to follow the prescription laid out by Barbara Geddes (1991), who argues "that the inability to accumulate theoretical knowledge will continue to plague us as long as we remain loyal to two time-honored traditions of comparative politics: trying to answer big ill-defined questions rather than trying to understand the fundamental processes which underlie them; and ignoring the basic principles of research design and hypothesis testing." I attempt to follow this advice by focusing on the processes by which "no taxation without representation" and other such demands translate into institutional practices and, ultimately, societal norms. Consideration of the history of extractive policies, namely taxation and conscription, in Europe, North America, and the Antipodes may provide some clue about the link between extraction and democratization.

The literature on the origins of representative institutions

The first question is when the government demand for extraction, which occurs virtually everywhere, entails the concession of representation and voting rights. There are two quite distinct literatures on the subject. One, labeled structuralist, comes from political sociology and history,

[1] To give Lipset his due credit, he argues that these and other factors "do shape the probabilities for democracy, but they do not determine the outcomes" (1994: 17).

and the emphasis is on independent variables that correlate with observable cross-national variations in institutions and practices. The second, labeled rational choice, offers a parsimonious theory built on simple assumptions about the preferences of rulers and of those with whom they must strategically interact.

This chapter builds on the rational choice accounts, but a brief review of the findings from the structuralist perspective illuminates some common conclusions as well as some sharp differences about key explanatory variables. The tradition of research created by Marx (1974 [1867]), Weber (1968), and Hintze (1994 [1906]) has, in the last several decades, stimulated an impressive body of work on state building and regime variation.[2] For Moore (1966), Bendix (1978), Wallerstein (1974), and Anderson (1974a and 1974b), pioneers in this revival of the classic questions of historical sociology, stress some combination of class structure and international system. Robert Brenner (see Aston and Philpin 1987) transformed the discussion by focusing on how differences in property rights produced significantly different village organizations and, thus, capacities to negotiate with agents of the central state or landlord class. Charles Tilly (1990) highlighted the critical importance of the way in which warmaking of rulers with different resource bases has implications for the form of the state (also, see Mann 1986 and 1993; Rasler and Thompson 1985). More recently, Hendrik Spruyt (1994), Brian Downing (1994), and Thomas Ertman (1997) have built on these authors to offer more nuanced accounts of state building, especially in medieval and early modern Europe.

The structural literature reveals several significant factors that might explain not only state building but also how and where democracy emerges. A common claim is that sufficient bargaining power by those facing extractions leads to an effective demand for representation. The best of this literature also clarifies some of the conditions and circumstances in which a class, group, or locality will gain such power. In almost every one of these works, there is a matrix that lays out the most important independent variables and then puts countries into the appropriate boxes. Some of the posited relationships seem quite powerful, but less compelling are the explanations for exactly why they are having the observed effects.

More convincing in terms of the logic of explanation are the accounts provided by rational choice scholars. The findings of this literature sometimes echo those of the structuralists, but not always. Although both literatures pay attention to structure and both to action, structuralist

---

[2] Ertman (1997: chap. 1) offers an excellent review of much of this literature.

theories concern the relationship between the macrovariables while, as a rule, rationalists theorize about strategic choices within the constraints given by the structure. More recently, however, largely as a result of the influence of North (1981 and 1990), rationalists have begun to theorize about how structural and institutional features of the environment change, but their models continue to commence with assumptions about the preferences of the key actors rather than with their resources.

For rationalists writing about extractive policies, the usual assumption is that rulers seek to maximize revenue within the context of constraints (see, e.g., North 1981; Levi 1988; Kiser 1994). Authors vary, however, over the most important constraints for explaining when rulers will permit or be compelled to allow the emergence and maintenance of representative institutions. One line of argument emphasizes the incentives of the ruler to grant representation when confronted with certain kinds of revenue-maximizing projects. Another emphasizes the incentives of the taxed to demand representation.

According to the investigations of Barzel and Kiser (Kiser and Barzel 1991; Barzel and Kiser 1995 and 1996) on proto-democracy,[3] it is the ruler who extends the franchise and other rights in order to promote joint ventures with subjects whose cooperation the ruler requires to maximize his own revenue. Voting rights provide subjects with a means to protect their investment and make the commitments of the ruler more credible. In this view, only secure and relatively powerful rulers will act in this way; insecure rulers will grant exemptions to those whose alliance is necessary to protect power. The Barzel and Kiser argument emphasizes the origin of representative institutions in the nature of the projects the ruler is undertaking and his discount rate rather than the relative bargaining power of those facing extractions, the kinds of arguments put forward in most structuralist accounts. In their words, "mutual benefit was often more important than power" (Barzel and Kiser 1996: 7). Olson (1993) adds a possible dimension to this claim when he posits that the more encompassing the interest of the ruler in the polity, the more likely it is that the rulers will provide public services and certain democratic rights in return for their extractions.[4]

It is not only the structuralists who give pride of place to the

---

[3] Proto-democracy involves granting voting rights to a subset of the population (but hardly full franchise) and the emergence of such institutions as an independent judiciary and other characteristics of the rule of law.

[4] Olson also posits that the more encompassing the interest of the ruler, the more likely it is that the tax system will provide the proper incentives for growth. At the least Olson lays to rest the old arguments of Tenney Frank (1927: 186) that democracies are more inefficient than autocracies. Frank's arguments are those of Olson's "village

bargaining power of the taxed. For example, Bates and Lien (1985) reflect on England and France in the late middle ages in order to develop a general argument that subjects with secure property rights (thus, neither Jews nor Italian bankers) who controlled mobile assets had more bargaining leverage with monarchs than those sectors of the economy that were less elastic. Rulers and potential taxpayers preferred collective negotiations concerning taxes on movables because of their relatively easy transferability. Collective negotiations reduced the transaction costs and increased the revenues to the ruler while assuring the taxpayers that others in similar circumstances were paying at the same rate.

Levi (1988), North and Weingast (1989), and Root (1994) likewise emphasize the bargaining power of the taxed. In particular, they focus on the unintended consequences of institutional arrangements that promote credible commitments by making congruent the self-interest of the negotiating parties. Levi (1988) finds that the early modern parliament enabled the English monarch to negotiate taxes that were acceptable to key constituents who then helped enforce them. The less constrained French monarchs could impose more taxes in principle but with less certainty and higher costs of collection. The conditional cooperation (Taylor 1987 [1976]) implied in parliamentary relations permitted sanctions against monarchs and other parliamentarians who reneged on agreements. Historian John Brewer (1989), in his major study of eighteenth-century Britain and France, reaches similar conclusions.[5]

North and Weingast (1989) also argue that in the eighteenth century the Crown's dependence on future parliamentary approval of its budgets significantly constrained the Crown's expenditure of public funds. Conversely, the multiple centers of power represented by Crown, Lords, and Commons tended to ensure strong elite endorsement and to increase popular support of policy change. The central argument of their paper is the value of parliament for ensuring the credible commitments of the Crown. The Crown did not want to cede so much authority to parliament, but it benefited none the less.

Another variant of the rational choice model is less concerned with the emergence of representative institutions than on the constraints they impose on rulers. Hoffman and Rosenthal (1997) and Rosenthal (1998) concur with Tilly (1990) on the role of warfare in creating the form and powers of the state in early modern Europe, and they are equally

monarchist": in autocracies, the elite perceive the kingdom as a possession to be respectfully managed; in democracies, there are diverse and numerous claimants.

[5] Also, see Hoffman and Norberg 1994 and Mathias and O'Brien 1976.

interested in the resources available to the dominant classes. However, their aim is to offer a simple model of the ruler's decision to go to war and the financial trade-offs implied in that decision. They offer a logic of the effects of elite dominance, ruler dominance, and elite–ruler division of the economy on the extractive and warmaking policies of the monarch. One of their most interesting findings is the reason why "political regimes differ in the type of wars they choose to fight" (Hoffman and Rosenthal 1997: 49). The greater the elite control of the economy and the more representative the institutions, the more the state is likely to encompass a wide range of interests. Consequently, it is less likely to go to war, more likely to have higher taxes, and more likely to have a productive economy. This last claim follows from the fact that the fiscal constraints on absolutist rulers lead to warmaking and regulations that produce income for the ruler but are inefficient for the economy as a whole. The Hoffman and Rosenthal model provides the fine-tuned argument that accounts for some of the correlations Tilly (1990) and Olson (1993) observe – despite their quite different approaches.

Both the structuralist and rational choice accounts capture significant features of the emergence of representative institutions. The structuralists bring breadth in terms of numerous cases and various periods of time but tend to neglect the microfoundations of the origin and maintenance of democratic institutions. The rationalists present models with general and testable implications, but they generally consider these models only in light of the English and French experiences or, at best, early modern Europe. They have not applied their findings to a sufficient range of cases to be as compelling as they might be. Neither of these criticisms are damning, and there are, increasingly, means for bridging the gulf between the two approaches.[6] The more damning critique is the failure of both of these literatures to explain the origins or maintenance of democratic institutions. They offer better and more convincing accounts of the emergence of proto-democracy than of democracy. They provide useful insights into the emergence of institutions that offer representation to elites and that ensure protection of elite property rights. They offer far less leverage on understanding full enfranchisement of the population or equal treatment under the laws.

The origin of democratic institutions

One way to conceptualize the conditions under which democratic rights emerge is to think of the problem in terms of a simple game between

---

[6] See, for example, the papers in Lichbach and Zuckerman 1997 or in Bates, Greif, Levi, Rosenthal, and Weingast 1998.

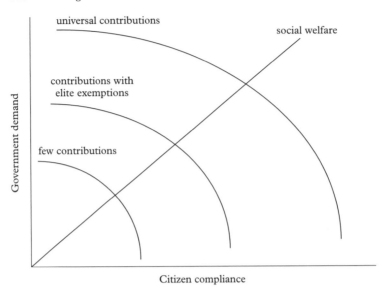

Figure 6.1 Demand for and supply of governmental extractions

government actors and citizens, in which, *ceteris paribus*, the government actors seek extractions and citizens agree to extractions only when each perceives that their benefits exceed their costs. The comparative statics of this simple game suggest the constraints on government demands for, and citizen supply of, extractions. Government demands rise with the requirements of war, the need to create infrastructure, or an increase in expenditures on private or public goods. The supply of money and men is a consequence of the costs of extraction relative to the benefits, that is, the transaction costs of monitoring and enforcing compliance with government demands. Given the costs of compliance, government actors will demand more money or men only when they calculate the costs justify the result. When the demands of a government are low, it may be able to rely on voluntary extractions or resort to coercion, but when its demands are high, it will require more in the way of willing compliance (see figure 6.1).

Given that rulers maximize revenue to the state subject to the constraints of relative bargaining power, transaction costs, and discount rates (Levi 1988), it then follows that insecure rulers will sacrifice extractions of revenue or men from those who can threaten the ruler's power, as Kiser and Barzel (1991) argue. However, it also follows that mutual benefit from the project the ruler is undertaking is only one of several reasons for the creation of voting and legal rights. Equally important may be exactly what almost all the structuralists and some of the rationalists claim: the capacity of certain groups to raise transaction costs by resisting extractions. Mutual benefits may well be the basis for representation and rule of law when the expected returns to those granted rights equal or exceed the material costs each is expected to pay. However, when the expected returns are diffuse and collective and when the individual return may be less than the individual extraction, the grant of representation and other rights is likely to be a function of the capacity of the group to resist. It is these kinds of cases that give rise to democratic, as opposed to proto-democratic, institutions. In both circumstances, however, ruler insecurity, which produces high discount rates, will lead to incomplete democratization in which certain constituents receive exemptions from extractions or other special privileges simply on the basis of their clout rather than on the basis of some universal principle.

To understand the process more fully, it is essential to separate out two different targets of extraction: elites and the general population. The arguments put forward by Barzel and Kiser (1995 and 1996, and Kiser and Barzel 1991), Hoffman and Rosenthal, Bates and Lien, and North and Weingast speak to the relative power of the elites, those who are most likely to get clear gains from joint projects. The importance of their cooperation gives rise to representative institutions perhaps but not contemporary democracy.

General citizen compliance, on the other hand, is a function not only of the actual demands placed upon the populace but also on the capacity of the citizens to resist extractions, the collective benefits they perceive from the specific institutionalization of extraction under negotiation, and, finally and more controversially, their perception of the fairness of the extractive procedures.

The quasi-voluntary compliance (Levi 1988) of citizens and subjects is contingent on assurances that government actors are able to make credible commitments concerning the provision of benefits for which extractions are being demanded and concerning procedures for ensuring that other citizens will also do their share. If government actors are unable to make such commitments or if they fail to live up to such commitments, citizens and subjects will withdraw their compliance or raise its costs significantly.

The demand for "no taxation without representation" implies more than quasi-voluntary compliance. All stable governments require some level of quasi-voluntary compliance, but stable government does not necessarily lead to democratic government. Democracy rests on a thick network of institutions that protect citizen rights and voice, and on a

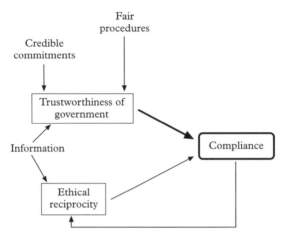

Figure 6.2 Model of contingent consent

more elaborated norm of fairness than the tit-for-tat of quasi-voluntary compliance. It generally requires evidence of government protection of "justice as impartiality" (Barry 1995). This means procedures that allow rational individuals to defend their actions to others by an appeal to having behaved reasonably and fairly; and of institutional arrangements that give them confidence that they, in turn, have been treated fairly by the government demanding their compliance.

In principle, the citizens of democracies must give their consent, albeit always contingently and usually indirectly, and not simply their compliance. Citizen consent rests upon a norm that compliance is the right thing to do, which is hardly the case for all citizens in all groups or all times. Thus, ethical reciprocity to comply among the relevant group of citizens is a necessary condition for the existence of contingent consent. However, even where a norm of compliance exists, consent remains contingent on evidence of government trustworthiness in terms of both the credibility of its commitments and establishment of fair and impartial procedures in making and implementing policy (see figure 6.2). Contingent consent is distinct from habitual obedience (in which citizens act from custom), ideological consent (which is driven by moral or political commitments), or opportunistic obedience (which involves a calculation only of direct and individuated costs and benefits).[7] Contingent consent involves a norm that sometimes means a citizen will act in a way counter to self-interest but only if she is convinced that she is

[7] For an elaboration of contingent consent, habitual obedience, ideological consent, and opportunistic obedience, see Levi 1997: especially chap. 2, 17–30.

not a sucker within her reference group and that government actors are acting in ways that promote democracy and its long-term benefits.

The issue of compliance, let alone consent, does not arise unless government actors make demands on constituents. This is why extractive practices may play a key role in the emergence of democratic institutions. In what follows, I explore the literature on the extraction of money and men to identify when government demands are met by a popular belief that government must meet the criteria of trustworthiness. Such a belief is consistent with the cry for representation and indeed should provoke such a demand.

When warmaking makes democracies[8]

Tilly's "warmaking as statemaking" (1990) captures the important role that war and military activity generally play in forging the infrastructure and capacity of governments (also, see Hooks and Mclauchlan 1992; Thomson 1995). To wage war requires economic resources, including the ability to tax subjects for money and men. Indeed, the initial insight of the political economic accounts of historical tax systems was, while obvious, none the less important: war permits increased government expenditure, which is sustained in peacetime (Schumpeter 1954 [1918]; Peacock and Wiseman 1961; Mann 1986: 483–90), and increased government expenditure implies increased taxation. Tilly (1990: 1–37), Finer (1975: 84–98), Barzel and Kiser (1996), and especially Downing (1994: 239–54) propose conditions under which the warmaking project is more likely to lead to authoritarian governments or constitutionalism, a prerequisite but hardly the *sine qua non* of democracy.

Certainly in the last century stable democracies have been relatively successful not only in terms of their economic development but also in terms of their capacity to fight wars. At least part of the explanation is that they are able to build wartime armies in which individuals want to serve. Key to this achievement is the combination of a popular voice in the decision to go to war and a means of extraction that ensures relative equality of sacrifice from the population.

In recent years, scholars attempting to develop a more adequate theory of the state have given considerable attention to the relationship between states and citizens in regard to social welfare and taxation (see, especially, Steinmo 1993). Variations in the form of the military obligation and the institutions that enforce this obligation have received some descriptive, but little or no theoretical, attention. Yet, military service is

---

[8] Much of the material in this section draws from Levi 1997 and 1998.

demonstrably as important an aspect of the state–citizen relationship as any that exists. There has not, of course, been total neglect. Several important historical and political sociologists have taken up the question to some extent but generally within the context of the role of the military in society (e.g., Huntington 1957; Enloe 1980; Janowitz 1980; Giddens 1985: chaps. 8 and 9; Mann 1986 and 1993; and Birnbaum 1988). There has been neither systematic investigation of how governments induce citizens to accept military service and relatively little consideration of the impact on democracy.

Research on the evolution of universal conscription indicates the factors influencing the form of the military service policy-makers propose. First, of course, is the demand for troops. The government of a country at war is likely to demand more troops than one at peace, *ceteris paribus*. Second is the likely level of compliance of the populations who must supply the troops. The bureaucratic capacity of the state, in particular its ability to actually identify, examine, and retain the eligible, clearly affect the level of compliance. However, as with the taxes, the costs of forced extraction are always higher than the costs of quasi-voluntary compliance. Thus, governments, non-democratic as well as democratic, try to arouse nationalism and other bases for a sense of duty as well as, often, exaggerating the costs of losing the war and the benefits of victory.

Those governments that claim to be democracies go even further and seem to be even more successful in achieving not only quasi-voluntary compliance but the more active contingent consent. They succeed by designing military service formats that, first, ensure relative equality of sacrifice and, second, provide a means for popular discussion and approval of the war and conscription policy. More often than not these more democratic moves were accomplished not through foresight but as revision of failed policies. With few exceptions, policy-makers first introduced conscription that provided discriminatory exemptions to powerful constituents and laid nearly the whole burden of warfare on those without the franchise or other form of political clout. They changed these policies only in response to legislative conflict, political protests, and actual draft riots, such as those in New York in 1863 or in Toulouse in 1868, acts which compelled policy-makers to revise their beliefs about the acceptability of permitting some part of the population to literally buy their way out of military service.

Warmaking requires not only personnel but also money. Here, too, government actors have learned that individuals are more willing to agree to extractions and even quasi-voluntarily comply with them when they have confidence that government is trustworthy, that its commitments are credible, and its procedures for making and implementing policy are relatively fair (Levi 1997: 21–4). The earlier discussion of taxation illuminated the exchange of resources to the state by elites in return for the capacity to at least veto and even determine the nature of tax policy. However, as warfare required more of the community to participate – be it in militias in defense of towns in the colonies or in large-scale nationalist campaigns such as the Napoleonic Wars – participation came at the price of a larger voice in policy-making, assurances that extractions were spread relatively evenly over the population, or both.

Prussia is the exception that proves the rule (Levi 1998). During the Napoleonic Wars, Prussia introduced universal military service. Reform seems to have resulted primarily from the demand for soldiers created by the wars with France, but the form of the policy reflected an ideology of fairness held by a small and powerful set of officials concerned with creating compliance with their policies at the least possible cost. The factor that is totally missing from this account is an active demand by the citizens for reform. Nor was there a simultaneous construction of democratic institutions that would permit them to express their opinions and demands. Finally, there is little evidence that they shared the ideology of fairness advocated by the ministers. Thus, it is not surprising that there is a postscript to this story. Later in the nineteenth century, Prussia reverted from the commitment to equality and fairness as a basis for universal service towards privileging the aristocracy and wealthy. The commitment to universalism and the recognition of the importance of contingent consent that motivated the Prussian reformers could not be sustained without democratic institutions.[9]

The extension of the franchise and other measures of democratization were not the inevitable result of an equalizing tendency, as the case of Prussia illustrates. Nor did large-scale warfare necessarily give rise to democracy, as is evidenced by the seesawing of French democracy throughout the nineteenth century. However, the experiences of Britain, the United States, New Zealand, Australia, and France are consistent with a model in which rulers deciding to go to war learn the advantages of democratic rights or are compelled to grant such rights to those who are bearing the costs but only if: (1) those individuals control significant resources required by the state; and, (2) those individuals have a view of fairness that implies relative equality of sacrifice and voice. This is, of course, a variant of the Hoffman and Rosenthal (1997) model. It adds an emphasis on the property rights and pre-existing institutions of the

---

[9] I thank Daniel Verdier for helping me to see this point.

populace as well as the elite, and it adds a concern with prevailing norms of fairness.

The emergence of democratic norms

If a norm is defined as an informal rule that circumscribes appropriate behavior in a particular context, then democracy depends on three quite different norms. These are tolerance of minorities and of difference, acceptance of electoral defeat, and political obligation. All depend to some extent on norms of fairness, which, first, establish the standards of fairness for government procedures and, second, define when members of a community have an ethic of reciprocity. Although countries striving to be democratic put in place institutions to enforce these norms, none the less a widespread belief in and support of these norms is essential for democracy to survive.

Countries that have become democracies have not generally entered nationhood with these norms in place; the norms emerge and evolve over time. The best extant model of normative change is Ensminger and Knight's bargaining model in which norms are presumed to have distributive consequences and in which relative bargaining power among relevant actors with different norms determines the dominant norm (1997: 4–6). This model has observable and testable implications, and it fits nicely with accounts of institutional change based on relatively high organizational capacity and other resources.

Two examples from the history of military service in democracies provide support for the bargaining model. The first concerns the nineteenth-century government practice of permitting certain recruits to buy their way out of military service (Levi 1997: chap. 4, 80–106). Commutation, substitution, replacement, and other devices for purchasing exemptions served the interests of the propertied who could afford the going market price and who had electoral or other influence with policy-makers. Nor, initially, was there much opposition. Buying out was Pareto optimal; those men who chose to become replacements or substitutes preferred military service to the alternatives. However, in France, the price of substitutes and replacements fluctuated widely, in response to regional labor markets and the number of troops required. When peasant proprietors could no longer afford to buy their sons out of the army and when more fathers gained the vote, a demand for change emerged. In the United States during the Civil War, substitution was retained because it served rural interests with clout in Congress, but commutation was abolished when draft riots crippled New York.

A second example is the parliamentary vote for conscription in

Canada in World War I (Levi 1997: 119–21, 139–53). The anglophone majority effectively imposed its standard of fairness on the francophone minority. Many francophones believed that the constitutions obligated them to fight only in a war of defense, when Canada itself was under attack. The anglophone advocates of conscription argued all should fight in a war Canada declared, and they appealed to the principle of equality of sacrifice. The historical record reveals how frustrated many anglophones were by the significantly lower level of participation among francophones. Conscription provided them with a means to impose their view of equity.

A bargaining model may account for most of the change in the norm of buying out or the imposition of conscription on francophones in Canada during World War I. It cannot possibly provide the explanation of the acceptance of conscientious objection or any other practice that requires tolerance by the majority of a minority's ethical position. Conscientious objection appears to violate the principle of equality of sacrifice, the very norm that had defeated buying out (Levi 1997: chap. 7, 165–99). Hostility was particularly strong in France, where the government prohibited it by law until 1962. In the Anglo-Saxon democracies, with their histories of dissenting religions, conscientious objection has almost always been legal. None the less, conscientious objectors were often subject to brutality and punishment. The current tolerance of conscientious objection did not really emerge until the middle of World War II.

The development of a norm of tolerance for conscientious objection seems to be an example of moral suasion by the few willing to pay the price for their convictions. However, other factors also contribute to the evolution of more pluralistic norms. Punitive reactions to a minority position often reflect government fear of non-compliance with a prevailing norm. Consequently, government actors (and other citizens) use sanctions to inhibit increasing deviations and, thus, an unraveling of the social cooperation a norm is meant to sustain. This reaction changes under quite different conditions. If the minority is recognized as having a position so distinct from the majority that it is unlikely to infect the majority (the Amish being a case in point), then the likelihood of social unraveling is significantly reduced. There is also a condition under which even those who might contribute to social unraveling, such as anti-war protesters, are tolerated. If institutions ensure that the decisions of government actors must appeal to reasons such as respect for civil liberties and if the processes of government are relatively open and participatory, then citizens have a means for making and winning their case for a different standard of judgment than equality of sacrifice.

Thus, where minorities have won such rights, one should also expect to find well-established constitutions and procedures for democratic decision-making. Moreover, the extension of rights and of institutional protections seems to teach individuals to have more tolerance on the one hand, and to demand more tolerance on the other. Such is certainly one of the lessons from the history of conscientious objection.

Yet this set of claims only pushes the question back. Just how did such institutions arise, and how are they maintained when those with coercive and, in wartime, extraordinary powers are strongly antagonistic to a minority position. The answer is the same answer for another necessary norm of democracy: acceptance of defeat in an election. As Przeworski (1991: 26–8) argues, the very definition of a democracy is the existence of losers who accept their losses without attempting to overthrow government or ignore election results (à la Myanmar or Algeria). Frankly, no one has yet provided a satisfactory explanation for an equilibrium in which losers accept their loss rather than take to their guns. Hopefully, this discussion reinforces the importance of searching for an adequate explanation.

There is some progress, however, on the prerequisites of a norm of acceptance. These include confidence that there will be another round, that the losers will win some as well as lose some, and that the losses they suffer, while possibly large, will be contained. How is such confidence to be achieved? Part of the answer lies in the creation of institutions that ensure credible commitments by government actors and trustworthy governments that will enforce the rights of citizens to voice their disaffection and give them future opportunities to vote and choose. However, there the cases reveal other factors as well. The first is the importance of demands for equitable treatment that emanate from civil society. The second is the recognition that there are human rights that are distinct from special privileges; that majority rule is not the only principle for making policy.

Government trustworthiness and norms of fairness that encourage citizens to respect and reciprocate with each other are also at the basis of political obligation. Empirically, political obligation rests on the citizen's perception that government actors and other citizens are trustworthy. This implies institutional arrangements that make promises and commitments credible and ensure long-term future interactions. The activation of political obligation in the form of contingent consent may also require extraordinary acts of compensation to overcome distrust based on past experiences. It implies government decision-making bodies that are not only representative of but also actively considerate of the diverse wishes of the population. It implies membership in a community of citizens who possess some common norms and standards about what it means to reciprocate with each other.

Norms of fairness concerning who pays, who is exempted, and the relative equality of contributions shift over time. What is particularly interesting is how the standard of fairness that emerges produces a demand for institutions designed to enforce this standard. When special treatment of some is revealed, this may evoke a political demand that the state equitably enforces compliance. In situations in which the majority, or at least a large percentage of the population, feels it should comply and a significant minority does not, the majority is more likely to demand rules that compel universal obedience. However, in situations that have allowed a democratic ideology to flourish, the ideology itself may alter the behavior of individuals who then press for institutional changes that are more consistent with their revised views for fairness and appropriate governmental practice.

Conclusion

From this brief account, what have we learned about the reasons why powerful actors in a society commit to democratic institutions or continue to sustain them? One key is the control of funds and personnel. As the demands on the state increase, due to warfare, welfare, or the economy, government actors have to find new means to elicit quasi-voluntary compliance. In order to extract sufficient resources from the polity, rulers need, first, to convince the suppliers they are getting something in return and, second, promote economic growth that increases their long-run return. Government actors can reduce their transaction costs of enforcement by encouraging citizens to willingly comply. To do this, government leaders must provide assurances that they will keep their policy promises and that they will see to it that everyone pays their share.

There is considerable collective knowledge about the conditions that lead to such credible commitments. Critical is a relatively long time horizon. Low discount rates will not emerge where there is civil war or tinpot dictators. Long time horizons may emerge, however, in relatively stable political systems where there is a payoff to the ruling elites from long-term investments both in the countryside and in long-distance trade. In the process of creating institutions that protect stability of rule and economic growth, political actors create, as a byproduct, some of the conditions for democracy. Most importantly, they reform bureaucracies, enlarge the budgetary and veto powers of legislators, and extend the franchise. Such institutions provide assurances that citizens will receive a return for their payments of money and labor, and that citizens may have a say in determining when governments have the right to make such extractions. These institutions form the necessary but not sufficient basis for the further extension of democracy.

Equally important is the evolution of a norm of fairness such as "justice as impartiality" (Barry 1995). This norm helps activate the demand for democratization, and the consequent creation of representative institutions and legal rights sustains and nourishes, and sometimes even generates, the norm. The diffusion of such a norm throughout the population makes it harder for government to curtail democratic rights.

This analysis raises questions about the emergence and maintenance of democratic institutions, both formal and informal. It suggests the beginning of an answer grounded in pre-existing institutional arrangements, relative bargaining power, and institutional change. It stresses the importance of norms in the determination of the extractive capacities of the state and the importance of the extractive requirements of certain government actors under certain conditions in generating a relative equality among the citizenry. The link between extraction, relative equality, and democracy exists neither everywhere nor at all times, but where it exists it can be a potent stimulus to democratic norms and practice.

REFERENCES

Anderson, Perry. 1974a. *Passages from Antiquity to Feudalism*. London: Verso.
    1974b. *Lineages of the Absolutist State*. London: Verso.
Aston, T. H. and C. H. E. Philpin (eds.), 1987. *The Brenner Debate: Agrarian Class Structure and Economic Development in Pre-Industrial Europe*. London: Cambridge University Press.
Barry, Brian. 1995. *Justice as Impartiality*. Oxford: Oxford University Press.
Barzel, Yoram and Edgar Kiser. 1995. "The development and decline of medieval voting institutions: a comparison of England and France." Institute for Economic Research, University of Washington, Seattle, Discussion Paper No. 95-11.
    1996. "Taxation and voting rights in medieval England and France." University of Washington, Seattle.
Bates, Robert H. and Da-Hsiang Donald Lien. 1985. "A note on taxation, development and representative government." *Politics & Society* 14(1): 53-70.
Bates, Robert H., Avner Greif, Margaret Levi, Jean-Laurent Rosenthal, and Barry Weingast. *Analytic Narratives*. Princeton: Princeton University Press.
Bendix, Reinhard. 1978. *Kings or People: Power and the Mandate to Rule*. Berkeley: University of California Press.
Birnbaum, Pierre. 1988. "The state and mobilisation for war." In Pierre

Birnbaum (ed.), *States and Collective Action*, pp. 55–66. New York: Cambridge University Press.

Brewer, John. 1989. *The Sinews of Power: War, Money and the English State, 1688–1783*. New York: Alfred A. Knopf.

Denzau, Arthur T. and Douglass C. North. 1994. "Shared mental models: ideologies and institutions." *Kyklos* 47(1): 3–31.

Downing, Brian M. 1994. *The Military Revolution and Political Change*. Princeton: Princeton University Press.

Enloe, Cynthia. 1980. *Police, Military and Ethnicity: Foundations of State Power*. New Brunswick, NJ: Transaction Books.

Ensminger, Jean and Jack Knight. 1997. "Changing social norms: common property, bridewealth, and clan exogamy." *Current Anthropology* 38: 1–24.

Ertman, Thomas. 1997. *Birth of the Leviathan: Building States and Regimes in Medieval and Early Modern Europe*. New York: Cambridge University Press.

Finer, Samuel. 1975. "State and nation-building in Europe: the role of the military." In Charles Tilly (ed.), *The Formation of National States in Western Europe*, pp. 84–163. Princeton: Princeton University Press.

Frank, Tenney. 1927. *An Economic History of Rome*. London: Jonathan Cape.

Geddes, Barbara. 1991. "Paradigms and sand castles in comparative politics of developing areas." In William Crotty (ed.), *Political Science: Looking Forward to the Future*, pp. 45–75. Boston: Northwestern University Press.

Giddens, Anthony. 1985. *The Nation-State and Violence*. Cambridge: Polity Press.

Hintze, Otto. 1994 (1906). "Military organization and the organization of the state." In John A. Hall (ed.), *The State: Critical Concepts*, Vol. I, pp. 181–202. London and New York: Routledge.

Hoffman, Philip T. and Kathryn Norberg (eds.). 1994. *Fiscal Crises and the Growth of Representative Institutions*. Stanford: Stanford University Press.

Hoffman, Philip T. and Jean-Laurent Rosenthal. 1997. "The political economy of warfare and taxation in early modern Europe: historical lessons for economic development." In John N. Drobak and John V. Nye (eds.), *The Frontiers of the New Institutional Economics*, pp. 31–55. San Diego: Academic Press.

Hooks, Gregory and Gregory Mclauchlan. 1992. "The institutional foundation of warmaking: three eras of U.S. warmaking, 1939–1989." *Theory & Society* 21: 757–88.

Huntington, Samuel P. 1957. *The Soldier and the State*. Cambridge, MA: Harvard University Press.

Janowitz, Morris. 1980. "Observations on the sociology of citizenship: obligations and rights." *Social Forces* 59(1): 1–24.

Kiser, Edgar. 1994. "Markets and hierarchies in early modern tax systems: a principal–agent analysis." *Politics & Society* 22(3): 285–316.

Kiser, Edgar and Yoram Barzel. 1991. "The origins of democracy in England." *Rationality & Society* 3(4): 396–422.

Levi, Margaret. 1988. *Of Rule and Revenue*. Berkeley: University of California Press.

1997. *Consent, Dissent and Patriotism*. New York: Cambridge University Press.

1998. "Conscription: the price of citizenship." In Robert H. Bates, Avner Greif, Margaret Levi, Jean-Laurent Rosenthal, and Barry Weingast, *Analytic Narratives*, pp. 109–47. Princeton: Princeton University Press.

Lichbach, Mark and Alan Zuckerman (eds.). 1997. *Comparative Politics: Rationality, Culture, and Structure.* New York: Cambridge University Press.

Lipset, Seymour Martin. 1994. "The social requisites of democracy revisited." *American Sociological Review* 59: 1–22.

Mann, Michael. 1986. *The Sources of Social Power: A History of Power from the Beginning to A.D. 1760*, Vol. I. London and New York: Cambridge University Press.

1993. *The Sources of Social Power: The Rise of Classes and Nation-States, 1760–1914*, Vol. II. New York: Cambridge University Press.

Marx, Karl. 1974 (1867). *Capital*, Vol. I. New York: International Publishers.

Mathias, Peter and Peter O'Brien. 1976. "Taxation in Britain and France, 1715–1810: a comparison of the social and economic incidence of taxes collected for the central government." *Journal of European Economic History* 5: 601–50.

Moore, Barrington. 1966. *Social Origins of Dictatorship and Democracy.* Boston: Beacon Press.

North, Douglass C. 1981. *Structure and Change in Economic History.* New York: Norton.

1990. *Institutions, Institutional Change, and Economic Performance.* New York: Cambridge University Press.

North, Douglass C. and Barry R. Weingast. 1989. "Constitutions and commitment: the evolution of institutions governing public choice in seventeenth-century England." *Journal of Economic History* 49(4): 803–32.

Olson, Mancur. 1993. "Dictatorship, democracy and development." *American Political Science Review* 87(3): 567–76.

Peacock, Alan T. and Jack Wiseman. 1961. *The Growth of Public Expenditure in the United Kingdom.* Princeton: Princeton University Press.

Przeworski, Adam. 1991. *Democracy and the Market.* New York: Cambridge University Press.

Putnam, Robert. 1993. *Making Democracy Work: Civic Traditions in Modern Italy.* Princeton: Princeton University Press.

Rasler, Karen and William R. Thompson. 1985. "War making and state making: governmental expenditures, tax revenues, and global wars." *American Political Science Review* 79: 491–507.

Root, Hilton L. 1994. *The Fountain of Privilege: Political Foundations of Markets in Old Regime France and England.* Berkeley: University of California Press.

Rosenthal, Jean-Laurent. 1998. "The political economy of absolutism revisited." In Robert H. Bates, Avner Greif, Margaret Levi, Jean-Laurent Rosenthal, and Barry Weingast, *Analytic Narratives*, pp. 64–108. Princeton: Princeton University Press.

Schumpeter, Joseph. 1954 (1918). "The crisis of the tax state." In Alan Peacock *et al.* (eds.), *International Economic Papers: Translations Prepared for the International Economic Association*, pp. 5–38. New York: Macmillan.

Spruyt, Hendrik. 1994. *The Sovereign State and Its Competitors.* Princeton: Princeton University Press.

Steinmo, Sven. 1993. *Taxation and Democracy.* New Haven: Yale University Press.

Taylor, Michael. 1987 (1976). *The Possibility of Cooperation.* Cambridge: Cambridge University Press.

Thomson, Janice E. 1995. *Mercenaries, Pirates, and State Sovereignty.* Princeton: Princeton University Press.

Tilly, Charles. 1990. *Capital, Coercion, and European States.* Cambridge, MA: Basil Blackwell.

Wallerstein, Immanuel. 1974. *The Modern World System.* New York: Academic Press.

Weber, Max. 1968. *Economy and Society.* Berkeley: University of California Press.

7   Democracy and development?

John Dunn

How democracy affects the prospects for development, and how development affects the prospects for democracy, are scarcely in themselves well-posed questions. It is far from easy, too, to see how they can readily be posed much better. What they lack in precision or stability of meaning, however, they more than make up for in urgency. On an optimistic view (of relatively recent plausibility) they form the central questions of modern politics, defining what is at stake in that politics, and indicating by their answers what real options it offers (Dunn 1990 and 1992; Fontana 1994). On what basis a state can hope to tax successfully, and on what terms it can rely in raising dependable and substantial armed forces, are much older questions, clearly antedating the modern state itself (Skinner 1989; Zagorin 1982) but unmistakably persisting with equal urgency well into the last century (Dunn 1980: chap. 9) in even the most prosperous and normatively preoccupied of modern states. Only with the changing military technologies of the last twenty-five years, and even then principally in societies which face no pressing external threat, has the latter concern relaxed decisively in face of the former. The relationship between perceived external military needs, public debt, domestic political constraint, and economic performance has been the core of the history of the modern state for well over three centuries (Hont 1990, 1993, and 1995; Sonenscher 1997; Shaviro 1997). Every element in this relationship is subject to highly imponderable political judgment. Most of the history of the modern world is potentially relevant to its assessment. This is not a domain in which to anticipate wholesale and reliable cognitive progress in a hurry.

The papers by Levi and Bardhan consider many interesting candidates for causal relations within these two huge but interconnected fields. Neither makes any strong or dogmatic claims about such relations. Bardhan gives a somewhat richer picture of the internal causal complexity of states, though Levi also clearly acknowledges this. Levi, as befits a student of taxation and conscription, conveys a stronger sense of the causal significance of popular agency (resistance, avoidance, even commitment) in reproducing or modifying the relations between states and their subjects. Both favor a cool and distanced vocabulary and conceptual apparatus for specifying such agency, in accordance with the conventional rhetoric of contemporary social science, although Levi also employs a number of somewhat more ambitious psychological categories, and gives at least some causal weight to the presence or absence of a norm of impartiality. Levi is certainly right to underline the practical significance of the relations she analyzes. Bardhan is wholly convincing in stressing the complexity of mediations which determine the developmental outcome of the operations of democratic polities, the multiplicity of sites within these polities at which there rests some real degree of political discretion over how they operate, and the eminently consequential impact of how that discretion is exercised (cf. Haggard and Webb 1994; Dunn 1996a, etc.). Both inductively and analytically it is hard to see how strong causal claims about the way in which such relations must work can be sustained.

Given the extraordinary practical importance of these questions, how dismaying should we find this? (This is intended as a question about rationality, not about temperament.) In the end, surely, not very. Fatalist political pathologies are genuinely politically alarming; but *ex ante* indeterminacy is simply the price of freedom. It is absurd to presume both that we truly are free to choose in politics and that we are also bound to choose benignly or intelligently. All polities allocate and constrain agency: the raw causal capacity to act and bring about effects by such actions. (This is Levi's own central and strategically compelling analytical presumption.) None eliminates agency. Agency, until proved otherwise, simply is free and mind-dependent. (This is a pragmatic, not a metaphysical point: Davidson 1980: esp. chap. 11.) On this view, the urgency of these issues rests, outside those polities which are fundamentally pathological, not with the institutional forms or underlying political economy of the state in question, but with the ways in which judgment is in fact exercised: within the historical field of political choice. Even within this field, purely cognitive questions of comprehension may be every bit as important as prior constellations of interests. There is some gross agreement today on the prerequisites for economic development (Lal and Myint 1996). But all particular judgments of strategy even in the long term are too heavily confounded with strictly political judgments, and too hard to bring to bear on the polity in question, to meet minimal standards of objectivity. The stipulative logic of economic models and the all too contingent practical causality of real economies articulate (where they articulate at all) at a level which is largely opaque.

If state building everywhere includes, as Levi says, the forging of governmental institutions capable of extracting ever more money and manpower from the population, it is scarcely surprising that democracy does not necessarily result from it. What is more striking is that democracy should ever result from it, and still more that, for the present, it should apparently result from it more often and more insistently than any other determinate state form.

The concepts of state and democracy have always been in some tension. It is certainly important to improve our understanding of why they have recently converged so sharply with one another in political practice (Dunn 1992, 1995, 1996a, and 1996b; Huntington 1991, and cf. Huntington 1996). If we envisage democracy as a concept, an intellectual instrument through which to apprehend and reflect upon politics (Dunn 1993: chap. 1, 1996c and 1998; Copp, Hampton, and Roemer 1993), we need to distinguish this as sharply as we can from democracy as the name for the political character of a miscellany of actually existing modern states: a disorderly and complex feature of the political history of the world.

State building is not well conceived as a process of forging governmental institutions capable of extracting ever more money and manpower from the population, except on a conjunction of provisos: (1) firstly, that the identification is essentially stipulative: that that is just exhaustively what a state is taken to be. Anything else must be something else. (2) Secondly that the capacity to do so is conceived as purely instrumental and exhibited over a very short time span. (3) Thirdly, that extraction in relation to money or other economic resources is conceived quite independently of the degree of discretion on the part of different agencies over how the extracted resources are subsequently deployed. (4) Fourthly, that a different sense is given to the idea of extraction in the cases of money and manpower. All these provisos are important and, taken together, they leave this conception of state building too threadbare to be intellectually serviceable. What a state really is is either an impossibly hard or a very ill-posed question. To equate a state with a process of extraction is incoherently realist, both excessively selective and injudiciously discreet over what renders such extraction possible. To do so is to turn our backs resolutely on the social and political imaginations of the state, its cadres, and its subjects.

Extraction of either or both resources is a steady concomitant of the history of anything we might now naturally call a state; but it is a poor candidate for what is common to all of them, and an even weaker candidate for what is most important about them. What makes the equation plausible is a picture of the state as an ever more elaborate apparatus for acting, with a powerful ideal charter, legal and ideological, to act as those who hold authority within it currently feel inclined. But the growing elaboration and intimacy of the apparatus for acting must operate over time in face of an always complex and constantly modifying array of powers on the part of other groups of agents, either to predis- cipline the directions in which the state can hope to act effectively, to obstruct its action to varying degrees at the receiving end, or to appro- priate the power of agency from the state and transform it into one of their own. More potent agency top down must contend throughout with more potent agency bottom up. The precise balance of power in this encounter can only ever be ascertained *ex post*. It shifts incessantly and transforms what the state really is by doing so. (This is, of course, only a suggestive handful of the pertinent considerations. For an example of a far richer range in action, see Meier 1996.) Democracy, however loosely defined, can reach a particular territory in the twentieth century by many routes: the departure of a colonial government, the arrival of a foreign army of occupation, a credible threat of international credit withdrawal, the loss of nerve by a domestic army of occupation, even the insurrection of an angry populace. Its relation to past and future tax levels, or to the directions in which such taxes have been or will be disbursed, will depend on how it arrives and on what has been going on in the economic, social, and even intellectual history of the society beforehand. It is hard to see how the question of the relation between democracy and extractive capacity in this very simple sense can be posed in a way which permits a reasonably, economical, clear and potentially valid answer. It plainly does so in all manner of ways. At this level of aggregation how it will prove to do so in practice is anyone's guess.

The last twenty-five years have seen two apparently contradictory theses about the relations between democratic institutions and tax extraction pressed with some vigor: that democracies are tendentially incapable of taxing adequately (compulsively fiscally profligate), or that they are congenitally incapable of refraining from over-taxing (com- mitted by their internal political properties to taking from the richer and fewer to give to the poorer and more numerous, or perhaps just to squander on themselves). As of today, the latter thesis has worn worse than the former as a short-term retrodiction; but this is very far from establishing that the former will turn out to be a smart prediction over any term at all. It was the latter – the propensity to expropriate – which was the classical complaint against democracy in Ancient Greece (before economic growth was even thought of), as it was for its corresponding enemies in eighteenth- and nineteenth-century Europe or in the recent past and present of East Asia. In the Greek case the complaint about abolishing personal debt and redistributing land was less about economic efficiency than about interclass justice. What it denounced was an affront to property right, not an error of macroeconomic policy. Even in the epoch of commercial society, since the late eighteenth century, what can reasonably be thought to menace economic efficiency is not the level of taxes exacted, but the ways in which these are subsequently disbursed: more especially how they are divided up between consumption and investment, whose consumption exactly they service and at whose expense, and how efficiently the investment they make possible is chosen and implemented. In the East Asian cases, for example, over the last half century relatively drastic and egalitarian land reform at one point in time, whatever its significance for interclass justice, is widely agreed to have greatly facilitated a development pathway of rapid growth funded by high savings rates and massive investment.

To understand the capacity (or otherwise) of states of different sorts to induce their subjects to come to the colors and fight, if need be, to the death for those who order them to do so requires the eliciting and ordering of a huge range of information, much of it on matters where the agents concerned have a clear interest in subterfuge (in concealing much of the relevant information and cloaking their own actions as effectively as they can). The search for a simple logic and a powerful explanatory structure in these cases is overwhelmingly likely to truncate inquiry prematurely and issue in stylized misunderstanding of a reality which is blearily specified in the first place, rather than in accurate assessment of what is really going on. Both in the cases of taxation and of conscription the history of well-institutionalized practices, often implemented in a context of recurrent policy dispute over the felicity or otherwise of the practice's present organization, gives, as Levi shows, both a sequence of change or persistence to be explained (a potentially clear and relatively neat explicandum) and a heuristically promising medium in which to seek for elements of its explanation. The resulting structure of understanding, however, privileges the express viewpoint of agents who may neither understand well what the other agents concerned are doing, nor be especially frank either with themselves or others as to quite why they in turn are acting as they are. They may, indeed, not really even know in any strong sense quite why they are acting as they are. (Who can be wholly confident, for example, that Bill Clinton or Gerhard Schröder quite know why they acted as they have? Who can even be confident that they can fully remember?) If it is hard for them to survey accurately even their own agency, they are still worse placed to assess accurately what prompts the responses of those whose actions they are attempting to control.

In the case of conscription, as with taxation, there is probably more causal weight in the perceived consequences of the extraction than in the internal fairness of the mode of extraction. Its history, therefore, cannot be adequately analyzed by focusing mainly on the institutions of tax extraction or conscription, but must extend over a much broader field, which is constituted by personal judgments of significance the whole way through. Within that field it is perfectly reasonable to view the relation between state controllers and those whom they tax or conscript as a bargaining game. But the formal properties of the game then depend on the judgments of significance and the judgments of significance depend upon imaginative contingencies which are conceptually prior to, and unanalyzable within, the logic of bargaining. (How exactly is a norm of impartiality to be incorporated into a logic of bargaining? cf. Barry 1989.) In the case of conscription, popular response throughout its history is structured through a vision of options practically open and personally appropriate, and, under democratic regimes more especially, the choice between fight or flight or plain defiance on the one hand and docility at the point of conscription followed by dedicated obedience within the ranks depends overwhelmingly on the perceived significance of the activities for which the conscription is occurring. Israel (perhaps even Iran for a period of time) could conscript wholesale and do so without needing to fear democratic inhibition. Iraq in the same span of time certainly could not have done so, had it needed to. Quasi-voluntary compliance needs to be counterposed to wholly voluntary compliance (volunteering) and the patterns of response which emerge need to be interpreted through the imaginative elements which would prompt each. Ideal considerations are inexpugnable from any realistic analysis of what is occurring, not merely in the, in practice, fairly marginal instance of conscientious objection, but right through the interpretation of the role of military manpower in warfighting for modern democracies or in sustaining or failing to sustain imperial authority. They can be expelled only at the price of incomprehension of what is occurring and of profound misjudgment of the political causality which underlies this. Even Hobbes assumed that it was incoherent to expel ideal elements from an understanding of conduct within military roles (Hobbes 1991 [1651]: Review and Conclusion, esp. 484–6; Baumgold 1988). No doubt he failed to capture quite what this implies; but it would be interesting to be told who since has succeeded in doing so in a clearer and epistemically more dependable manner.

What can one say positively about the relation between democracy and development on the basis of a skeptical, historical approach which sees normative categories as inexpugnable from the understanding of political causality? Firstly, that we must separate sharply our analysis of the causality of economic development from that of the causal dynamics of democratic polities, and articulate the two with the greatest intellectual care only when we have carried each as far as we can. This requires very vigorous and controlled abstraction from history in the first instance. In the second place, once we have judged as best we can who at present does best understand the strictly economic dynamics of given territorial and demographic units today, then we must develop and deploy a conception of what a democratic polity is which is appropriate to grasping its causal dynamics. This is overwhelmingly much harder to do than political scientists have yet fathomed.

No polity (and still more, no state) is or could be democratic *tout court*. Any approach to grasping the causal dynamics of putatively democratic polities needs to be ultra-sensitive to the degree to which the description of a polity as democratic is descriptively illuminating and the degree to which it is simply politically impertinent. There is a great deal more impertinence in the predication of the term to any modern state than there is descriptive precision (Dunn 1992: Conclusion). In so far as the predication is descriptively accurate rather than impertinent, the key to deep understanding is to recognize that in a democracy political structure *ex hypothesi* gives no guidance whatever on the deliberative content of its politics. It is that deliberative content, however politically implemented (however the game-theoretical problems of coalition formation and commitment are solved within it), which gives the outcome of democratic political choice. It cannot be validly explained from the outside (as it were, from underneath, something more fundamental) or from what came before (historically). It can only be explained from within the deliberative sequence itself. Democracy, on this understanding, is, stipulatively, a system in which a miscellany of free agents deliberate freely with one another and choose interactively what is to be done through the apparatus of public choice and what must be left severely to one another outside that apparatus. The point of the metaphor of a bargaining game is to flatten out and render tractable this seething and disorderly complexity. But adopting the metaphor always risks eliminating most of the content in the first instance, and in a manner profoundly imaginatively at odds with what democracy in this sense is. Under democracy it is not pregiven interests that determine political outcomes. Rather, democracy itself, deliberatively and heuristically, defines the content of interests. This is every bit as true, and as muddling in practice, in the case of taxes or conscription as it is over any of the more elevated spiritual concerns which those who are revolted by the lowness of contemporary capitalist democracies wish somehow or other to haul back more effectively into collective deliberation. To accept it is a concession to political realism, not a flight into political sentimentality. To reject it is either to reject the presumption that democracy in this sense is a causal possibility or that it is a practically coherent concept. Perhaps we should reject this presumption; but, if so, we should surely do so consciously and frankly, not by inadvertence.

REFERENCES

Barry, Brian. 1989. *Theories of Justice*. Hemel Hempstead: Harvester-Wheatsheaf.
Baumgold, Deborah. 1988. *Hobbes's Political Theory*. Cambridge: Cambridge University Press.
Copp, David, Jean Hampton, and John E. Roemer (eds.). 1993. *The Idea of Democracy*. Cambridge: Cambridge University Press.
Davidson, Donald. 1980. *Essays on Actions and Events*. Oxford: Clarendon Press.
Dunn, John. 1980. *Political Obligation in its Historical Context*. Cambridge: Cambridge University Press.
(ed.). 1990. *The Economic Limits to Modern Politics*. Cambridge: Cambridge University Press.
(ed.). 1992. *Democracy: The Unfinished Journey*. Oxford: Oxford University Press.
1993. *Western Political Theory in the Face of the Future* (2nd edn). Cambridge: Cambridge University Press.
(ed.) 1995. *Contemporary Crisis of the Nation State?* Oxford: Blackwell.
1996a. "How democracies succeed." *Economy and Society* 25: 511–28.
1996b. "The transcultural significance of Athenian democracy." In Michel Sakellariou (ed.), *Democratié Athénienne et Culture*, pp. 97–108. Athens: Academy of Athens.
1996c. "Does separatism threaten the state system?" In Trude Andersen, Beate Bull, *et al.* (eds.), *Separatism*. Bergen: C. Michelson Institute.
1999. "Situating democratic accountability." In Adam Przeworski (ed.), *Democratic Accountability*. Cambridge: Cambridge University Press.
Fontana, Biancamaria (ed.). 1994. *The Invention of the Modern Republic*. Cambridge: Cambridge University Press.
Haggard, Stephan and Steven B. Webb (eds.). 1994. *Voting for Reform*. Oxford: Oxford University Press (for the World Bank).
Hobbes, Thomas. 1991 (1651). *Leviathan*. Edited by Richard Tuck. Cambridge: Cambridge University Press.
Hont, Istvan. 1990. "Free trade and the economic limits to national politics: neo-machiavellian political economy reconsidered. In John Dunn (ed.), *The Economic Limits to Modern Politics*, pp. 411–20. Cambridge: Cambridge University Press.
1993. "The rhapsody of public debt: David Hume and voluntary state bankruptcy." In Nicholas Phillipson and Quentin Skinner (eds.), *Political*

Discourse in Early Modern Britain, pp. 321–48. Cambridge: Cambridge University Press.

1995. "The permanent crisis of a divided mankind: contemporary crisis of the nation state in historical perspective." In John Dunn (ed.), *Contemporary Crisis of the Nation State?* pp. 166–231. Oxford: Blackwell.

Huntington, Samuel P. 1991. *Democratization: The Third Wave*. Norman: University of Oklahoma Press.

1996. *The Clash of Civilizations and the Remaking of World Order*. New York: Simon & Schuster.

Lal, Deepak and Myint, H. 1996. *The Political Economy of Poverty, Equity and Growth*. Oxford: Clarendon Press.

Meier, Christian. 1996. *Caesar*. Translated by D. McKlintock. Cambridge, MA: Harvard University Press.

Shaviro, Daniel. 1997. *Do Deficits Matter?* Chicago: University of Chicago Press.

Skinner, Quentin. 1989. "The state." In Terence Ball, James Farr and Russell Hanson (eds.), *Political Innovation and Conceptual Change*, pp. 90–131. Cambridge: Cambridge University Press.

Sonenscher, Michael. 1997. "The nation's debt and the birth of the modern republic: The French fiscal deficit and the politics of the Revolution of 1789." *History of Political Thought* 18.

Zagorin, Perez. 1982. *Rebels and Rulers 1500-1660*. 2 vols. Cambridge: Cambridge University Press.

8   State, civil society, and social justice

Iris Marion Young

Recent interest by political theorists in the concept and practices of civil society has been spurred by the revolutionary events in Eastern Europe, South Africa, and several Latin American countries, where apparently well-ensconced authoritarian regimes crumbled after being hollowed out by resistance movements of ordinary citizens in voluntary associations who withdrew their tacit support. Rediscovery of the concept of civil society, however, goes beyond these moments of opposition to authoritarian rule. Many claim for civil society a central role in promoting democracy and social welfare under liberal regimes as well. Some theorists and political commentators even suggest that civil society is better equipped than the state to further social justice and solidarity. On this view, state institutions should be restricted in order to allow the flourishing of associational life to effect all these goods.

This chapter has three purposes.[1] First, I aim to clarify the idea of civil society by distinguishing it from both state and economy, and by distinguishing three levels of associative activity. Second, I support claims for the unique virtues of networks of civic associations and public spheres in promoting democracy and justice. Specifically, civic associations and public spheres outside state and economy allow self-organization for the purposes of identity support, the invention of new practices, and the provision of some goods and services. Perhaps even more important, public spheres thriving in civil society often limit state and economic power and make their exercise more accountable to citizens.

Despite these virtues of civil society in supporting democracy and solidarity, my third purpose is to criticize tendencies to regard civil society as an alternative to state-constituted regulatory, service, and

[1] An earlier version of this chapter was presented to the Fellows Seminar at the Center for Human Values, Princeton University, December 1996. I am grateful to the seminar members for their comments and criticisms: Neera Badhwar, Robert Gooding-Williams, Amy Gutmann, Casey Haskins, David Heyd, George Kateb, Donald Morrison, and Jeremy Waldron. I am also grateful to David Alexander, David Plotke, Carlos Forment, and Michael Walzer for comments on earlier versions.

welfare institutions. State institutions and actions have their own unique virtues in promoting democracy and social justice. Both civil society and the state should be strengthened and made more democratic; together with a private-sector market economy, each can limit and support the others. Thus social movements seeking greater social justice and well-being should work on both these fronts, and aim to multiply the links between civil society and states.

Thus the question of this essay is this: what is the role of autonomous associational life within the context of societies guided by a rule of law that recognizes basic liberties, but where structural injustice nevertheless exists? No society with a liberal democratic political regime is free of structural injustice, and many are grossly unjust. I define injustice in terms of domination and oppression. Domination consists in institutional conditions which inhibit or prevent people from participating in decisions and processes that determine their actions and the conditions of their action. Persons live within structures of domination if other persons or groups can determine without reciprocation the conditions of their actions, either directly or through the structural consequences of their actions (cf. Pettit 1997 and this volume). I name the aspect of social justice that domination denies "self-determination." In a large-scale society with intricate webs of economic and social interdependence, the value of self-determination can be realized for the most part only collectively through democratic practices. Oppression, the second aspect of injustice, consists in systematic institutional processes which prevent some people from learning and using satisfying or expansive skills in socially recognized settings, or which inhibit people's ability to play and communicate with others or to express their feelings and perspective on social life in contexts where others can listen. I name the aspect of social justice that oppression denies "self-development" (Young 1990: 38; cf. Sen 1993). While the values of self-determination and self-development overlap in particular circumstances, they are irreducible to one another.

My argument for the distinct virtues of state capacities over and above those of civil society assumes this two-part definition of social justice in terms of self-determination and self-development. The associational life of civil society can do much to promote self-determination. Precisely because of its plurality and relative lack of coordination, however, civil society can only minimally further values of self-development. Because many of the structural injustices that produce oppression have their source in economic processes, state institutions are necessary to undermine such oppression and promote self-development.

The idea of civil society

"The words 'civil society,'" says Michael Walzer, "name the space of uncoerced human association and also the set of relational networks – formed for the sake of family, faith, interest, and ideology – that fill their space" (Walzer 1995: 7). This is a good enough beginning to a definition of the concept, but, like most other definitions of civil society, it seems to include almost everything we know as social. Indeed, the idea of civil society does include a great deal, making attempts at a simple sentence definition inevitably vague. Theoretical elaboration of the idea of civil society requires not a sentence definition, but rather distinguishing and articulating terms describing social life. Accordingly, this section "defines" the social phenomena often referred to by the term "civil society," in two steps. I argue that activities of voluntary associational life are usefully distinguished from those of both state and economy. State and economy are distinguished from associational life because they coordinate action differently, and because state and economy exercise kinds of systematic power. I then distinguish three levels of associational life relatively autonomous from state and economy: private association, civic association, and political association.

In classical modern usages "civil society" referred to the entirety of social life outside state institutions (Chandhoke 1995; Tester 1992). Civil society referred to the diverse and particular activities, institutions, and associations regulated and unified by the general legal and coercive apparatus of the state. Activities of private enterprise and market transaction, in this classical usage, enjoyed a central place in civil society. The concept of civil society has evolved in the last century and a half, however, in response to significant changes in both states and the institutions and associations outside the state. While some theorists continue to mean by "civil society" all of social life outside the state, many political theorists now distinguish the activities of voluntary associational life from both state and economy (Cohen and Arato 1992; Habermas 1996: chap. 7; Walzer 1995; Nielsen 1995). Distinguishing voluntary associational life from economy as well as state helps refine the guiding question of this essay, namely: what is the role of civil society in promoting social justice?

"State" refers to activities and institutions of legal regulation, enforcement backed by coercion, legislatively mandated coordination and public services, along with the managerial and technical apparatus necessary to carry out these functions effectively. In distinguishing economy from state I assume a capitalist economy, that is, an economy in which at least a large part of the society's goods and services are supplied by private enterprise operating through markets. Economic activity is profit- and market-oriented. "Civil society" refers to a third sector of private associations relatively autonomous both from state and economy. They are voluntary, in the sense that they are neither mandated nor run by state institutions, but spring from the everyday lives and activities of communities of interest. The associations of this third sector, moreover, operate not for profit. Most participate in economic activity only as consumers, fund-raisers, and sometimes employers. Even those activities of the third sector that involve providing goods and services for fees, however, are not organized toward the objectives of making profit and enlarging market shares.

It is useful to distinguish civil society from both state and economy in two respects. For the first I follow Cohen and Arato (1992) in relying on Habermas's distinction between "system" and "lifeworld" (Habermas 1984). State, economy, and civil society correspond to three distinct ways of coordinating action, the first through the medium of authorized power, the second through the medium of money, and the third through communicative interaction. State and economy are each *systemic* inasmuch as the actions of thousands or even millions of people are conditioned by system imperatives of bureaucratic routine or profit making, and those coordinating their actions need not directly communicate with one another. Both state and economy are systemic inasmuch as they bring together disparate people, places, and particular goals in action networks mediated by authorized power or money, where the particular actors are constrained by the imperatives of each to accomplish their particular goals within the system. They are systemic also inasmuch as each tends to extend its influence or effects, bureaucratizing or commodifying human needs and relationships ever more deeply.

Habermas designates as "lifeworld" those activities and institutions which are structured primarily through communicative interaction rather than by systemic imperatives in relation to which actors reason instrumentally and strategically. "Civil society" corresponds to associative activities of the lifeworld. In the associations of civil society people coordinate their actions by discussing and working things out, rather than by checking prices or looking up the rules. Civil society includes a vast array of activities, institutions, and social networks outside state and economy, from informal clubs, to religious organizations, to non-profit service providers, to cultural producers, to political action groups.

The first reason to distinguish civil society from both state and economy, then, is to notice differing forms of the coordination of social action. The second reason is connected, but bears more directly on the issue of whether and how activities in this social sector can promote democracy and social justice. Recent political theory of civil society analyzes how organizations and activities relatively autonomous from the state can limit state power, and make its exercise more accountable and democratic. If a purpose of theorizing the functions of civil society is to describe the possibilities of free self-organization and their potential for limiting power and democratizing its exercise, however, then it is important to distinguish civil society from economy as well as state. Private firms, some of which are larger and more powerful than many states, dominate economic life in contemporary capitalist societies. Their internal organization is typically far less democratic than most governments, and persons whose lives are affected by the policies and actions of such economic institutions often lack the means to confront them. The structural consequences of market imperatives and profit-orientation as followed by these powerful economic actors, moreover, severely limit the options of individuals, groups, and sometimes states.

Theorists of civil society often use spatial or substantial language to define the concept, characterizing it as a realm, sphere, or space, distinct from spheres of economy and state. Such spatial language suggests that society has three distinct parts that do not overlap. It also tempts us into placing each social institution into one, and only one, of these social spheres. I suggest that a more process-oriented understanding of what civil society names, however, better enables us to use the concept to understand complex social reality. Rather than think of state, economy and civil society as distinct spheres or clusters of institutions, we should think of them as distinct *kinds of activities*. When we understand state, economy, and civil society as kinds of activity, we can see how many institutions include all three activities. Institutions where state or economic activities dominate may also contain or promote significant activities of voluntary association.

Thus far I have refined Walzer's definition of civil society only to the extent of distinguishing "the space of uncoerced human associations and also the set of relational networks that fill their space" from systems of state and economy. This leaves a vast undifferentiated range of social life. To answer how activities of this associative lifeworld support democracy and promote social justice, it is helpful to distinguish levels of associative activity: private association, civic association, and political association.

Private association is self-regarding, in the sense that it is activity for the participants or members of the association. Families, social clubs, private parties and gatherings, many of the activities of religious organizations, are all examples of private association. More often than not, private association concerns enjoyment and suffering – light sociability, personal caretaking, consumption, entertainment, grieving, and spiritual renewal. Such activities are private in the Arendtian sense that they concern basic matters of life, death, need, and pleasure, which in the extreme cannot be shared, and in the sense that the social relations carrying out these activities are usually more or less exclusive. Private associations tend to be inward looking and particularist. I go to this club's functions because it is my club, where I know the other individuals and they know me; our meetings and events include only us and others whom we invite, and our purpose is to have a good time, or care for one another.

Civic associations, on the other hand, are primarily directed outward from those engaged in them to others. Activities with a civic purpose aim to serve not only members, but also the wider community. Civic associations claim to make some contribution to the collective life of the neighborhood, city, country, or world. What is distinctive here is that when civic associations claim to contribute to some community good, their participants assume that at least some of the beneficiaries are strangers, anonymous others who live in the community or who pass through, or others in far-away places. Thus a civic association that organizes volunteers to cut the vines that are choking the trees in a public park wishes to preserve the lushness of the park both for themselves and others who might wander into it. The neighborhood crime watch, the community arts center, battered women's services, and journals of information and opinions about events and issues in the community, are all shaped and justified as knitting relations among strangers as well as acquaintances and friends. Unlike private association, civic association tends to be *inclusive* in this sense that it is open in principle to anyone.

A healthy civil society has a huge array of such civic activities and associations, not only small, ad hoc, and short lived – such as some crime-watch groups or neighborhood clean-up crews – but also large, well funded, and institutionalized over generations, such as the United Way. Most civic associations rely on volunteer work even when they employ paid staff, and all rely on donations of money and other resources to carry out their work. Some civic activities advance a partisan "cause" and in this sense may be proto-political, such as associations working against the death penalty, promoting recycling, or wishing to save the spotted owl.

Robert Putnam (1993) famously argues that a rich associational life strengthens democratic institutions and culture. His concept of associationalism, however, appears to include a great variety of groups and activities, from church groups to unions to reading the newspaper. He makes no distinctions between kinds of associations, nor does he try to account for just *how* some or all of them allegedly enhance democracy. I believe that it is important to distinguish between private and civic association, as I have done, between more inward-looking and outward-looking forms of association. Such a distinction shows how some kinds of association may not enhance democracy very much or help change those structures that inhibit capabilities. There is little reason to think that soccer clubs or bowling leagues, for example, do very much to enhance democracy or contribute to a solidarity of strangers. To be sure, members of such groups might develop skills in organizing schedules and leading meetings that non-joiners lack, and such skills may contribute to one's ability to be a citizen. Private clubs such as these, however, belong to that vast layer of associational life where people do something they enjoy, in the company of friends, for the sake of that enjoyment. Such private association is a wonderful thing, but it contributes little to the good of the wider society.

Private association, moreover, is sometimes depoliticizing or brazenly self-regarding. Some people and groups with a rich private associational life are indifferent to public life and restrict themselves to an enclosed group of family, friends, and career contacts. Whole communities or groups withdraw into associational privatism and even create defensive walls in the effort to keep the political and social concerns of the wider society at bay. There is nothing wrong with private association per se in a big and free society, as long as citizens and associations respect one another and are willing to do their part to contribute to the wider society. Too much private association relative to civil and political association, however, may weaken democracy and concern for social justice, because people and groups may care little for outsiders, and indeed may be hostile to others (cf. Levi 1996).

Political association is distinct from both private and civic association, in that it self-consciously focuses on claims about what the social collective ought to do. Political activity consists in voicing issues for public debate about what ought to be done, what principles and priorities should guide social life, what policies should be adopted, how the powerful should be held accountable, and what responsibilities citizenship carries. It allows conflict to surface, and proposes means of adjudicating conflict.

Many political associations aim to influence state policy formation or implementation, for example, parties and lobbying organizations, and special-interest associations organizing to influence or protest state policy. Political association also refers to organized forms of public challenge directed at primarily economic institutions without using state policy. Thus a direct demand on The Gap to cease employing poorly paid teenagers in Central America is a political demand, even though it does not involve a claim on the state. Political activity is any activity whose aim is to *politicize* social or economic life, to raise questions about how society should be organized and what actions should be taken to address problems or do justice.

I refer to private, civic, and political association as *levels* of associational activity to indicate the ease of movement from one to another. Some voluntary associations are founded explicitly to move on all three levels. Others shift easily among levels even though they define their mission on one of them primarily. A gay bar, for example, usually serves as a site for private socializing. When it becomes a meeting place and constituency for planning a rally in support of a city ordinance banning discrimination against gays and lesbians, however, it participates in political association. Civic associations often move to a political level when they find that their ability to achieve their civic goals is inhibited by the policies and practices of powerful agents in the state or economy, or when their activities come under public criticism or produce conflict. On the other hand, members of civic or political associations also often engage in private activity of enjoyment or mutual support.

Functions of civil society

To examine the uses and limits of associative activity for democratization and bringing about social justice, we need to move from an ontology of civil society to analysis of how civil society activities effect changes in state, economy, and civil society itself. Cohen and Arato (1992) propose what they call a dualistic theory of civil society with "defensive" and "offensive" aspects. The first aspect refers to the way associations and social movements develop forms of communicative interaction that support identities, expand participatory possibilities, and create networks of solidarity. I call this aspect "self-organization." In the second function, associational activity aims to influence or reform state, and less often corporate, policies and practices. Along with those like Cohen and Arato who work within a broadly Habermasian framework, I refer to this aspect of civil society as the activity of "public spheres" (Cohen and Arato 1992: 523–32; Rodger 1985). Distinguishing the functions of self-organization and public exposure and debate helps clarify how the activities of the associational lifeworld contribute to supporting democracy and social justice.

This two-leveled interpretation of civil society maps onto the three-leveled interpretation I made in the previous section roughly as follows. The *self-organizing* level discussed here includes some activities of *private association*, but not all. Many of the activities of *civic association* belong to the self-organizing aspect, but some belong to or serve as conditions for public spheres. The second set of functions discussed in this section, *public spheres*, largely corresponds to *political association*, but includes some activities of civic association.

Self-organization

In a free society people are liable to form all kinds of associations with diverse identities and goals. Recent praise for civil society often neglects to acknowledge how many of such associations, even when voluntarily entered, are hierarchical or authoritarian in their rule. Associations founded with the intention of being democratic, moreover, are often even more susceptible to autocratic takeover than governments. A great number of voluntary associations, however, are directly democratic. People form and run them according to rules they collectively adopt. To this extent even private associations can be schools of self-government.

Beyond such general virtues of participation, the self-organizing activities of civil society contribute to self-determination, and, to a lesser degree, self-development, by supporting identity and voice, facilitating innovative or minority practices, and providing some goods and services.

Associations and networks of the lifeworld outside state and economy facilitate the meeting of people according to communities of interest, value, or social group perspective. Associations supporting cultural expression grounded in particular communities are especially important for such support of identities and particular social voice. By allowing opportunities for relatively excluded or marginalized people to find each other, meet together, pursue private and civic activities, civil society makes possible the development of voice and idiom for the expression of their experience, interests and needs in public spheres.

In voluntary associations where people coordinate their action by discussion, people sometimes reach for new ideas and practices. Perhaps some people are dissatisfied with the prevailing conventions or they are simply attracted to saying or doing something differently. Whether organic farming, herbal healing, evangelical religious worship, or car pooling, people often form associations in order to develop alternative practices. Many of these turn out to be crank or idiosyncratic; through their dissemination in the public spheres, however, many others come to be widely adopted, thereby facilitating social changes outside any legislative or legal mandates.

Associations of civil society provide many goods and services outside the framework of the state or profit-oriented economy. Non-profit social services, such as tenants' advocates, health services, homeless or battered women's shelters, literacy centers, immigrant or exile settlement support services, after-school youth centers, and so on, are often democratically organized, connected to their communities, and more empowering for clients than state-run services. While producer and consumer cooperatives rarely escape market forces and pressures, they often introduce democratic decision-making or other substantive non-market values into the business process. Many experts and activists in less-developed countries regard civic organizations as important promoters of development: they improve the lives of some disadvantaged people by involving them directly in participatory projects such as small producer cooperatives, credit associations, and self-help housing construction. Civic associations worried about the revitalization of deteriorating inner cities in wealthier societies also aim to meet needs through non-profit, non-governmental associational activity. In the United States non-profit associations such as Community Land Trusts or Habitat for Humanity have supplied units of decent, affordable housing when both government and private developers apparently abandoned the task. Democracy and social justice would be enhanced in most societies if civic associations provided even more goods and services.

Not all of the identities, practices, or goods and services that flourish in civil society are necessarily good; nor do they coexist without conflict. By means of voluntary associations, however, people can take some control over the conditions under which they live and act, support affinities, develop practices, and provide goods and services in ways more under their direct control than activities of state and economy. In these ways civil society directly realizes the value of self-determination, and to a lesser extent self-development.

Public spheres

A major and unique function of civil society is incubation of information, ideas, and images by supporting public fora and media. Places, writings and other cultural expression, and media are *public* in so far as they are in principle accessible to anyone. Public information and opinions aim to communicate to anyone who might see or hear them. Print, visual, and electronic media provide the vital infrastructure for such public discussion. Public spheres crucially support and enlarge democracy by enabling the effective expression of criticism and dissent, pressuring for policy change, and disseminating new social practices.

Ian Shapiro reminds us that, although recent political theory of democracy often fails to thematize the fact, "democracy is as much about opposition to the arbitrary exercise of power as it is about collective self-government" (Shapiro 1996: 582). Public spheres help limit arbitrary power by exposing it, and holding powerful actors accountable. Researchers, journalists, and activists publicize what is going on in the halls of government, and less often in the boardrooms, and expose connections between decisions and consequences (Melucci 1989). An affordable housing coalition demands to know why the city council has approved subsidized loans to developers of downtown office space instead of using the city's money and power to promote affordable housing development. Events that people might have thought of as inevitable thus begin to appear as products of decisions that serve powerful interests.

When civic movements expose power in public discussion and demand that the powerful give an account of themselves, they sometimes simply assert particular interests against others. Often, however, they make moral appeals about justice, rightness, or the collective good, rather than couching their criticism in self-interested terms. Sometimes the force of public moral appeals made by otherwise powerless people effects a change of policy because the powerful agents have been successfully shamed.

In June 1992 tens of thousands of environmental activists from all over the world created a critical civic public in the parks, streets, and hallways of Rio de Janeiro. Their purpose was both to discuss environmental issues among themselves, and to pressure officials at the UN conference to adopt more far-reaching international resolutions to protect species, trees, and people from the damage of pollution and over-consumption. Among other things, they demanded that George Bush, then President of the United States, attend the conference. Rowdy demonstrations witnessed on televisions all over the world accused him of snubbing the world body and not caring about future generations. The protestors did not achieve all their objectives, of course, but their moral appeal did succeed in bringing Bush to Rio, and many analysts credit the non-governmental public sphere in Rio with influencing some of the language of the treaties and resolutions adopted at the conference. Public shame is sometimes the only weapon ordinary citizens have against private economic actors, but sometimes that weapon is powerful. Mexican employees of a US company subsidiary travel north to the site of a board of directors meeting to protest their horrid working conditions, and the press is there. Not long after, the directors take actions aimed at improving conditions.

The critical and oppositional functions of the public spheres of civil society perform irreplaceable functions for democracy. Nearly every society can benefit from enlargement of such critical public activity. Publicly criticizing state or corporate actions, however, is often easier than recommending positive action. Public spheres function to promote democracy and justice also to the extent that they facilitate discussion and debate about what ought to be done, both by the state, economic actors, and groups and individuals in civil society itself. In public spheres organized citizens often debate collective problems and what should be done about them, and organize to influence the policy-makers.

Sometimes public spheres aid social change projects without directly targeting the state or economy. Associational life enables people to experiment with ways of living and doing things, interacting or produc-ing goods and distributing them, and with new norms of symbolic expression, or different ways of organizing associations. Sometimes people believe that these alternative norms and practices would be generally better for the society or some particular disadvantaged group if they were widely adopted. Public spheres then serve to spread the ideas and practices of this alternative.

Many of the changes wrought by the contemporary feminist move-ment, for example, have had this form. Feminists effectively criticized the strong sexual division of labor in the family that makes men the public breadwinner and women the private domestic workers. While sexual equality in the family has by no means been achieved, decades of public discussion of the fairness of traditional arrangements have con-tributed to changes in attitudes and practices by many women and men. One might argue along similar lines that issues such as pornography are best dealt with by means of intrasocial transformation rather than by means of legislation. Attempting to regulate or forbid the publication of books and movies degrading to women is fraught with problems of definition and application, thus endangering legitimate liberty. Femin-ists cannot take a "live and let live" attitude toward such cultural products, however. Public discussion, demonstration, and boycott are useful ways of calling directly on the public for people to examine their behavior and desire.

To summarize, people collectively exercise positive power through civil society in many ways. People acting in civil society develop and disseminate new ideas and practices, organize public criticism of and opposition to state and economic power, form solidarities for both the privileged and the relatively disadvantaged, and invite members of the society to discuss and debate problems either in order to influence change in state or corporate policy, or to foster change in society directly. All these activities refer to the value of self-determination, the primary aspect of social justice that associative activity outside state and economy promotes. To the extent that associative activity enables public expression and recognition of particular cultures and forms of life and provides goods and services, it also contributes to promoting the value of self-development.

The limits of civil society

The rediscovery of civil society, I have suggested thus far, is an important development both in contemporary political theory and practice. Especially when we understand civil society as a third sector outside of and anchoring both state and economy, the theory of civil society reveals powerful means of enhancing democracy and social solidarity. These functions have been relatively neglected by political theorists concentrating on state and economy. Current interest in civil society, however, coincides with new expressions of doubt about, and disaffection with, state institutions. Anti-state sentiment in many parts of the world has helped create conditions for dismantling many state enterprises, regulatory and planning functions, and welfare services. Coincidentally, some political analysts regard civil society more highly than the state as a means for citizens to pursue social justice and well-being.

In this section I challenge this tendency to regard civil society as an alternative site for the performance of public-spirited, caring, and equalizing functions that have long been associated with governments. While civil society can promote democracy, social justice, and well-being in ways I have outlined, there are limits to what citizens can accomplish in civil society alone. Some argue that the fragmentation and plurality of civil society can undermine the trust and solidarity necessary for self-determining democracy (e.g., Levi 1996), and I think that there is merit to this argument. Here I will be more concerned with limits to the ability of civil society to address issues of justice as self-development. Especially because profit- and market-oriented economic activities inhibit the self-development of many people, citizens must rely on states to take positive action to undermine oppression and promote justice. While state power must always be subject to vigilant scrutiny by citizens alert to dangers of corruption and domination, democratic state institutions nevertheless have unique and important virtues for promoting social justice.

I assume that none of those critical of state institutions today deny that states are important for policing, adjudicating conflict, and enforcing basic liberties. Nevertheless, many consider state institutions as necessary evils, which ought to be kept to a minimum and are not to be trusted. We should not look to states, on this view, to take more expansive and substantial action to further the well-being of persons and groups. It is always good to reduce suffering or injustice, solve social problems, and promote well-being; but we should not depend on states to do it. There are at least three kinds of arguments for the claim that citizens should reject reliance on state institutions to solve social problems and promote justice as the equal opportunity for everyone to develop and exercise capacities: libertarian, communitarian, and post-Marxist. I will reconstruct each of these arguments, and then respond to them together.

The libertarian argument is familiar. Maximizing the liberty of individuals and organizations to pursue their own ends is the primary principle of justice. Coercive state institutions are justified only in order to enforce liberty, that is, to prevent some agents from interfering with others' legitimate exercise of their liberty. A society may contain many social and economic problems, many conflicts, injustices, and harmful inequalities. These are more properly addressed by voluntary cooperation in settings of private enterprise and civil society, however, than by means of state regulation. It is wrong to use state institutions to try to produce substantive social outcomes in the way of resource use, income distribution, or the allocation of social positions. Aiming to do so, moreover, is likely to produce irrational or inefficient consequences. Minimizing the reach of state institutions is thus the social ideal.[2]

The communitarian argument differs from the libertarian in its positive concern for substantive values of caring, solidarity, and civic virtue. While communitarians endorse the value of liberty, protection of liberty is but one among several principles that ought to guide moral and political life, and may be overridden for the sake of promoting values of community. Communitarian morality, moreover, aims at fostering and nurturing substantive ends of mutual aid and shared cultural symbols and practices. In preferring institutions of civil society to state institutions for pursuit of the ends of mutual aid, caring, and social justice some communitarians suggest the following grounds. State bureaucratic institutions that provide social services, redistribute income, regulate economic activity, and so on, break down and distort local communities because they universalize and formalize these activities and curtail local autonomy. Government regulatory, redistributive, welfare and social

---

[2] I derive this argument primarily from Milton Friedman (1962). For the idea that it is wrong for state institutions to aim to produce distributive patterns, however, I am thinking of Robert Nozick's argument in *Anarchy, State and Utopia* (Nozick 1974).

service bureaucracies, moreover, transform citizens into passive followers of orders and clients of services. State efforts to promote citizen
well-being, furthermore, allow individuals and communities to shirk
their personal and particular responsibilities to contribute to the well-
being of community members. State actions break up the civic sources
of mutual aid and solidarity. Government programs that aim at substantive ends of equality or self-development generate an "entitlement"
mentality, according to which citizens' clamor for particular benefits to
serve their interests without being willing to make social contributions,
thus ultimately overloading and incapacitating the state. Good citizens
are independent and autonomous, rather than dependent on others, at
the same time that they manifest a commitment to promote the well-
being of others and of the institutions and values of the community.
Thus, rather than create and sustain bureaucratic state institutions to
promote the well-being of citizens, public policy should devote itself to
supporting civic education to instill in citizens a sense of obligation to
others and the skills to organize civic institutions of solidarity and
mutual aid.[3]

I call "post-Marxist" those writers and activists in the socialist tradition who continue to be critical of capitalist economic processes and
who argue for radical democracy, but who also criticize some aspects of
historic Marxism. Post-Marxists express several reasons for turning to
civil society as the arena for pursuing democracy and social justice, and
for taking a distance from the state.

Most socialists traditionally have understood their political project to
consist in using state institutions to control the means of production and
direct them to meeting needs and developing capacities. Some post-
Marxists question this state socialist project because it assumes that the
state can be a single agent outside society, directing its operations as a
whole, instead of understanding the state as part of society. Even if it
holds democratic ideals, moreover, state socialism collapses the distinction between state and economy which helps the lifeworld of civil society
to maintain its freedom and autonomy from coercive regulation (Cohen
and Arato 1992: 40–72, 418, 466, 481). The radical anti-capitalist
pursuit of justice is better thought of as a project of democratizing both
the state, corporate economy, and civil society than bringing all the
production and distribution of goods under democratic state direction.

---

[3] This argument is my own reconstruction which I derive from contemporary public
policy rhetoric in the United States, and from the writings of Amitai Etzioni (1993) and
William Galston (1991). Neither Etzioni nor Galston, however, would be likely to
endorse the complete anti-state formulation I have attributed to the communitarian
position here. Certain versions of African-American community-based self-help discourse might also be said to fall within this general communitarian position.

While most post-Marxists support existing social insurance and welfare programs, they also raise critical questions about capitalist welfare states. Interventionist and redistributive policies in the context of capitalism can be sustained under conditions of rapid growth and relative insulation from foreign competition. Without these conditions, the fiscal and managerial tensions of supporting large welfare states become manifest, and states retreat from economic regulation and welfare provision (Offe 1984; Cohen and Arato 1992: 462–8; Young 1990: chap. 2). Activities to meet needs and provide social services that come under the bureaucratic rationality of the state, moreover, disorganize the democratic communicative potential of family and community, replacing them with normalizing, dominating, and pacifying regulatory regimes to which clients must submit or do without help (Habermas 1984; Fraser 1989).

Like traditional Marxists, finally, some post-Marxists argue that in capitalist societies states do not neutrally represent all social sectors, but rather respond most to the imperatives of capital accumulation. States that try to control investment and service provision in ways that conflict with the interests of big economic actors are faced with capital strike and disinvestment. When states are thus dominated by economic power, social change movements of environmentalists or economic egalitarians are bound to be coopted if they try to work within the state. Movements for social justice should thus limit their activity to pressuring state and economy from outside civil society, and to enlarge the activity of democratic associations and economic cooperatives in that independent sector (Dryzek 1996a and 1996b).

Each of these arguments gives primary value to self-determination. The libertarian position above all values individual self-determination defined as the negative liberty of persons and enterprises. Both communitarians and neo-Marxists hold that libertarians do not recognize how the power of large organizations often seriously inhibits an individual's self-determination, and how the interdependence of modern social life transforms the meaning of self-determination. Because individual well-being depends on communicative and associative relations with others, and because social and economic processes generate collective problems, individuals can determine the conditions of their action primarily as participants in democratic decisions about community affairs. In my view, all three of these arguments tend to forget that social justice involves not only self-determination but also self-development.

I interpret the value of self-development along lines similar to the values Amartya Sen calls equality as capabilities. Just social institutions provide conditions for all persons to learn and use satisfying and expansive skills in socially recognized settings, and enable them to play and communicate with others or express their feelings and perspective on social life in contexts where others can listen. Self-development in this sense certainly entails meeting people's basic needs for food, shelter, health care, and so on. It also entails the use of resources for education and training. With Sen (1993), however, I find focus on the distribution of goods on income per se too limited a way of evaluating justice or well-being (Young 1990: chap. 1). Not only do the different circumstances of people mean that they may need different amounts of goods or income to enable equal levels of capability, but there are aspects of this value of self-development which are only accidentally related to goods or income. Using satisfying skills and having one's particular culture, modes of expression, and ways of life recognized depend on the organization of the division of labor and the structures of communication and cooperation. While self-development is thus not reducible to the distribution of resources, market- and profit-oriented economic processes particularly impinge on the ability of many to develop and exercise capacities. Because this is so, pursuit of justice as self-development cannot rely on the communicative and organizational activities of civil society alone, but requires positive state intervention to regulate and direct economic activity.

Before making that argument, I should make clear that I agree with the post-Marxist critique of state socialism for its totalizing tendencies. State power threatens freedom and self-determination, and should be limited by markets and independent economic enterprise on the one hand, and strong independent networks of civic and political associations, on the other. Confining state institutions to enforcing agreements, adjudicating disputes, and protecting private liberties, however, cedes too much scope for economically based oppression. Social justice requires the mutual limitation of state, economy, and civil society.

Profit- and market-oriented economic processes impede the ability of too many people in most societies and vast numbers worldwide from developing and exercising capacities, due to at least the following factors. Business cycles, along with technological and organizational changes aimed at reducing labor costs, regularly throw people out of work. Commodity markets increasingly favor big producers over the small farmer or craftsperson. Vast numbers of people are thereby economically marginalized, without meaningful work and means of subsistence. Many unemployed people are so worried about survival that they have little time and energy for volunteer contributions to their communities, and many employed people also lack the time. Many currently employed people live at the edge of economic insecurity. This might not count as remediable injustice if there were no resources in the society; both locally and globally, however, there are such vast inequalities of wealth, comfort, and privilege that structural change could enable more people to develop and exercise capacities. Rationalization of production or service delivery to minimize costs per unit often mechanize work or divide it so minutely that performing it does not require learning and using satisfying skills even when the work requires significant concentration. Market-driven investment and pricing decisions encourage the proliferation of gadgets and cheap entertainment at the same time that they fail to provide housing, health care, quality education, and training affordable to everyone. At the same time, markets produce numbers of harmful or socially costly consequences as "externalities" difficult to charge to particular responsible parties, such as pollution, congestion, the need to travel greater distances, despoilation of city and countryside, and other damage to the collective quality of life.

If promoting social justice means that society should aim to make conditions for self-development available for everyone, then these endemic consequences of profit- and market-oriented economic processes ought to be corrected. The most direct and rational response entails, on the one hand, socially directed investment decisions to meet needs, provide education and training, create and maintain quality infrastructure, parks, pleasant and well-lit streets, and other such public spaces; and on the other hand, the organization of the necessary, useful, and artful work of the society so that everyone able to make social contributions has the opportunity to do so.

The associations of civil society certainly can respond to the failures of firms and markets to enable the development exercise of capacities. Civil society alone, however, cannot do the major work of directing investment toward meeting needs and developing skill and usefully employing its members. Ensuring investment in needs, infrastructure, and education and training enough to support self-development for everyone and the organization of the work of society so that everyone who is able does meaningful work requires much society-wide decision-making and coordinated action. Precisely the virtues of civil society, however – voluntary association, decentralization, freedom to start new and unusual things – mitigate against such coordination. Indeed, the activities of civil society may exacerbate problems of inequality, marginalization, and inhibition of the development of capabilities. For persons and groups with greater material and organizational resources are liable to maintain and even enlarge their social advantages through their associational activity. Especially to the extent that their associational life is private, as distinct from civically oriented, their associational activities often reinforce unequal opportunities for developing capabilities. Associations of civil society, moreover, cannot mobilize the amount of resources necessary to create conditions for the self-development of everyone.

State institutions in principle are the most important means of regulating and directing economic life for the sake of the self-development of everyone. Well-organized states accomplish large-scale collective goals and enable individuals and groups to contribute resources and action to collective goals by facilitating social coordination. To manage such coordination states must be centralized and regulative, they must gather useful information, monitor implementation and compliance, and rely on coercion in case of non-compliance. Only states can facilitate the coordination required for a society to ensure investment in needs, skill development and quality infrastructure and environment for everyone, and to organize many necessary and useful occupations so that those not self-employed or working for private enterprise have options for meaningful work. Democratically legitimated states are not necessary evils, but potentially and sometimes actually exhibit uniquely important virtues to support social justice in ways no other social processes do (cf. Goodin 1995).

The claim that citizens ought to promote justice as self-development as well as self-determination, and that state institutions are the most important means of doing so, raises many questions about how this should be done. I have already rejected trying to absorb the entire economy and civil society into the state, because the costs in freedom and efficiency are too great. The social welfare policies of most states, however, fall far short of addressing the issues of social investment priorities and setting conditions so that everyone is able to develop and exercise capacities. Welfare policies tend only to compensate for the social failures to do these things, rather than actually to do them, and this is one of the reasons that welfare states have come under fiscal and moral strain. This chapter aims to make a moral argument for the value and necessity of state-coordinated collective action to complement markets and civil society, and compensate for the harms they can do. Rather than take up questions of policy options in the space remaining, however, I shall close by posing a few objections to this virtuous state position, and briefly answer them.

Libertarians, of course, object that use of the state to promote particular social outcomes wrongly interferes with the liberty of individuals, organizations, and firms. I have assumed that social justice requires that everyone has an equal opportunity to develop and exercise capacities. I have argued that such opportunities are by no means guaranteed by the workings of private enterprise and civil society, and further that profit- and market-oriented economic activity contributes to the inhibition of the capacities of many. As Goodin (1995) argues, the libertarian claim that each should be allowed to attend to his or her own business without interference does not apply where discharging a moral obligation is the business of nobody in particular. Under such circumstances, the collective must discharge the obligation through the state, and it is permissible for the democratic state to do what is necessary to compel everyone to contribute to those moral priorities.

From both communitarians and post-Marxists might come the dependency-domination objection. If states coordinate investment and the division of labor in ways to ensure that everyone can develop and exercise capacities, they do so at the cost of making citizens dependent on state action and submitting them to bureaucratic rules. Society-wide coordination of action through the state does generate formal regulation and bureaucracy which can have pacifying and dominating effects. The proper response to such dangers is not to reject state action to achieve objectives best achieved by governments, but rather to couple that action with the flexibility and critical accountability of civil society. Theorists such as Joel Rogers, Joshua Cohen, and Paul Hirst have offered models of formal and legal regulation of economic activity for the sake of justice and well-being that call for devolving implementation onto participatory civic associations (Rogers and Cohen 1995; Hirst 1993). While I question elements of each of these models, this is nevertheless a useful direction for policy-makers and social movement activists to look for alternatives to a totalizing state that pacifies citizens.

One of the post-Marxist arguments for restricting the pursuit of social justice to activities in civil society may work most directly against the image of the virtuous state I have offered. Do I not assume that the state is a neutral instrument citizens can use to coordinate their collective lives toward particular ends? Is it not rather the case that the very economic powers I argue ought to be regulated for the sake of ensuring social investment in self-development and well-being themselves control and direct states in ways that serve their particular interests? There is considerable truth in this claim, especially in these days of globalization when the ability of most states to fashion policies that will promote the self-development of their citizens is severely hampered by economic powers larger and more powerful than states. Multinational corporations, trade agreements, and financial institutions such as the International Monetary Fund exercise significant power to influence the policies of many states in ways that often make ordinary working and poor people worse off. To the extent that this is a global reality it should be recognized, but not accepted as either necessary or good.

At this point, however, we return to the role of civil society, as the lived world where social and systemic problems are felt, and the world of communicative organizing that, by protest and persuasion, shifts public opinion and the forces that influence state policies. Both social movement activists such as Zapatistas and scholars of international relations appeal to expanded activities of an international civil society as a means for citizens to respond to the economic powers that transcend states. People organized across borders can expose the power of transnational economic actors and work to develop and strengthen democratic international regulation and cooperation. Both within and across societies, strengthening the associative life of civil society for the sake of promoting self-determination and self-development for everyone remains a crucial project. I have argued in this chapter that civil society performs unique functions of social solidarity, identity support, and criticism of state and economic actors. To perform these functions associations must remain independent of, and potentially opposed to, states. I have also argued, however, contrary to a prevalent anti-statist spirit, that the slogan "society against the state" should be matched by "society for the state." We who live in liberal democratic societies with deep injustices cannot address these injustices through free associational life alone. We need strong regulative and coordinating programs mandated through state institutions, strongly linked to participatory and critical civic organizations.

REFERENCES

Cohen, Jean and Andrew Arato. 1992. *Civil Society and Political Theory*. Cambridge, MA: MIT Press.
Chandhoke, Neera. 1995. *State and Civil Society*. Berkeley, CA: Sage Publications.
Dryzek, John. 1996a. "Political inclusion and the dynamics of democratization." *American Political Science Review* 90(1): 475–87.
  1996b. *Democracy in Capitalist Times*. Oxford: Oxford University Press.
Etzioni, Amitai. 1993. *The Spirit of Community*. New York: New York Times Books.
Fraser, Nancy. 1989. "Struggle over needs." In Nancy Fraser (ed.), *Unruly Practices*, pp. 161–90. Minneapolis: University of Minnesota Press.
Friedman, Milton. 1962. *Capitalism and Freedom*. Chicago: University of Chicago Press.
Galston, William. 1991. *Liberal Purposes*. Cambridge: Cambridge University Press.
Goodin, Robert. 1995. "The state as a moral agent." In Robert Goodin,

Utilitarianism as a Public Philosophy, pp. 28–46. Cambridge: Cambridge University Press.

Habermas, Jürgen. 1984. *Theory of Communicative Action*, Vol. II. Boston: Beacon Press.

——— 1996. *Between Facts and Norms*. Translated by William Rehg. Cambridge, MA: MIT Press.

Hirst, Paul. 1993. *Associative Democracy*. Amherst: University of Massachusetts Press.

Levi, Margaret. 1996. "Social and unsocial capital: a review essay of Robert Putnam's *Making Democracy Work.*" *Politics and Society* 24(1): 45–55.

Melucci, Alberto. 1989. *Nomads of the Present: Social Movements and Individual Needs in Contemporary Society*. London: Radius Publishers.

Nozick, Robert. 1974. *Anarchy, State and Utopia*. Cambridge, MA: Harvard University Press.

Nielsen, Kai. 1995. "Reconceptualizing civil society for now: some somewhat Gramscian turnings." In Michael Walzer (ed.), *Towards a Global Civil Society*, pp. 41–68. Providence: Berghan Books.

Pettit, Philip. 1997. *Republicanism*. Oxford: Oxford University Press.

Putnam, Robert. 1993. *Making Democracy Work: Civic Traditions in Modern Italy*. Princeton: Princeton University Press.

Offe, Claus. 1984. *Contradictions of the Welfare State*. Cambridge, MA: MIT Press.

Rodger, John J. 1985. "On the degeneration of the public sphere." *Political Studies* 32: 203–17.

Rogers, Joel, and Joshua Cohen. 1995. *Associations and Democracy*. London: Verso.

Sen, Amartya. 1993. *Rethinking Inequality*. Cambridge, MA: Harvard University Press.

Shapiro, Ian. 1996. "Elements of democratic justice." *Political Theory* 24(4): 124–51.

Tester, Keith. 1992. *Civil Society*. London: Routledge.

Walzer, Michael. 1995. "The idea of civil society." In Michael Walzer (ed.), *Toward a Global Civil Society*, pp. 7–27. Providence: Bergham Books.

Young, Iris Marion. 1990. *Justice and the Politics of Difference*. Princeton: Princeton University Press.

9   Republican freedom and contestatory democratization

Philip Pettit

The apparatus of the state may often have the effect of reducing violations of freedom by non-governmental agents and agencies; a standard rationale of government is precisely that it secures such a result. But even if the state reduces non-governmental violations of freedom, there is a question as to whether it itself is a source of distinct infringements. Does its possession and exercise of coercive powers mean that even if it reduces overall violations of freedom, for example, it does so by virtue of itself reducing people's freedom in certain regards? Does it mean that, however beneficent in its ultimate effects on the enjoyment of freedom, the state as such is unfriendly to freedom?

One tradition, associating democracy and freedom, suggests that democratizing government – bringing government under the control of the governed – is a means whereby the freedom-friendliness of the state can be promoted and even perfected. The idea is that, putting aside the matter of how well a state does in reducing violations of freedom by other, private agencies, a properly democratized state will necessarily be freedom-friendly: the coercive actions it takes will not offend against the freedom of those coerced, or at least not offend in the manner of coercion by a private agent or an undemocratic state.

This chapter addresses the question of whether there is anything in this thought. I take it for granted that a democratized state may or may not do better than an undemocratized one in reducing violations of liberty by other, private agents and in promoting overall freedom. I ask whether a democratized state, just in virtue of being democratized, will itself represent a lesser assault – or perhaps even no assault at all – on the liberty of its citizens.

The chapter is in three sections. The first examines the impact of construing the question, first under the modern conception of freedom as non-interference, and then under the older, republican conception of freedom as non-domination; the argument here is that only the republican conception holds out any hope for sustaining the claim that democratization can make government freedom-friendly. The second looks at how far electoral democratization can make for friendliness towards republican freedom, emphasizing the limitations of what can be achieved along this route. Then the third section introduces the notion of contestatory democratization and argues that making a democracy contestatory as well as electoral would be bound to make government more freedom-friendly (see Pettit 1997: chap. 6; see too Pettit 1996). Government would continue to restrict the range of activity in which people can enjoy freedom – in the way natural obstacles may restrict it – but government would not tend to violate that freedom in the primary sense of violation: it would condition people's freedom, as I put the distinction, but not necessarily compromise it.

The contestatory mode of democratization that I describe relates to the electoral in the way that editorial control of a text – say, a newspaper article – relates to the control enjoyed by an author. Under electoral democracy the collective people are the authors, direct or indirect, of public decisions. Under the contestatory mode, they would enjoy the power of contesting such decisions in relatively impartial forums – though in an individual, not necessarily a collective, capacity – and they would thereby have the opportunity to edit rather than to author the laws. The contestatory mode of democratization will have interest, I hope, for people in a variety of traditions and will appeal on a number of different grounds. But my own argument for it here will be grounded entirely in how it connects with republican freedom (for a more general defense, see Pettit, forthcoming).

1   The question of democracy and freedom

Three concepts of liberty

Isaiah Berlin (1958) is famous for the distinction that he drew between two concepts of individual liberty, one negative, the other positive (see also Berlin 1969). Under the negative concept, liberty requires the absence of interference by others, where interference is understood broadly to mean any intentional form of obstruction or coercion. Under the positive concept, liberty requires a presence rather than an absence: the presence, in particular, of self-mastery. This ideal of self-mastery is variously interpreted. Sometimes it connotes the psychological ability to master passion with reason, the lower self with the higher self. At other times it is taken to mean the right to participate in the democratic self-determination of the local community; it corresponds to the liberty of the ancients that Benjamin Constant (1988) had contrasted, early in the last century, with the liberty of the moderns: in effect, with negative liberty. This allegedly ancient liberty is sometimes given a Rousseau-esque cast under which it represents the ability to master particular inclinations with a general, socially orientated will; hence its connection with the notion of self-mastery.

I believe that Berlin's dichotomy, and indeed the narrower dichotomy with which Constant worked, both overlook the traditional republican way of thinking about liberty. The republican conception of liberty is akin to the negative one in maintaining that what liberty requires is the absence of something, not necessarily the presence. It is akin to the positive conception, however, in holding that that which must be absent has to do with mastery rather than interference. Freedom consists, not in the presence of self-mastery, and not in the absence of interference by others, but rather in the absence of mastery by others: in the absence, as I prefer to put it, of domination. Freedom just is non-domination.

One person is dominated by another, so I shall assume, to the extent that the other person has the capacity to interfere in their affairs, in particular the capacity to interfere in their affairs on an arbitrary basis. The capacity to interfere on an arbitrary basis is the sort of capacity that a master has in relation to a slave or subject. It is the capacity to interfere in a person's life without regard to their perceived interests. In the most salient case it is the capacity to interfere as the interferer's wish or judgment – their *arbitrium* – inclines them.

If freedom means non-domination, then such freedom is compromised whenever a person is exposed to the arbitrary power of another, even if that power is not used against them. Unlike freedom as non-interference, then, it is inconsistent with subjugation to another. It is inconsistent with being anyone else's slave or subject, even the slave or subject of a person who never actually interferes. That, indeed, is the primary contrast between the two ideals. A person's expectation of freedom as non-interference may be at a maximum in a situation of vulnerability to a particular, other person: that other may be an effective protector against third parties and may be benign enough never to be inclined toward interference themselves. But the person's expectation of freedom as non-domination is hardly going to be maximized under such a benevolent protectorate. Although unlikely to interfere, the protector still retains the power of interfering, and of interfering on an arbitrary basis. However improbable such arbitrary interference may be, it remains accessible to the protecting agency and so that agency represents a dominating presence in the life of the person protected: that person depends on the good will of the protector and lives, in effect, at his or her mercy.

But if freedom means non-domination, then there is also going to be a secondary contrast with the negative concept of liberty. Freedom as non-interference is compromised by any form of interference, even the interference of an agency that is not arbitrary: an agency that is constrained to interfere only in a way that accords with the perceived interests of the person interfered with. Freedom as non-domination, however, will not be lost under such an arrangement. The person may suffer interference but so far as the interference is really constrained to track their perceived interests – so far as it does not come of an arbitrary power – to that extent it does not represent a form of domination: the interferer does not stand over them in the way a master stands over a slave or subject.

Why associate the conception of freedom as non-domination with the republican tradition (see Pettit 1997)? This is the broad tradition associated with Cicero at the time of the Roman republic; with Machiavelli – "the divine Machiavel" of the *Discourses* – and various other writers of the Renaissance Italian republics; with James Harrington, Algernon Sydney, and even "old liberals" such as John Locke, in and after the period of the English civil war and commonwealth; and with the many theorists of republic or commonwealth – with the commonwealthmen, as they were often called – in eighteenth-century England, America, and France (Pagden 1987; Pocock 1975; Raab 1965; Robbins 1959; Skinner 1978; Worden 1991). It was eighteenth-century thinkers of this republican stamp who were responsible for the publication of texts such as *Cato's Letters* and *The Federalist Papers*. They included less radical individuals such as Montesquieu and Blackstone – the author of the famous commentary on the laws of England – as well as the anti-monarchists responsible for the United States Constitution and for the various declarations emanating from revolutionary France. If they did not seek a political republic, settling instead for a constitutional monarchy, they still espoused a complex of ideas – in particular, I would argue, a conception of freedom as non-domination – that linked them with the republican tradition.

Quentin Skinner and other historians have shown that the long republican tradition did not embrace the positive concept of liberty, despite what Berlin and Constant may have suggested (Skinner 1984 and 1990). In particular, they did not embrace a concept of liberty under which being free is just being part of a self-determining democracy; they did not embrace the liberty of the ancients, as Constant described it. The important point to register is that notwithstanding later reconstruals of the tradition as Athenian in origin and as committed to one-eyed enthusiasm about democracy and participation, the tradition was essentially neo-Roman in character (Skinner 1997). It originated in an enthusiasm for the Roman republican constitution, with its complex web of checks and balances – a web in which democratic participation was but one element – and in a distaste for the pure democracy represented in many minds by classical Athens: this was always likened, in Polybius's metaphor, to a ship without a captain, buffeted by the winds of public opinion (Sellers 1995; Pettit 1998).

But though the republican tradition did not embrace the positive concept of liberty, still it is hard to ascribe the negative concept of liberty to republican or commonwealth authors. In the broad way of thinking that is shared among such authors we find a pair of themes that reveal a conception of freedom, not as non-interference, but as non-domination (Pettit 1997; see too Skinner 1997).

The first theme is that even the non-interfering mastery of the kindly boss is sufficient to take away a person's freedom: the slave is a slave, and therefore someone unfree, no matter how gentle the yoke. As Algernon Sydney (1990 [1751]: 441) put it, "he is a slave who serves the best and gentlest man in the world, as well as he who serves the worst," or as it was put by Richard Price (1991: 77–8) in the eighteenth century, "Individuals in private life, while held under the power of masters, cannot be denominated free, however equitably and kindly they may be treated."

The second theme is that, even if non-interfering mastery is inimical to freedom, non-mastering interference is not: in particular, the non-mastering interference that the tradition associated – rightly or wrongly – with certain forms of law is not sufficient to compromise people's freedom. The laws of a well-constituted republic may reduce the number of choices available to a person – they may reduce the range of territory over which the person enjoys their freedom – but so far as they are not arbitrary, so far as they are required to track people's common perceived interests, they will not compromise people's freedom. They may condition the exercise of liberty in the manner of natural limitations and obstacles but they will not violate that liberty in the sense of dominating people; unlike the laws of an absolute monarch, so these authors all urge – this claim shall be illustrated later – they will not represent the presence of an arbitrary power in people's lives.[1]

---

[1] Freedom as non-interference is compromised by interference but it is conditioned by natural obstacles: these reduce the scope for exercising the freedom. Freedom as non-domination is compromised by domination but it is conditioned by any factors that reduce the scope for exercising it without actually occasioning domination; these factors will include non-mastering forms of interference – perhaps certain forms of law – as well as natural obstacles. Theorists of freedom as non-interference recognize this distinction when they distinguish formal and effective or real freedom: the latter requires resources with which to overcome certain natural limitations as well as the absence of interference. See Van Parijs 1995.

So much by way of introducing Berlin's two concepts of liberty and the republican alternative. The question with which we are concerned here is whether there is any mode of democratization that is bound to make government more freedom-friendly. And that question, so we can now see, can bear different interpretations. This question will be discussed here under the republican interpretation only but in order to help justify that focus I shall first examine its interpretation under the negative concept of liberty. This examination will provide an important background for what follows and it will also help to show why the republican version of the question is of particular interest.

Democratization and freedom as non-interference

Suppose we interpret freedom, then, in the negative sense of non-interference. Is there any mode of democratization such that democratizing government in that way would necessarily increase its friendliness to freedom as non-interference? The received wisdom on this question is that democracy and negative freedom are quite distinct ideals and that there is no necessary connection of the kind envisaged. It may be true as a matter of contingent fact that democratic governments violate people's freedom less, say because there is less corruption and less abuse of power. But as Berlin (1969: 130) himself formulates the orthodoxy, "there is no necessary connection between individual liberty and democratic rule."

Some recent authors are more optimistic than Berlin about finding a certain connection between democratization and freedom-friendliness, in particular friendliness to freedom as non-interference. Stephen Holmes (1995: 206) has argued that any feasible mode of democratization – any mode of democratization that does not place an impossible burden on public decision-making – will have to give people the private rights associated with negative liberty, thereby taking issues of private life off the public agenda. And Jürgen Habermas (1996: 142) has urged that a proper, deliberative form of democracy is bound to give such rights to the citizenry, since they are a *sine qua non* of deliberative participation in government.

But whether or not we go along with this limited optimism, there is one striking respect in which Berlin's pronouncement remains correct. If we think of freedom as non-interference, then we have to say that all forms of coercive law themselves represent types of interference – coercion, under standard views, is a form of interference – and we have to admit that democratizing the laws does nothing in itself to reduce this particular way in which government is unfriendly to negative freedom.

The observation is important because those who first introduced the negative way of thinking about freedom did so with a particular relish in this result. They exulted in the fact that if freedom is non-interference, then all law is pro tanto an offence against freedom. This enabled them to say, as they all wished to say, that from the point of view of freedom there is no important difference between republican and arbitrary – or between democratized and undemocratized – forms of law.

Thomas Hobbes was the first important thinker to represent freedom as non-interference and he was also the first to exploit this fact. Wishing to defend the law of a more or less despotic *Leviathan* – the only guarantee, as he thought, of effective peace – his definition of liberty as non-interference enabled him to point out that freedom exists only in the silence of the laws and that the democratic form of law that we find in a republic such as Lucca is no more friendly towards freedom than the arbitrary sort that exists in a despotism such as Constantinople. "Whether a Commonwealth be Monarchical, or Popular, the Freedome is still the same" (Hobbes 1968 [1651]: 266).

Hobbes's redefinition of freedom was used to a similar, anti-democratic effect in two other important interventions in seventeenth- and eighteenth-century politics. In defending absolute monarchy, Sir Robert Filmer relied on the redefinition to make an explicit case against democracy: "there are more laws in popular estates than anywhere else, and so consequently less liberty" (Filmer 1991 [c. 1635]: 275). And John Lind, an apologist for Lord North's government, used it to justify British rule in the American colonies. Richard Price and others in the commonwealthman tradition had argued that the power of British law in America was arbitrary and dreadful because the British parliament, however benignly disposed, could act as it willed in colonial affairs. Lind countered that all law is dreadful, being inimical to freedom – freedom as non-interference – and that the Americans were no worse off than the British themselves. "Dreadful as this power may be, let me ask you, Sir, if this same power is not exercised by the same persons over all the subjects who reside in all the other parts of this same empire? – It is" (Lind 1776: 114).

The conception of freedom as non-interference first became associated with a progressive movement in the work of utilitarians such as Jeremy Bentham and William Paley. In correspondence with Lind, Bentham claimed to have discovered this way of thinking about freedom and saw it from the first as a cornerstone of his system (Long 1977: 54). Like Hobbes, he was always clear that if freedom is non-interference then every coercive law, no matter how democratic in provenance, represents in itself a violation of freedom; Bentham was content to tolerate such violations to the extent that they made for fewer offences overall and for a higher level of aggregate utility. "As against the coercion applicable by individual to individual, no liberty can be given to one man but in proportion as it is taken from another. All coercive laws, therefore ... and in particular all laws creative of liberty, are, as far as they go, abrogative of liberty" (Bentham 1843: 503).

Whether or not Holmes and Habermas are right, then, it remains a fact that the negative conception of freedom as non-interference forces us in one important respect to say that democratization is not bound to make government more freedom-friendly. On the contrary, as was emphasized in the earliest uses of the conception, it is bound to be the case that democratization does nothing to relieve the essential enmity that exists between coercive law or government, on the one hand, and individual freedom on the other.

Democratization and freedom as non-domination

With this result in hand, let us turn now to the significance of our question when freedom is interpreted, not as non-interference, but rather as non-domination. Is there any mode of democratization available such that it is bound to make government more friendly to the freedom of people in this republican sense? Is there any form of democratization that is bound to reduce or even remove the possibility of government itself being arbitrary and dominating in its treatment of individuals?

There is no conceivable form of democratization that would be bound to reduce the interference – the violation of freedom as non-interference – inherent in coercive legislation: all coercive legislation, democratic or otherwise, is unfriendly as such to freedom as non-interference. But no parallel lesson, no similar impossibility result, goes through for democratization and freedom as non-domination. For it is not the case that all coercive laws are unfriendly as such to freedom as non-domination. On the contrary, laws will be friendly to people's freedom as non-domination – they will not themselves dominate people – so far as they are forced to track the perceived interests of those on whom they are imposed and do not represent an arbitrary form of interference. Thus democratization is bound to make government more freedom-friendly if it can increase the non-arbitrariness of legislation, adjudication, and administration.

The point has an important historical resonance. In their anti-republican arguments, Hobbes was opposed by the great republican, James Harrington; Filmer was opposed by the hero of the later commonwealthman tradition, John Locke; and Lind was explicitly opposed, of course, to the pro-American commonwealthman, Richard Price. And these opponents uniformly insist, against the drift of their respective adversaries, that far from being inherently inimical to freedom, law – they always have coercive law in mind – is an essential part of its infrastructure. The idea is not the Benthamite theme that while law as such compromises liberty, still it may do more good than harm: it may prevent more violations than it perpetrates. The idea, rather, is that law need not exemplify the sort of thing that compromises liberty; in particular, it need not exemplify the presence of arbitrary power.

Harrington (1992 [c. 1771]: 8) sets himself squarely against the Hobbesian vision in arguing that there is a world of difference between the non-dominating empire of laws and the arbitrary empire that men may exercise over one another. Thus he sees a contrast, not a commonality, in the positions of people who live in despotic Constantinople and republican Lucca: "whereas the greatest bashaw is a tenant, as well of his head as of his estate, at the will of his lord, the meanest Lucchese that hath land is a freeholder of both, and not to be controlled but by the law" (Harrington 1992 [c. 1771]: 20).

More than thirty years later Locke sets himself equally strongly against the position of Filmer. He argues for a "freedom from Absolute, Arbitrary Power" as the essential thing in a good polity (Locke 1965 [1681]: 325), and, in explicit opposition to Filmer, he sees law as creative of freedom: "that ill deserves the Name of Confinement which serves to hedge us in only from Bogs and Precipices . . . the end of Law is not to abolish or restrain, but to preserve and enlarge Freedom" (Locke 1965 [1681]: 348).

The commonwealthmen who provided Lind's opposition are just as insistent on the theme in the century following. Price (1991: 81), Lind's avowed adversary, is particularly forthright. "Just government . . . does not infringe liberty, but establishes it. It does not take away the rights of mankind but protect(s) and confirm(s) them."

Let us take it, then, that whereas coercive law is inherently unfriendly to freedom as non-interference, it is not inherently unfriendly to freedom as non-domination. Coercive law may condition the exercise of liberty in the manner of natural limitations and obstacles, as we noted earlier, but it need not violate or compromise that liberty in the sense of dominating people. So far as law and government can be made non-arbitrary in character, to that extent they will not constitute a form of domination and will not represent a compromise of republican freedom.

This observation means that the question about democratization has real potential when freedom is interpreted in the republican way. We can ask whether there is a mode of democratization which is bound to make government more freedom-friendly, and we can ask this with an open mind. We need not succumb to the sort of impossibility theorem on which Hobbes and Filmer and Lind were so anxious, for their different strategic reasons, to insist.

2   Electoral democratization and its limitations

The benefits of electoral democratization

Let us assume that in any society that is fit to become a polity there is a potential for certain common, perceived interests to crystallize; if there were not, then it is hard to see how political organization could serve any purpose other than the suppression of some by others.[2] These interests will presumably encompass unobjectionable public goods – goods from which no one can readily be excluded – such as external and internal peace, a stable framework for commercial and civic relations, a sustainable but high level of economic activity, and so on.

The assumption means that from the point of view of freedom as non-domination, it is always better to have an arrangement under which the possibility of government's being indifferent to the common, perceived interests of ordinary people is reduced or removed. Thus the great anathema in the republican tradition is the rule of a prince who is capable, if only within certain broad limits, of doing as he wills. Such a ruler is free to ignore the common, perceived interests of people in the coercive legislation and taxation to which he subjects them and so he will hold a dominating position in the society. Tom Paine's (1989 [1794]: 168) complaint against monarchy catches the point very nicely: "It means arbitrary power in an individual person; in the exercise of which, *himself*, and not the *res-publica*, is the object."

For similar reasons there is absolute resistance within the tradition to the idea of foreign or colonial government, however benign. This resistance is well expressed in Joseph Priestley's articulation of the complaint made by the American colonists against government from London. On his reading of that complaint, it is little consolation that the government may be fairly benign, taxing the Americans only for "one penny"; the problem is that this government has the power, without

---

[2] In Pettit 1997 I argue that a relevant image of the collective interests of those in any society – the common good – can be derived from the needs of providing each with the fullest enjoyment possible of freedom as non-domination. That is to say that I invoke the republican ideal of freedom, not just to derive the forms – democratic and other – that government ought to instantiate, but also to derive the goals that it ought to pursue. See Pettit forthcoming for a different approach.

being forced to look to the interests of Americans, to tax them for their "last penny."

Q. What is the great grievance that those people complain of? A. It is their being taxed by the parliament of Great Britain, the members of which are so far from taxing themselves, that they ease themselves at the same time. ... For by the same power, by which the people of England can compel them to pay *one penny*, they may compel them to pay the *last penny* they have. (Priestley 1993: 140)

The need for government to be forced to track the common, perceived interests of citizens argues for an electoral form of democratization. Under such democratization, the occupants of certain key positions in government are determined by periodic elections that have a popular character: in general, no competent adult is excluded from participating in them – no one is prevented from standing or voting in the elections, for example, or from speaking about election issues – and no one's vote is worth more than anyone else's. And the rules whereby those in government operate – and are periodically and popularly elected – are themselves subject to popular control: they can generally be altered by popular referendum or by the determination of the popularly elected representatives.

Setting up such an electoral regime involves democratizing government – bringing it under the control of the governed – so far as the governed are given the power to choose and reject a government: in particular, to do so on the basis of its actual or expected performance in identifying and furthering collective interests. The republican argument for such a regime – and of course the regime is subject to many variations – is that it holds out a good prospect of forcing government to track the common, perceived interests of the populace. It puts government under a constraint that ought to guard against arbitrariness in that respect. Under a popular, periodic electoral system, whatever its other features, those in government will be unlikely to be re-elected if they display indifference to common, perceived interests. And in that respect there is a deep contrast with dictatorial or colonial regimes. Indeed, there is also a contrast with the sort of regime under which officers of government would be appointed by lot.

The limitations of electoral democracy

This attitude to electoral democracy may explain why the achievement of parliamentary rule, after the execution of Charles I, was much celebrated – and had, of course, been sought – by thinkers within the republican or commonwealthman tradition. Some even suggested that nothing more was needed to ensure that no one – or at least no one among the effective citizenry of propertied, mainstream males – was dominated by government. They argued that "Kings seduced may injure the commonwealth, but that Parliaments cannot." Why so? Because "the Parliament men are no other than our selves," so that "their judgment is our judgment, and they that oppose the judgment of Parliament oppose their own judgment" (Morgan 1988: 64).

This line of thought, if sound, would provide an argument for thinking that electoral democratization is not just an advance over dictatorial or colonial rule, but that it is sufficient in itself to ensure that government is freedom-friendly towards electors: to ensure that the coercive actions of government do not represent, even pro tanto, an assault on the freedom of those people. Letting the alleged identity of parliament and people pass, we might cast the reasoning in the following syllogistic form.

1. People will not be dominated by a government to the extent that it is under their control.
2. Under elective democratization, direct or representative, the people effectively control the government: they govern themselves.

Conclusion. And so in such a democracy it cannot be that people are significantly dominated by government.

But the line of thought encapsulated here is not sound. The word "people" in the first premise and in the conclusion is understood differently from how "the people" is naturally taken in the second premise. "People," without the article, refers to individuals taken severally or distributively – to individuals taken one by one – whereas "the people" with the article refers to a collectivity. Thus the syllogism is undermined by a fallacy of equivocation. For all that the reasoning shows, it is quite possible that the people, understood collectively, should dominate the people, understood severally; the collective people can be as uncontrolled an agency, from the point of view of at least some individuals, as the divinely endorsed king.

The problem with the argument can be put more pointedly. Electoral democracy may mean that government cannot be wholly indifferent to popular perceptions about common interests and that it cannot fail altogether to try and advance those interests. But it is quite consistent with electoral democracy that government should only track the perceived interests of a majority, absolute or relative, on any issue and that it should have a dominating aspect from the point of view of others.

The reasoning in the democracy syllogism did not prove to be persuasive, even in the seventeenth century. Royalists, as might be expected, argued that the collective people can be an arbitrary, even a wayward, agency: a body "in continuall alteration and change, it never continues one minute the same, being composed of a multitude of parts, whereof divers continually decay and perish, and others renew and succeed in their places" (Morgan 1988: 61). But the point was also taken on the republican side. Thus a leader of the Levellers argued that the purpose of government was the "severall weales, safeties and freedomes" of people – the word "severall" is important – and that their protection required checking the power of the people in their collective, parliamentary incarnation (Morgan 1988: 71).

The idea here, and it became a centrepiece of commonwealthman thought, was that from the point of view of some individuals the majoritarian people could be a tyrant in the same way – if not with the same ease or over the same range – as the absolute monarch. It was well expressed in the last century in a dissertation prepared by the great historian, F. W. Maitland. Commenting on what he called the conventional theory of government, according to which the people are the only source of authority – there is no divine right of kings – he wrote: "If the conventional theory leads to an ideally perfect democracy – a state in which all that the majority wishes to be law, and nothing else, is law – then it leads to a form of government under which the arbitrary exercise of power is most certainly possible. Thus, as it progresses, the conventional theory seems to lose its title to be called the doctrine of civil liberty, for it ceases to be a protest against arbitrary forms of restraint" (Maitland 1981: 84).

The tyranny of the majority

The mistake that Maitland identifies is often characterized by saying that the elective mode of democratization, direct or representative, can lead to a tyranny of the majority. The problem is not confined to a divided society in which one and the same majority – a religious or ethnic or ideological formation – dictates to others on a wide variety of issues. The problem in question arises even in societies that are relatively homogeneous and cohesive. It consists in the fact that, constituted as an agent by electoral arrangements, the collectivity has the power to treat certain individuals in a way that does not necessarily track their perceived interests. It stands over individuals in the way a master stands over a slave or subject.

Of course every government will fail to track some of the perceived interests of citizens. For it may be presumed that from the point of view of any individual, their perceived interests would be served best of all if government made a favourable exception in how they were treated: if it taxed others but not them; if it punished others for certain crimes but not them; and so on. The problem in the tyranny of the majority is not that this may happen: that would scarcely constitute a tyranny, given that there is no way of satisfying people's shared, perceived interest in having a common government without frustrating such special, unavowable interests.

We should distinguish between the politically avowable, perceived interests of people from their unavowable ones. The politically avowable interests are those, roughly, that are consistent with the desire to live under a shared scheme that treats no one as special (cf. Barry 1995; Scanlon 1982). They are the interests that those who are expected to give a system of government their allegiance may reasonably expect government to track. The problem with the tyranny of the majority is that government may be so constituted that in identifying or pursuing common interests, it is not forced to take account of the avowable, perceived interests of a minority. It can ignore these and be driven solely by the concerns of a majority. It can identify interests that only involve that supportive majority as common interests; it can take its cue only from the perceptions of the majority in identifying common interests; or it can pursue common interests – perhaps common, perceived, interests – in a manner that lays most of the costs of the pursuit on the minority.

The tyranny of the majority gives the lie to any suggestion that the elective mode of democratization is bound fully to ensure the friendliness of government to freedom, in particular to freedom as non-domination. Electoral democracy may amount to nothing short of an "elective despotism," as James Madison described it in 1787 (Madison, Hamilton, and Jay 1987 [1787–8]) or an "elective dictatorship" (Hailsham 1978: 127). There are three more or less obvious ways – I do not say that they are exhaustive – in which an absolute or relative majority may form on any issue and may dominate others in the society: that is, may impose a form of treatment on those others that is indifferent to perceived interests that have just as good a call to be heeded as their own. The collectivity may tyrannize certain individuals under a regime of majoritarian interest, majoritarian passion, or majoritarian righteousness.

Majoritarian interest rules when, regardless of the cost to others, a suitable number of people find their interest directing them to vote a certain way or to support representatives who are disposed to vote that way. For an example imagine that a majority of people do not have open fires in their homes and that they vote out of environmental considerations to ban such fires, oblivious to the perceived interests of a perhaps small minority – we may suppose, a poor minority – for whom open fires are the only source of heat. I pick the example to emphasize the fact that majoritarian interest may rule, not just in cases where self-seeking lobbies manage to carry the day – not just when factional interest groups prevail (Sunstein 1993a) – but even in cases where people are distinctively public-spirited.

Majoritarian passion rules when, regardless of long-term, aggregate effects, popular enthusiasm or outrage leads a majority of voters to adopt or demand a governmental line that imposes arbitrarily on a certain minority of individuals. For an example consider how the occurrence of heinous offences, say by offenders on parole, can lead to a progressive, often counterproductive stiffening of penal sentences and practices. In this particular case the tyranny of the majority becomes, in Montesquieu's (1989 [c. 1748]: 203) memorable phrase, a "tyranny of the avengers."

Majoritarian righteousness rules, finally, when each voter in a referendum or election uses their vote primarily as a way of expressing their personal, often heartfelt stand on some issue of moral or religious significance: say, on whether brothels should be legal, on whether soft drugs should be allowed, or on whether abortion should be available. When people vote in this way they do not take account of the fact that often the stand in question will never be successfully implemented as a social policy and that the attempt to implement it will result in an extremely bad situation from the point of view of many people: a situation in which prostitutes become the slaves of pimps, those dependent on drugs become vulnerable to suppliers, and women who want abortions are forced to put their lives in the hands of back-street, unregulated clinics.

This last form of collective tyranny is particularly threatening, since there are grounds for arguing that in a large-scale, secret election or referendum, the most rational stance for a voter to take is to use their vote for the pleasure of expressive satisfaction. Their chance of affecting the outcome in a large-scale poll is close to zero and a secret vote does not provide an opportunity for engaging with others. Being instrumentally and socially insignificant, then, the only prospect of satisfaction that the vote may represent is the satisfaction of voting according to personal feeling and commitment (see Brennan and Lomasky 1993; Brennan and Pettit 1990).

I stress the various forms in which the tyranny of a majority may materialize in order to underscore the real danger involved and to rescue a recognition of that threat from the jading effects of the cliché. What makes the danger particularly significant is that however arbitrary the collective majoritarian will may be on any issue, it is a will which we may have real discursive difficulty in challenging and criticizing. If you oppose that will, after all, you expose yourself to the charge of being elitist and of not having faith in the wisdom of ordinary people. By a curious irony, the language of egalitarian respect for ordinary people gives a sort of moral immunity to a force that may represent the most serious threat of all to the freedom as non-domination of certain individuals.

3   Towards contestatory democratization

The notion of contestatory democratization

We saw that so far as it is meant to show that electoral democracy will eliminate all domination, the democracy syllogism is vitiated by a fallacy of equivocation. The elimination of domination would require, not just that the people considered collectively cannot be ignored by government, but also that people considered severally or distributively cannot be ignored either. Otherwise put, it would require not just that the majority are heard in determining what common, perceived interests ought to be pursued by government, but also that relevant minorities also get a hearing: their politically avowable, perceived interests are not just ignored and flouted. So the question is whether there is any way of subjecting government to a mode of distributive or minority control in order to balance the electorally established mode of collective or majority control.

There is one salient mode of democratization under which people in the several or distributive sense would have control of government. This is the arrangement under which each would have a veto on any public decision, and each could ensure that public decisions tracked their perceived interests, or at least their avowable, perceived interests (see Buchanan and Tullock 1962). While the vetoing mode of democratization would certainly make government more friendly towards freedom as non-domination, however, it does not have more than an abstract, purely academic interest. The reason is that no vetoing scheme of things has the remotest chance of being instituted; it is a wholly infeasible mode of public decision-making.

The reason the vetoing scheme is infeasible is that it would undermine the possibility of compromise.[3] Suppose that the common, perceived interests of a community clearly require a certain line of action: say, erecting a power plant, providing a needle-exchange centre for drug addicts, or closing down certain schools. There is no way of achieving

---

[3] For an attempt to show the importance of compromise in a republican conception of deliberative democracy, see Bellamy forthcoming.

such a goal without some people faring worse than others: no one wants to have a power plant or a needle-exchange centre on their doorstep and few will want their neighborhood school to be closed down. If the common interest is to be advanced, therefore, the decision-making procedure has to allow for some people to be treated less well than others. And a vetoing scheme would hardly fit the bill, since it would enable those from every quarter to rule out anything that damaged them.

If there is to be a feasible way of subjecting government to distributive or minority control, therefore, it had better allow for the possibility that there are winners and losers in many public decisions. But won't the losers be dominated under any such decision-making procedure and won't their freedom be to that extent undermined? Not necessarily. If the procedure is impartial, in the sense of not being stacked in favour of any of the relevant, conflicting interests – if the decision is made just on the basis of what course of action would best promote the shared goal – then those who come off worse are unlucky but they are not subject to interference on an arbitrary basis: their avowable interests will be taken into account just as much as the interests of those more fortunate, in the process that leads to the decision.

There is an enormous gulf between being subject to a will that may interfere in your affairs without taking your perceived interests into account and being subject to a process such that, while it takes your interests and those of others equally into account, it may deliver a result – for reasons you can understand – that favours those others more than you (Spitz 1995: 382–3). In the first case, you must see yourself as living at the mercy of another; in the second, you can see yourself as simply unlucky. You can treat the setback you suffer as something on a par with a natural misfortune. The world, it transpires, does not enable you simultaneously to satisfy your interest in having government establish a power plant, for example, and your interest in not having that power plant near your backyard.

Is there any procedure that would empower the avowable perceived interests of individual members of the community, even those in relevant minorities, but not to the same self-defeating extreme as the vetoing proposal? The obvious candidate is a procedure that would enable people, not to veto public decisions on the basis of their avowable, perceived interests, but to call them into question on such a basis and to trigger a review; in particular, to trigger a review in a forum that they and others can all endorse as an impartial court of appeal: as a forum in which relevant interests are taken equally into account and only impartially supported decisions are upheld. I describe this alternative arrangement, which allows of many possible variations, as a contestatory regime.

The power that people would have under a contestatory regime is weaker than a veto but still of considerable significance. It is a power of contesting public decisions on the grounds that they do not answer adequately to certain avowable, perceived interests – they do not answer adequately to perceived interests that are consistent with the desire to live under a shared, non-discriminating system of government – and that they impose arbitrarily on the bearers of those interests. The complaint is not that the bearers fare less well than others under such a decision – some are bound to lose out – but that the decision was taken in a way that did not take their interests equally into account. The assumption behind the complaint is that if those interests had been taken equally into account, then the ultimate decision would have been different.

The electoral mode of democratization represents public decisions as democratic and to that extent legitimate because they originate, however indirectly, in the collective will of the people. The people are the ultimate authors of the decisions. The contestatory mode of democratisation would represent public decisions as democratic in a further sense – and to a further extent legitimate – so far as they are capable of withstanding individual contestation, in particular contestation in forums and under procedures that are acceptable to all concerned. Where the electoral mode of democratization gives the collective people an indirect power of authorship over the laws, the contestatory would give the people, considered individually, a limited and, of course, indirect power of editorship over those laws.

The feasibility of contestatory democratization

The appeal of the contestatory proposal is that, while enjoying similar attractions to the vetoing arrangement, it does not suffer the same problems of feasibility. The proposal will be more feasible than the vetoing arrangement to the extent that it empowers people in the assertion of their perceived interests but does not set them up as dictators with an individual capacity to negate any public decision.

But there is another question of feasibility that has to be raised in relation to the contestatory proposal. This is the question of whether it will ever be possible to establish procedures and fora of appeal that almost everyone can regard as impartial. Of course, there is unlikely to be any hope of finding the perfectly compelling process of appeal and review. But the crucial question is whether we can hope for the feasibility of a process that will satisfy the following constraint: that surviving the process reinforces, and that failing the process reduces, the reasons that an ordinary individual has available for believing that a decision is consistent with taking people's avowable, perceived interests equally into account.

People will have reason to believe that a public decision is likely to be consistent with equal consideration of such interests so far as it is salient that the decision-makers and decision-testers lack the opportunity or incentive for unequal consideration and have the opportunity and incentive for equal. So the question, then, is whether any feasible contestatory regime would shift the salient opportunities and incentives in the appropriate direction. We may consider this question in relation to the familiar avenues for contestation. These include: challenging a public decision in the courts on the grounds that it is illegal or unconstitutional; challenging it before a public commission or parliamentary inquiry on the grounds that it is improper in some way; or challenging it before an administrative appeals tribunal, or complaining about it to an ombudsman, on the grounds that it is not adequately supported.

Wherever a court or inquiry or appeals board hears public challenges and reviews a decision, then that means that the opportunities and incentives shift in an appropriate direction. The striking feature about any such contestatory process is that in cases where it is activated the relevant opportunities and incentives are relatively favourable from the viewpoint of equal consideration of people's interest. It may be in such cases that the original decision-makers in the legislature or administration had the incentive and the opportunity to ignore the avowable, perceived interests of a certain minority. But it is unlikely that the reviewing agency will have the same opportunity and the same incentive.

The reviewing agency may have to do or report its business in public, for example, in which case it will probably not have the same opportunity to ignore the minority interests: it will have to consider explicitly how they are served by the decision. And it will almost always be subject to quite a different array of incentives. Where those elected to government may have an interest in securing re-election by satisfying their particular backers, for example, those involved in review will usually have quite different – if in some cases, still electoral – incentives. They may be free of self-serving interests and be all the more susceptible to considerations of fair play – this, by analogy with what we expect of juries (Abramson 1994) – or they may have an interest in enhancing their reputation as knowledgeable and even-handed among their professional colleagues or in the community at large (Brennan and Pettit 1993; Pettit 1997: chap. 8).

The best test of whether a contestatory regime is likely to be feasible is this. Are people disposed to endorse processes of review and resolution that find against their own particular views? Are they willing to think that if a decision stands up under such a process, for example, then however unwelcome the result, it is not arbitrary from their point of view: it is not generated in any necessary part by a neglect of their avowable, perceived interests?

There are many social divides such that people on different sides may not be willing to have their rival views on certain issues decided by any independent process; if the process goes against them, and if its finding rules, then they may be unable to believe that their avowable, perceived interests were taken equally into account. In such cases, the promotion of freedom as non-domination will require us to look at possibilities of secession for one or another side, or to explore the prospect of separate jurisdictions for the different groups, or to think about a federal structure in which each gets its own territory, or to make room for rights of conscientious objection on the part of the group that is negatively affected. Or at least it will require this so far as other things are equal: so far as such emergency measures would not in other ways have more damaging effects on people's freedom as non-domination.

But many issues on which people divide are not so intractable as this. And in these cases the evidence is that, yes, people in general are often willing to think that contestatory processes that deliver unwelcome results are still fair – they do not ignore their avowable, perceived interests – and are to that extent acceptable: they do not represent the presence of an arbitrary power in their lives. According to Tyler and Mitchell (1994: 746), "research indicates that the key factor affecting the perceived legitimacy of authorities is procedural fairness. Procedural judgments have been found to be more important than either outcome favorability – whether the person won or lost – or judgments about outcome fairness" (see too Lind and Tyler 1988).

One of the most difficult of issues in contemporary democracy concerns the legalization of abortion on demand. Here Tyler and his associates found that US citizens regard the Supreme Court as legitimate in its handling of abortion decisions, and defer to those decisions in a measure that is mainly determined by whether they think that the decision-making procedures followed by the Court were fair. "Institutional legitimacy is more important than is agreement with either past Court decisions in general or past Court decisions about the specific issue of abortion" (Tyler and Mitchell 1994: 789). Nor is the effect confined to the courts. In a recent book summarizing overall research in the area, the authors write: "people's evaluations of group authorities, institutions, and rules have been found to be influenced primarily by procedural-justice judgments. This is found in studies of legal, political, and managerial authorities" (Tyler, Boeckmann, Smith, and Huo 1997: 83).

Historical antecedents

The notion of making a democracy contestatory is not a newfangled idea that I have just dreamt up. It has been a theme in democratic thinking right back to the seventeenth century, although it has generally been overshadowed by the emphasis on the collective, popular control of government that electoral regimes are designed to make possible.

Pasquale Pasquino (1996) has argued recently that we find in Locke a notion of popular sovereignty distinct from the model of collective control that had already figured in Hobbes. This associates popular sovereignty with the fact that government is a trust, in Locke's (1965 [1681]) legal metaphor, and that the people – the trustors, as we might say – retain the right to resist and reject government – the trustee – in the event of that trust not being properly discharged. This model gives the notion of popular sovereignty an essentially contestatory cast, though it emphasizes only the limit possibility of contestation by resistance.

But the model of government as trustee, people as trustors, was widely invoked in the seventeenth century – it was not Locke's invention (Gough 1950: 161) – and it was associated with more routine ways of challenging government than armed resistance. It gave the judiciary a means of calling the authorities, even authorities established by the Crown, to book: "whatever the source of their power and position, if their offices existed to perform a public service (to discharge public duties) theirs were offices of 'trust and confidence concerning the public'" (Finn 1995: 11). And it enabled the Levellers to argue that even an elected parliament should be subject to the terms of an agreement that would enable the people to know when they could legitimately challenge their government. "Parliaments are to receive the extent of their power, and trust from those that betrust them; and therefore the people are to declare what their power and trust is, which is the intent of this Agreement" (quoted in Morgan 1988: 83).

The idea in the trust model of government is that the democratic role that enables people to ensure control over law is not their creative, law-making role, assuming they have that, but rather an oppositional one: a role, ideally, that would "give a separate and superior institutional voice to the people, to protect them as subjects from themselves as governors" (Morgan 1988: 83). This oppositional idea has survived, side by side with the growing emphasis on popular election, down to the present day. One of its best-known expressions, of course, is the recurrent emphasis on the need for constitutional guarantees, akin to the terms of the Levellers' Agreement, whereby people can be given power over government. It is unfortunate that, far from being seen as expressive of a notion of democratic control of government (a contestatory model of control), that emphasis is sometimes presented, even by its defenders, as an anti-democratic device that is needed to guard against the control of the people (Riker 1982; see also Holmes 1988).

The oppositional idea of democratic control has survived also in other forms, as the work of political scientists and political theorists demonstrates. Political scientists have long recognized that "contestation," as Robert Dahl (1956) describes it, is just as important a feature of democracy as participation or representation (see too Lijphart 1984 and 1991). It is significant that Barrington Moore (1989: 8), for example, maintains that the defining criterion of democracy is "the existence of a legitimate and, to some extent effective, opposition." Ian Shapiro (1994 and 1996) reflects this background of analysis in his prescriptive recommendation for a democratic scheme under which the institutionalization of opposition plays an equal role with collective self-government.

In arguing for a contestatory element in the interpretation of democracy, then – in arguing, specifically, that freedom as non-domination requires a contestatory as well as an electoral mode of democratizing government – we are not defending a novel and untested notion. The idea of making government answerable to the challenges of individuals and groups has been there from the earliest formulations of democracy and is there still in most democratic practice.

But while this idea has not disappeared, it has consistently played a secondary role to the idea of putting government under popular, collective control and it has ceded to that other idea a semantic connection with the word "democracy." To our contemporary ears a democratic regime is one in which the people collectively govern themselves, whether directly or via representatives. And so to our ears any proposal to constrain government by instituting individual rights or by setting up possibilities of individual challenge – any proposal to put limits on what can be decided either by the legislature or in a referendum – looks like a trimming of the democratic sails (as in Riker 1982). This, from my perspective, is the product of a serious conceptual loss. Sensible political theorists all agree that popular, collective control needs to be restricted in various ways. What they should also recognize is that the case for this

limitation is not just pragmatic in character. It derives from the principles of democracy when democracy is interpreted in an electoral-cum-
contestatory manner. It derives from the principles of democracy under
the only interpretation that properly connects democracy with the
requirements of individual freedom.

The significance of the contestatory turn

What, finally, is the significance for democratic theory of adopting the
perspective defended here and of taking democracy – or at least
democracy in the sense in which it would serve republican freedom – to
have two dimensions, one electoral, the other contestatory? What is the
payoff for taking the contestatory turn in democratic theory? I see two
benefits and I conclude with a brief mention of these; I hope to elaborate
them more fully elsewhere (see Pettit forthcoming).

The first benefit of giving democracy a contestatory as well as an
electoral cast is that by doing so we can make sense of a range of features
which most of us take to be desirable in any democratic regime.
Consider the following list of democratic desiderata, for example:

political control, legislative and executive, should leave people each
with a sphere of autonomous decision-making: it should be limited
in scope;

political control should be exercised under the constraints of certain
constitutional procedures and restrictions;

political control should conform to a rule of law, with laws framed in
general terms, not directed to named individuals;

political control should be exercised on the basis of publicly accessible, parliamentary deliberation;

political control should be exercised in a bicameral fashion, with each
house of parliament representing distinctive interests;

judicial functions, or at least certain ones, should be filled by statutory
appointment, not by electoral means, and should be exercised
without legislative or executive direction;

some executive decision-making – for example, in drawing electoral
boundaries – should be depoliticized and put in the hands of
statutorily appointed officers and bodies;

executive decisions should be generally open to inspection, justified
by documented reasons, and subject, on appeal, to review by the
courts or by certain statutory officers or bodies.

These desiderata may not be of equal importance and one or two may
not be given much weight by some democratic theorists. But they do

figure in most political thought as features that are intimately associated with the notion of democracy. Someone who defended democracy but rejected one or more of these desiderata would certainly feel obliged to comment on the fact and to try and justify it.

This being so, it would be good to have a conception of democracy that made sense of why the features in question are generally thought to be important to the democratic ideal. And here the striking thing is that if we think of democracy as having a contestatory as well as an electoral aspect – as requiring individualized as well as collective control of government – then we can immediately explain why the features so often figure as democratic desiderata.

It would be possible to have an electoral democracy, even one that made government effectively answerable to an electorate, without having all, even perhaps any, of the features mentioned. There is no reason why electoral democracy should be limited in scope, constitutionally restricted, forced to operate by rule of law, based on public deliberation rather than private accommodation, and so on. But it would hardly be possible to have a contestatory democracy without building such features into the design. Some of the features would serve to restrict government decision-making in a way that ought to reassure the public and remove patterns that might prompt unnecessary contestation; others would help to facilitate the possibility of contestation where contestation does indeed prove to be necessary.

Consider features such as the limitation of the scope of political control; the constitutional restriction on political control; the rule of law and bicameral requirements; and the use of statutorily appointed officers and bodies in both executive and judicial or quasi-judicial roles. These all make sense as features designed to remove patterns of government that would cause public anxiety and prompt a great deal of contestation. The prospect of unlimited, unrestricted, legally particularistic and electorally hypersensitive government is a hideous specter from the point of view of anyone who wants to make government contestable. Such government would leave extraordinary scope for those in power to pursue their private goals and not take people's interests equally into account; it would open the gate to widespread domination.

Consider now the other features on the list given above: the requirements that parliamentary democracy be deliberative and that governmental decisions should be generally open to inspection, justified by documented reasons and subject, on appeal, to review by the courts or by certain statutory officers or bodies. As the first set of features are designed to remove prompts towards contestation, these features can be seen as designed to facilitate contestation itself. If democratic decisions were just bargained accommodations between different interest groups, then there would be no ground on which ordinary people could contest them. And if governmental decisions were taken in camera or without reference to reasons, or if there were no avenues of appeal and review, then contestability would be wholly undermined.

I have been suggesting that a first benefit in the contestatory turn is that it would enable democratic theory to derive from the democratic ideal certain features that are generally seen as desiderata and that would otherwise have to be taken as exogenous constraints. The second benefit that I see in the contestatory turn I must record without documentation. This is that once the features mentioned are unified as requirements of a contestatory democracy, then we may begin to think about how they can be extended and improved in the service of promoting contestability. The contestatory turn does not merely provide us with a more encompassing grasp of the democratic ideal, it also suggests a research program of elaborating the institutional means whereby the contestatory dimension of democracy might be enhanced.

Constitutional lawyers and theorists have always given enormous attention to questions of constitutional restriction, and recently there has been a good deal of investigation among political theorists into the best means of making democracy more deliberative (Cohen 1989; Habermas 1984 and 1994; Sunstein 1993a, 1993b, and 1993c; Young 1993). But discussion of the other contestatorily justified features of democratic systems has been desultory and undirected. Everyone tends to agree that they are indeed justified but few have looked into how best they might be institutionalized and into whether they suggest further ways of developing democratic institutions. Thus, while there is widespread agreement that depoliticization of certain functions is often a good idea in government, there has been little or no discussion of how far it should be extended. Many agree that there should be a depoliticized electoral commission and perhaps a depoliticized central bank but there has been no systematic study of how depoliticization can be achieved, of when it is feasible or of when it is desirable: of when it serves contestability well, for example, without undermining electoral control (see Waldron forthcoming).

I believe that if we take the contestatory turn in thinking about democracy, then such questions should quickly present themselves as both important and tractable. They should assume the profile of a compelling research program. That research program would not be novel, given the attention devoted to related, institutional questions in the writings of theorists from Machiavelli to Montesquieu and the American founders. But it would make for a new and interesting departure in the work of contemporary political theory, or at least contemporary political philosophy.[4]

REFERENCES

Abramson, Jeffrey. 1994. *We, the Jury: The Jury System and the Ideal of Democracy.* New York: Basic Books.

Barry, Brian. 1995. *Justice as Impartiality.* Oxford: Oxford University Press.

Bellamy, Richard. Forthcoming. *Liberalism and Pluralism.*

Bentham, Jeremy. 1843. "Anarchical Fallacies." In J. Bowring (ed.), *The Works of Jeremy Bentham.* Edinburgh: W. Tait.

Berlin, Isaiah. 1958. *Two Concepts of Liberty.* Oxford: Oxford University Press.
    1969. *Four Essays on Liberty.* Oxford: Oxford University Press.

Brennan, Geoffrey and Loren Lomasky. 1993. *Democracy and Decision: The Pure Theory of Electoral Preference.* Oxford: Oxford University Press.

Brennan, Geoffrey and Philip Pettit. 1990. "Unveiling the vote." *British Journal of Political Science* 20: 311–33.
    1993. "Hands invisible and intangible." *Synthese* 94: 191–225.

Buchanan, James and Gordon Tullock. 1962. *The Calculus of Consent.* Ann Arbor: University of Michigan Press.

Cohen, Joshua. 1989. "Deliberation and democratic legitimacy." In Alan Hamlin and Philip Pettit (eds.), *The Good Polity.* Oxford: Blackwell.

Constant, Benjamin. 1988. *Constant: Political Writings.* Edited by B. Fontana. Cambridge: Cambridge University Press.

Dahl, Robert. 1956. *A Preface to Democratic Theory.* Chicago: University of Chicago Press.

Filmer, Sir Robert. 1991 (c. 1635). *Patriarch and Other Writings.* Edited by J. P. Sommerville. Cambridge: Cambridge University Press.

Finn, Paul. 1995. "A sovereign people, a public trust." In Paul Finn (ed.), *Essays on Law and Government. Vol. I: Principles and Values.* Sydney: The Law Book Company.

Gough, J. W. 1950. *John Locke's Political Philosophy.* Oxford: Oxford University Press.

Habermas, Jürgen. 1984. *A Theory of Communicative Action,* Vol. I. Cambridge: Polity Press.
    1989. *A Theory of Communicative Action,* Vol. II. Cambridge: Polity Press.
    1994. "Three normative models of democracy." *Constellations* 1: 1–10.
    1996. "Postscript to *Between Facts and Norms.*" In M. Deflem (ed.), *Habermas, Modernity and Law.* London: Sage.

Hailsham, Lord. 1978. *The Dilemma of Democracy: Diagnosis and Prescription.* London: Collins.

[4] I presented earlier versions of this chapter in the Research School of Social Sciences, Australian National University, in Columbia University, Hong Kong University, and at the Yale conference on Rethinking Democracy. I am most grateful for the many helpful challenges that I received in those discussions, especially from my Yale commentators, Philippe Van Parijs and Steve Holmes. I was helped by independent conversations with Steve Bottomley, Geoff Brennan, Josh Cohen, David Held, Barry Hindess, Rob Sparrow, Jean-Fabien Spitz, and Iris Marion Young.

Harrington, James. 1992 (c. 1771). *The Commonwealth of Oceana and A System of Politics*. Edited by J. G. A. Pocock. Cambridge: Cambridge University Press.

Hobbes, Thomas. 1968 (1651). *Leviathan*. Edited by C. B. MacPherson. Harmondsworth: Penguin Books.

Holmes, Stephen. 1988. "Gag rules or the politics of omission." In Jon Elster and Rune Slagstand (eds.), *Constitutionalism and Democracy*, pp. 19–58. Cambridge: Cambridge University Press.

1995. *Passions and Constraint: On the Theory of Liberal Democracy*. Chicago: University of Chicago Press.

Lijphart, Arend. 1984. *Democracies: Patterns of Majoritarian and Consensus Government in Twenty One Countries*. New Haven: Yale University Press.

1991. "Majority rule in theory and practice: the tenacity of a flawed paradigm." *International Social Science Journal* 43: 483–93.

Lind, Allen E. and Tom R. Tyler. 1988. *The Social Psychology of Procedural Justice*. New York: Plenum.

Lind, John. 1776. *Three Letters to Dr Price*. London: T. Payne.

Locke, John. 1965 (1681). *Two Treatises of Government*. Edited by P. Laslett. New York: Mentor.

Long, Douglas C. 1977. *Bentham on Liberty*. Toronto: University of Toronto Press.

Madison, James, Alexander Hamilton, and John Jay. 1987 (1787–8). *The Federalist Papers*. Edited by Isaac Kramnik. Harmondsworth: Penguin.

Maitland, F. W. 1981. "A historical sketch of liberty and equality." In H. A. L. Fisher (ed.), *Collected Papers*. Buffalo: W. S. Hein and Company.

Montesquieu, Charles de Secondat. 1989 (c. 1748). *The Spirit of the Laws*. Edited by A. T. A. M. Cohler, B. C. Miller and H. S. Stone. Cambridge: Cambridge University Press.

Moore, Barrington, Jr. 1989. *Liberal Prospects under Soviet Socialism: A Comparative Historical Perspective*. New York: The Averell Harriman Institute.

Morgan, Edmund S. 1988. *Inventing the People: The Rise of Popular Sovereignty in England and America*. New York: Norton.

Pagden, Anthony (ed.). 1987. *Languages of Political Theory in Early Modern Europe*. Cambridge: Cambridge University Press.

Paine, Tom 1989 (1794). *Political Writings*. Edited by Bruce Kuklick. Cambridge: Cambridge University Press.

Pasquino, Pasquale. 1996. "Popular sovereignty. What does it mean?" *CREA, Ecole Polytechnique* (ms).

Pettit, Philip. 1996. "Freedom and antipower." *Ethics* 106: 576–604.

1997. *Republicanism: A Theory of Freedom and Government*. Oxford: Oxford University Press.

1998. "Reworking Sandel's republicanism." *Journal of Philosophy* 95: 73–96.

Forthcoming. *Democracy, Contestatory and Electoral*. NOMOS.

Pocock, J. G. A. 1975. *The Machiavellian Moment: Florentine Political Theory and the Atlantic Republican Tradition*. Princeton: Princeton University Press.

Price, Richard. 1991. *Political Writings*. Edited by D. O. Thomas. Cambridge: Cambridge University Press.

Priestley, Joseph. 1993. *Political Writings*. Edited by P. N. Miller. Cambridge: Cambridge University Press.

Raab, Felix. 1965. *The English Face of Machiavelli. A Changing Interpretation 1500–1700*. London: Routledge & Kegan Paul.

Riker, William. 1982. *Liberalism against Populism*. San Francisco: W. H. Freeman and Co.

Robbins, Caroline. 1959. *The Eighteenth Century Commonwealthman*. Cambridge, MA: Harvard University Press.

Scanlon, Thomas M. 1982. "Contractualism and utilitarianism." In Amartya Sen and Bernard Williams (eds.), *Utilitarianism and Beyond*. Cambridge: Cambridge University Press.

Sellers, M. N. S. 1994. *American Republicanism: Roman Ideology in the United States Constitution*. New York: New York University Press.

Shapiro, Ian. 1994. "Three ways to be a democrat." *Political Theory* 22: 124–51.

1996. "Elements of democratic justice." *Political Theory* 24: 579–619.

Skinner, Quentin. 1978. *The Foundations of Modern Political Thought*. 2 vols. Cambridge: Cambridge University Press.

1984. "The idea of negative liberty." In R. Rorty, J. B. Schneewind and Q. Skinner (eds.), *Philosophy in History*. Cambridge: Cambridge University Press.

1990. "The republican ideal of political liberty." In G. Bock, Q. Skinner and M. Viroli (eds.), *Machiavelli and Republicanism*. Cambridge: Cambridge University Press.

1997. *Liberty before Liberalism*. Cambridge: Cambridge University Press.

Spitz, Jean-Fabien. 1995. *La Liberte Politique*. Paris: Presses Universitaires de France.

Sunstein, Cass R. 1993a. *The Partial Constitution*. Cambridge, MA: Harvard University Press.

1993b. *Democracy and the Problem of Free Speech*. New York: The Free Press.

1993c. "The enduring legacy of republicanism." In S. E. Elkin and K. E. Soltan (eds.), *A New Constitutionalism: Designing Political Institutions for a Good Society*. Chicago: University of Chicago Press.

Sydney, Algernon. 1990 (1751). *Discourses Concerning Government*. Edited by T. G. West. Indianapolis: Liberty Classics.

Tyler, Tom R. and G. Mitchell. 1994. "Legitimacy and the empowerment of discretionary legal authority: the United States Supreme Court and abortion rights." *Duke Law Journal* 43: 703–815.

Tyler, Tom R., R. J. Boeckmann, H. J. Smith, and Y. Y. Huo. 1997. *Social Justice in a Diverse Society*. Boulder, CO: Westview Press.

Van Parijs, Philippe. 1995. *Real Freedom for All*. Oxford: Oxford University Press.

Waldron, Jeremy. Forthcoming. *Law and Disagreement*.

Worden, Blair. 1991. "English republicanism." In J. H. Burns and M. Goldie (eds.) *The Cambridge History of Political Thought*. Cambridge: Cambridge University Press.

Young, Iris M. 1993. "Justice and communicative democracy." In R. Gottlieb (ed.), *Radical Philosophy: Tradition, Counter-tradition, Politics*. Philadelphia: Temple University Press.

10 Contestatory democracy versus real freedom for all

Philippe Van Parijs

Since the mid-1970s the United States and a number of other industrialized countries have experienced a dramatic increase in income inequality and a steep fall in the standard of living for the lower layers of the income distribution. These trends are, in a plausible sense, the outcome of greater freedom. They are also, in an even more plausible sense, a deadly threat to the freedom of many. To tackle this threat, to reverse the underlying trends, democracy is essential, but not just any form of democracy. Philip Pettit's contribution to this volume is helpful, not merely because it helps clarify the conceptual relationship between freedom and democracy, but because it also makes us think about how to reshape our democracies to preserve or create as truly free a society as is possible. I warmly welcome this, as political philosophy has never been for me an idle game played for the pleasure of making subtle distinctions and smart points, but a crucial part of the urgent task of thinking up what needs to be done to make our societies and our world less unjust than they are, or even simply to avert disaster.

I fully agree with Pettit that making our democracies more contestatory is urgently required, not as an aim in itself, but in order to promote freedom. Yet I also believe that making them as contestatory as possible would, under present circumstances, handicap their pursuit of the ideal of freedom in the most defensible interpretation of that ideal. To explain, some preliminary conceptual clarification is in order.

Three distinctions

On the freedom side, Pettit's key distinction is between freedom as non-interference and freedom as non-domination, also called republican freedom. How does this distinction relate to the old (and often confusing) distinction between negative and positive freedom? How does it relate to my own favorite distinction between formal and real freedom, at which Pettit briefly hints (see footnote 1, p. 167, above). If positive freedom is interpreted (as it is by Pettit on p. 164) either as psychological self-mastery or as political participation, it definitely lies outside the scope of both Pettit's distinction and my own. Both of these rather operate within the domain of negative freedom, broadly understood as not being prevented from doing what one may wish to do. But they differ in the cut they make between different characterizations of what counts as freedom-restricting.

Though a variety of negative freedom in the broad sense just stated, republican freedom is crucially distinct from negative freedom in the narrower sense of absence of interference, i.e., absence of intentional coercion or obstruction. Republican freedom is the absence of domination, i.e., the capacity to interfere in an arbitrary way, or in a manner that is not "without regard to [the interferee's perceived interests]" (Pettit, p. 166, above). There can be domination without interference (when the capacity is left unused) and there can be interference without domination (when it is not arbitrary).

Republican freedom, so defined, is not strictly more demanding than formal freedom, characterized along standard libertarian lines as the existence of a consistent and well-enforced system of property rights which incorporates universal self-ownership. This is not because any law is coercive and "coercion, under standard views, is a form of interference" (Pettit, p. 168, above). Property-rights-protecting legislation is not formal-freedom-restricting even if it is, in this plausible sense, coercive. The reason is rather that there can conceivably be non-arbitrary, and hence non-dominating, government interference in breach of the citizens' self-ownership, for example in the form of conscription for the defence of the republic. The extent to which a concern with republican freedom will fall short of guaranteeing formal freedom to all is crucially dependent on what counts as non-arbitrary power, or power that is "forced to track the perceived interests of those on whom they are imposed" (Pettit, p. 170, above), and so is a fortiori the extent to which the promotion of republican freedom can be relied upon to give citizens, at the highest level enjoyable by all, the *real* freedom – the actual possibility, encompassing the means and not just the right – to do what they may wish to do.[1] Conversely, no degree of formal or real freedom for all citizens entails, by definition, that they enjoy republican freedom.

---

[1] This rough characterization will suffice for present purposes. For a detailed discussion of real freedom and its metric, see Van Parijs 1995: chaps. 2–4; Barry 1996; Vallentyne 1997.

Convergence?

In the light of these distinctions, it is clear that the ideal of freedom is conceptually different, depending on whether it is interpreted in terms of republican freedom for all or in terms of real freedom for all (in a sense that incorporates but does not reduce to formal freedom). But this conceptual distinction would be of negligible practical importance if a strong convergence could safely be expected between the requirements of the ideal under both interpretations. Whether this is the case hinges on susbtantive implications of the key criterion of "non-arbitrary power" which enters the definition of republican freedom. The quickest way of spelling them out is to turn to the link Pettit's central thesis establishes between republican freedom and contestatory democracy.

When freedom is understood as non-domination, democracy, understood as collective rule, is neither necessarily inimical to freedom, nor necessarily freedom-friendly. But it can be made more freedom-friendly as a matter of necessity, according to Pettit, by being shaped on a contestatory model. The latter is one of two models of democracy that could block, or at least sharply reduce, the possibility of an elective democracy degenerating into collective tyranny, arbitrary power exercised by the collectivity over its members. The first and most straightforward of these models is unanimitarian democracy, which gives each citizen a veto on any public decision. But this model does not have more than an abstract, purely academic interest. "The reason is that no vetoing scheme of things has the remotest chance of being instituted; it is a wholly infeasible mode of public decision-making" (Pettit, p. 178, above).

The second model, contestatory democracy, does not share this defect. It consists in "a procedure that would enable people, not to veto public decisions on the basis of their allowable, perceived interests, but to call them into question on such a basis . . . in a forum that they and others can all endorse as an impartial court of appeal" (Pettit, p. 179, above). This model is far more feasible than the first one to the extent that, in actual fact, "it empowers people in the assertion of their perceived interests, but does not set them up as dictators with an individual capacity to negate any public decision" (Pettit, p. 180, above). Democracy is here defined not as government by the people (collectively) but as contestability by the people (distributively) and therefore as intrinsically freedom-friendly if freedom is defined as the absence of arbitrary power, which it is in the essence of contestability to undermine.[2]

---

[2] I interpret the necessity of this connection as a conceptual rather than factual one. Pettit emphasizes the conceptual possibility of domination by private agents (and hence republican unfreedom) even under a fully contestatory democracy. But can anything

In the final section of his contribution, Pettit describes a number of illustrative features of how a contestatory model would work in practice. One crucial feature is "the requirement that parliamentary democracy be deliberative and that governmental decisions should be generally open to inspection, justified by documented reasons" (Pettit, p. 186, above). To make contestation possible, legislation must take place in a context of debate to which all sides are represented, and only those reasons which are acceptable in such a debate can be recognized as relevant.

Pettit is not explicit about the set of socio-economic institutions that would be likely to emerge from such a process. But other theorists of deliberative democracy (e.g., Cohen 1996; Gutmann and Thompson 1996) have allowed themselves to sketch the substantive principles that can be expected to systematically underlie the resulting legislation. Unsurprisingly, the tracking of both the interests and the opinions of all turns out to lead, in a pluralist society, to liberal–egalitarian principles involving both a strong protection of fundamental liberties and a strongly egalitarian (be it maximin) distribution of the means each is given to pursue her conception of the good life. Once the notion of an acceptable or compelling reason is duly specified and a number of uncontroversial empirical facts are taken into account, it seems that any well-functioning contestatory democracy should gently converge on a set of institutions that will express adequate concern for all its citizens' formal and real freedom, and the contestatory model of democracy should therefore be just about as congenial to the real-libertarian as to the republican-libertarian.

A trade off?

This expectation of a convergence is comforting, but it should not blind us to the possibility of a conflict between the optimal realization of republican freedom and the pursuit of the greatest real freedom for all. Let me illustrate this possibility with one example, that is particularly close, for reasons that will soon be obvious, to some of my current concerns. Pettit (p. 182, above) mentions that there are cases in which contestatory democracy will hardly be less paralyzing than giving everyone a veto: "There are many social divides such that people on different sides may not be willing to have their rival views on certain issues decided by any independent process ... In such cases, the

establish the presence of political domination (and hence of politically generated republican unfreedom) apart from the observation of a departure from the procedures of contestatory democracy?

promotion of freedom as non-domination will require us to look at possibilities of secession for one or another side, or to explore the prospect of separate jurisdictions for the different groups, or to think about a federal structure in which each gets its own territory." In particular, in a linguistically heterogeneous polity, with limited or sometimes no knowledge of each other's language, there is a strong fear that the weaker voices will not be heard, that the debates and arguments that hold sway in the minority-language areas will simply be ignored.

In recent negotiations on the future shape of the European Union's institutions, this was one of the reasons given by the Swedish government in favour of maintaining a veto right at the Council of Ministers for each member state, however small its population: the purpose is not, it was argued, that minority interests should enjoy absolute protection but that arguments be heard (see Gustavsson 1998). As such a veto right is often paralyzing, some alternatives have been proposed that would precisely exemplify the move from a unanimitarian to a contestatory model, in the sense of enabling member states "not to veto public decisions on the basis of their avowable, perceived interests, but to call them into question on such a basis and to trigger a review" (Pettit, p. 180, above). For example, the "alarm bell mechanism," which is already used in some federal systems, would enable a member state to get a decision suspended and reconsidered on another occasion when it can plausibly argue that some of its vital interests are at stake (see Dehousse 1994: 121–3).[3]

Yet, in the light of the recent experience of a multilingual country such as my own, Belgium, it is overwhelmingly clear to me that a smoothly running contestatory democracy is far more difficult to achieve in a linguistically heterogeneous polity: the screening of proposals and arguments so that they are acceptable to every citizen, not just to those who happen to speak the speaker's language, the ability to get one's voice heard, to scrutinize legislative and administrative processes effectively, and the disposition to accept verdicts as impartial are all systematically weakened in such a context. Republican freedom, therefore, is far safer in a unilingual republic, and if it were the overarching aim, I could not think of any persuasive argument in favour of preserving or developing multilingual states such as Belgium or the European Union.

But republican freedom is not the overarching aim. In my view, it is just an important means, not to something other than freedom, but to a conception of justice as maximin real freedom, and this aim may justify

---

[3] Since 1970, Belgium's Constitution gives each linguistic community the power to force reconsideration of a decision if three-quarters of its parliamentary representation find it detrimental to its interests. (See, e.g., Karmis and Gagnon 1996: 457–8.)

getting along with less republican freedom than could be durably achieved. In my example, dismantling the Belgian federal state so as to enable each of its linguistically more homogeneous components to achieve greater republican freedom, would mean splitting up a common social security system that redistributes massively from richer to poorer areas. It would also mean conferring to the components a fiscal autonomy that would soon lead (for reasons exacerbated by the peculiar geographical situation of largely francophone Brussels surrounded by Flemish territory) to cut-throat fiscal competition and hence also far lower redistribution within each of the components. For the sake of real freedom for all, or any other substantive principle of justice, the scales at which one locates the democratic process, contestatory or otherwise, are of crucial importance. Nothing guarantees that the scales that such a conception of justice recommends that we select are also the ones that are optimal for the sake of republican freedom. When there is a conflict – as I believe there is in my example – the choice of scales should be made with a view to the sustainable achievement of justice, while doing one's best, on each of the selected scales, to make democracy as contestatory as possible.[4]

Struggles ahead

Let us return on this background to the growing inequalities which I mentioned at the very beginning. Should we simply accept them as the necessary correlates of economic freedom or of efficient incentive structures? I militantly believe that our concern for freedom, properly interpreted, should make us resist this pitiful shrinking of the agenda. We do not need to claim that reducing inequality would not affect incentives. There are strong efficiency-based arguments in favor of more equality, but many of them stress the effect on overall capacities (to become or remain healthy and skilled) rather than on incentives.[5] More-over, even if there were a net cost in terms of overall growth, this would not need to make a fairer distribution of resources unachievable. Making democracy more contestatory is certainly part of the answer, for example, especially in the US, by making the voices of the poor less inaudible compared to wealthy campaign sponsors. [6] Once the effects of

[4] I develop this theme in Van Parijs 1997.

[5] See, e.g., Glyn and Miliband 1993 and Bowles and Gintis 1998.

[6] The liberty-based constitutional argument that has so far blocked any attempt to impose significant limits on campaign spending provides a crystal-clear example of how a totally implausible notion of freedom can undermine the prospects of a free society, and there is now plenty of good argument around (e.g., Dworkin 1996 and Okin 1996), it seems to me, to blow up the constitutional blockage.

this massive wealth bias are finally under check, one can reasonably hope, for the sake of a fairer distribution of real freedom, that the US political system will have acquired the capacity to react to the crisis of the welfare state, not through running it down, through making it ever stingier and more selective, but through universalizing its provisions, for example as regards health care and child benefits.

But making democracy more contestatory, promoting republican freedom for all, is not enough. The growth of factor income inequality in advanced democracies is a deep-rooted trend. I am not sure much can or should be done to reverse it. I do, however, believe that much can and should be done to prevent this gross inequality from translating into net inequality, post-tax-and-transfer inequality in standards of living (in a broad sense that encompasses not only consumption, but also security, environmental quality and participation in social and economic life). How much this "much" is crucially depends on the democratic capacity to get hold of an increasingly concentrated economic rent in order to permanently distribute it widely across the whole population, not only in cash but also in the form of expenditure on education, public health, the environment, etc. This in turn depends on the extent to which the payers and recipients of this economic rent are able to play off against each other the redistributive polities. The easier and cheaper it is to move a commodity, a business, a deposit, a highly skilled worker's workplace or residence, from one jurisdiction to another, the weaker the grip of the democratic will, contestatory or otherwise, on the resources that can help make freedom more real for all. In a context in which technological and institutional impediments to mobility keep melting, this prompts a strong case for limiting the fiscal autonomy of individual states in existing federations and for scaling down the fiscal autonomy of the nation states in order to build up a supranational redistributive authority.

This sounds most freedom-unfriendly in at least three ways: it would bridle the collective freedom of each state; it would diminish the richer people's freedom to protect their wealth and incomes from what they regard as confiscatory taxation; and it would arguably depress the overall level of republican freedom, as important decision-making powers are moved away from the people's contestatory reach to a more centralized, less accountable level. Yet it is for the sake of freedom that we should move that way as fast as we can, for the sake of freedom as tangible, real freedom for all, the only freedom that matters to justice as such and for which the other freedoms I have discussed are sheer means.

REFERENCES

Barry, Brian. 1996. "Real freedom and basic income." *Journal of Political Philosophy* 5: 242–76.

Bowles, Samuel and Herbert Gintis. 1998. *Recasting Egalitarianism: New Rules for States, Communities and Markets.* London: Verso.

Cohen, Joshua. 1996. *Deliberative Democracy.* Cambridge, MA: MIT, typescript.

Dehousse, Renaud. 1994. "Community competences: are there limits to growth?" In Renaud Dehousse (ed.), *Europe After Maastricht: An Ever Closer Europe?* Munich: Law Books in Europe.

Dworkin, Ronald. 1996. "The curse of American politics." *The New York Review of Books* 17: 19–24.

Gustavsson, Sverker. 1998. "Double asymmetry as normative challenge." In Andreas Follesdal and Peter Koslowski (eds.), *Democracy and the European Union*, pp. 108–31. Berlin and New York: Springer.

Gutmann, Amy and Dennis Thompson. 1996. *Democracy and Disagreement.* Cambridge, MA: Harvard University Press.

Karmis, Dimitrios and Alain-G. Gagnon. 1996. "Fédéralisme et identités collectives au Canada et en Belgique: des itinéraires différents, une fragmentation similaire." *Canadian Journal of Political Science* 29(3): 435–68.

Okin, Susan M. 1996. Comment on Robert Dahl, "Equality and inequality: facts and causes in a normative perspective", APSA Conference, San Francisco, 31 August.

Vallentyne, Peter. 1997. "Self ownership and equality: brute luck, gifts, universal dominance, and leximin." *Ethics* 107(2): 321–43.

Van Parijs, Philippe. 1995. *Real Freedom for All. What (if anything) Can Justify Capitalism?* Oxford: Oxford University Press.

   1997. "Should the European Union become more democratic?" In Andreas Follesdal and Peter Koslowski (eds.), *Democracy and the European Union*, pp. 287–301. Berlin and New York: Springer.

Index

accountability 31–9, 80–1, 94, 102–6
affirmative action 107–9
Allende, Salvador 34
Anderson, A. B. 76
Anderson, Perry 114
Arato, Andrew 144, 148
Arendt, Hannah 146
Arrow, Kenneth 6–7, 26, 70, 71, 72, 73
associations 143–4, 145–8, 149–150,
    158–159, 160
asymmetrical information 75–9
authoritarianism 7–10, 80–1, 94–6,
    108–9

Béteille, André 78
Bardhan, Pranab 8–10, 132, 133
Barro, R. J. 88
Barry, Brian 57, 59, 60, 65, 67
Barzel, Yoran 115, 118, 119, 121
Bates, Robert 116, 119
Benabou, R. 107
Bendix, Reinhard 114
Bentham, Jeremy 169–70, 171
Bergson, A. 71
Berlin, Isaiah 14, 164, 165, 166, 168
Black, Duncan 29, 30
Blackstone 166
Bobbio, Norberto 23, 47
Bolton, Patrick 103
Brenner, Robert 114
Brewer, John 116
Bryce, James 48
bureaucracy 100–1

Campos, Nauro 93
capitalism 4, 41–3, 143–4, 157–8
checks and balances 44, 102–3
Cicero 166
civil society 12–14, 125–6, 141–61
    and social justice 12–14, 141–2, 145,
        153–61
    and state 141–2, 153–61
Cohen, Jean 144, 148

Cohen, Joshua 30, 48, 58–9, 62, 67, 160
communitarianism 7–10, 77–9, 103–6,
    154–5, 156
compliance 117–28
    with extraction 117–21, 122–3,
    with military service 121–4, 136–7
Condorcet 26, 48, 72
Condorcet jury theorem 26–31, 72, 73–4,
conscientious objection 125–6, 137
conscription 121–4, 136–7
Constant, Benjamin 164, 165, 166
constitutionalism 39, 44, 108, 185–6
Conte, Stephen 107
contestatory democratization 179
contractarianism 58–62
corporatism 99–100
corruption 100–1
credible commitment/government
    trustworthiness 122–3, 126–8,
    see also precommitment
Crook, Richard 105

Dahl, Robert 15, 23, 25, 32, 69–70, 71,
    73, 79, 184
Dasgupta, Partha 6–8, 73–4
deliberation 30, 48, 138–9, 185–7
deliberative democracy 58–9, 65, 138–9,
    168, 187, 194
development 81–9, 93–109
    cross-country statistical inquiry vs case-
        by-case 81–2, 93–4
Di Palma, Guiseppe 12
domination 1, 13, 14, 142
Downing, Brian 114, 121
Drèze, Jean 104
Dunn, John 11–12, 29
Durlauf, Steve 107

economic equality 3–4, 5–6, 40–3, 62–8
economy (distinguished from civil society)
    143–4
elections, causal effects of 23–50, 172–8
Elster, Jon 98

emergence of norms 124–8
Engels, Friedrich 49
enlightened understanding 69
Ensminger, Jean 124
Ertman, Thomas 114
Estlund, David 29, 30
ethnicity 106–9
Evans, Peter 96
extraction 117–21, 122–3, 134–6

Farrell, Joseph 103
Feld, Scott 27, 30
Ferejohn, John 37
Filmer, Robert 14, 169, 170, 171
Finer, Samuel 121
Fiorina, Morris 37
freedom 163–90, 191–2
    conceptions of 14, 16, 164–8, 191–3

Gauthier, David 57
Geddes, Barbara 96–7, 113
Goodin, Robert 160
Grofman, Bernard 27, 30
Grossman, Herschel 37

Habermas, Jürgen 144, 148, 168, 170
Hacker-Cordòn, Casiano 72
Hamilton, Alexander 36
Hardin, Garrett 7, 75
Hardin, Russell 46
Harrington, James 166, 170, 171
Hecht, S. 76
Hintze, Max 114
Hirschman, Albert 30
Hobbes, Thomas 169, 170, 183
Hoffman, Philip 116, 119, 123
Holmes, Stephen 168, 170
Howe, J. 78
Huntington, Samuel 12

identity politics 106–9
impartiality 5–6, 10–11, 57–68, 120,
    122–4, 124–8, 133, 137, 176,
    180–2
incomplete information 75–9
infant survival rate 83–9
infant-industry protection 98–9, 107–8
Inkeles, Alex 93
interethnic equity 108–9

Jodha, N. S. 76
justice 5–6, 16, 12–14, 56–68
    procedural vs end-state 57–8, 62, 142,
    153–61

Karl, Terry Lynn 24, 32

Katzenstein, Peter 99
Kelsen, Hans 24, 29, 48
Key, V. O., Jr. 37
Kiser, Edgar 115, 118, 119, 121
Kissinger, Henry 34
Klare, Karl 56
Knight, Jack 124

Ladha, Krishna 28
Levi, Margaret 10–11, 12, 116, 132, 133
libertarianism 154, 156, 191–7
Lien, Da-Hsiang, Donald 116, 119
life expectancy 83–9
Lijphart, Arendt 108
Limongi, Fernando 44, 93, 95
Lind, John 169, 171
Lippman, Walter 35
Lipset, Seymour Martin 49, 112, 113
literacy 83–9, 104
local common-property resources 7, 9,
    75–9, 106
local democracy 7–10, 79, 103–6
Locke, John 15, 166, 171, 183
Lowry, Glenn 107

Macaulay, Thomas 40
Machiavelli 166, 187
Mackintosh, James 40
Madison, James 38, 176
Maitland, F. W. 175
majority rule 26–31, 31–9, 69–74
Manin, Bernard 30, 35
Manor, James 105
Marx, Karl 26, 40, 114
Maskin, Eric 6–8, 73–4
May, Kenneth 71
May, P. 76
median-voter model 4–5, 41, 42–3
Michnik, Adam 109
Mill, John Stuart 24
Miller, Nicolas 29, 30
Mitchell, G. 182
Montesquieu 166, 177, 187
Moore, Barrington 15, 114, 184
mutual advantage 57–8

Netting, R. McC. 77
Noh, Suk Jae 37
North, Douglass 112, 115, 116, 119
Nozick, Robert 57

Olson, Mancur 101, 115, 117
opposition 15, 183–5
oppression 1, 13, 14, 142
Ostrom, Elinor 76–7
Owen, Guillermo 27

Paine, Thomas 175
Paley, William 169
Pareto principle 73
parliamentarism 50
participatory democracy 79, 103–6
Pasquino, Pasquale 183
Persson, Torsten 44
Pettit, Philip 13–15, 16, 17, 191–5
Piketty, Thomas 65–7
Pitkin, Hanna 33
Ploeg, Rick van der 43
political and civil liberties 83–9, 93, 94, 125–6, 153–4
political competition 79–81
Polybius 167
Popper, Karl 23, 45, 50
populism 8–9, 14, 95–7, 108–9
post-Marxism 155–6, 157, 160
precommitment 97–9, 103
presidentialism 50
Price, Richard 167, 169
Priestley 172
procedural vs end-state 57–8, 62, 142, 153–61
property rights 41–3, 95
Przeworski, Adam 3–5, 12, 17, 43, 44, 58, 60, 93, 95, 108
public spheres 148, 150–3
Putnam, Robert 112, 113, 146

Ramseyer, Mark 100
Rasmusen, Erik 100
rationality 25–31
Rawls, John 57, 65, 67
real income per head 83–9
reasonable disagreement 60–2, 64–7
representation 2–3, 31–9
    mandate conception of 32–3, 34–6,
    retrospective view of 32–3, 34–9
    see also retrospective voting model
representative democracy 69–70, 71, 71–2, 79–81
republicanism 13–15, 163–90, 191–7
retrospective voting model 36–9
Ricardo, David 40
Riker, William 32
Robinson, James 101
Rodrick, Dani 97
Roemer, John 5–6, 12, 43, 44
Rogers, Joel 160
Roland, Gerard 44

Rosenthal, Jean-Laurent 116, 117, 119, 123
Rousseau, Jean-Jacques 2, 26, 29
Rout, Hilton 116
rule of law 95

Sah, Raaj 96
Saran, Mrinalini 104
Scanlon, Thomas 58–9, 59–62, 67
Schleifer, Andrei 100
Schmitter, Philippe 24, 32
Schumpeter, Joseph 2, 4, 12, 23, 24, 33, 35, 47
Seabright, Paul 71
Sen, Amartya 13, 102, 156, 157
separation of powers 44
Shapiro, Ian 15, 24, 72, 151, 184
Sirowy, Larry 93
Skinner, Quentin 23, 166
social capital 76, 104–6, 107
social movements 151–2
socialism 56
Spitz, Jean-Fabien 179
Spruyt, Hendrik 114
state 43–4, 114–18, 121–2, 134–5, 141–2
Stigler, George 33
structural dependence of the state on capital 4, 41–3
Sydney, Algernon 166, 167

Tabelini, Guido 44
Tilly, Charles, 114, 116, 117, 121
Tocqueville, Alexis de 14
Tyler, Tom 182
tyranny of the majority 175–8

utilitarianism 57

Van Parijs, Philippe 16–17
Vishy, Robert 100
voting 23–50

Wade, R. 78, 104
Waldron, Jeremy 29, 30
Wallerstein, Immanuel 114
Wallerstein, Michael 43
Walzer, Michael 143, 145
Weber, Max 114
Weffort, Francisco 24
Weingast, Barry 116, 119

Young, Iris Marion 12–14, 15